BETWEEN THERAPISTS

The Processing of Transference/ Countertransference Material

2nd Edition

by Arthur Robbins, Ed.D.
Director and Training Analyst,
Institute for Expressive Analysis,
Faculty and Training Analyst,
National Psychological Association
for Psychoanalysis,
Professor of Art Therapy,
Pratt Institute, Brooklyn, NY

Jessica Kingsley Publishers
London and Philadelphia

The right of Arthur Robbins to be identified as author of this work has been asserted by him in accordance with the Copyright, Designs and Patents Act 1988.

Originally published in 1988 by Human Sciences Press Inc.

Second edition published in 2000 by
Jessica Kingsley Publishers Ltd,
116 Pentonville Road, London
N1 9JB, England
and
325 Chestnut Street,
Philadelphia PA 19106, USA.

www.jkp.com

Library of Congress Cataloging in Publication Data
A CIP catalog record for this book is available from the Library of Congress

British Library Cataloguing in Publication Data
Between therapists : the processing of transference/countertransference
material 1. Transference (Psychology) 2. Countertransference (Psychology)
3. Therapist and patient
I. Robbins, Arthur, 1928-
154.2'4

ISBN 1 85302 832 0

Printed and Bound in Great Britain by
Athenaeum Press, Gateshead, Tyne and Wear

CONTENTS

Foreword to New Edition   7
Foreword   9
Acknowledgments   12

1. COUNTERTRANSFERENCE LEARNING AND THE ROLE OF THE
   PROFESSIONAL ANALYST   13
   The Therapist as "Container"   13
   The Group: An Alternative Mode   14
   The Focus on Countertransference Material   14
   The Role of Group Members   16
   An Aesthetic View of Professional Training   17
   The Particularity of the Groups   21

GROUP ONE
2. DON: THERAPEUTIC COLLUSION   24
   Prologue: The Challenger   24
   The Session: The Ideas of January   25
   Reciprocal Exploration   38
3. JULIE: CAST IN THE ROLE OF THE HEALER   42
   Death Guidance   42
   Simonton: Pros and Cons   42
   "I Don't Need This"   46
   A New Therapeutic Alliance   56
4. GEORGE: HOMOSEXUAL ANXIETY   60
   Creating the "Holding Environment"   60

The Case of "Arcade Joe"   62
The Problem of the Paranoid Patient   78
5. REIKO: A MIRRORING STANCE FLOWS INTO FUSION   **82**
Twinship and Separation   82
"We Don't Do That to People"   92
Transcultural Recognition   100

GROUP TWO
6. DAISY: GREED AND THE THERAPIST   **103**
No Perfect "Parent," No Powerless Patient   103
The Session: Giving and Getting   104
The Insatiability of Depression   123
7. DAISY: EXPLORING THE MALE ELEMENT
IN THE FEMALE THERAPIST   **127**
A High-Functioning Woman   127
The "Bridal" Patient   135
Varieties of "Performance Anxiety"   146
8. JANICE: EXPANDING TRANSITIONAL SPACE   **149**
To Dance or Not to Dance   149
The "Magic" Mirror and the Mother Within   172
9. JANICE: THE THERAPIST AS A WHORE   **176**
A Study in Contrast   176
The Presentation: A "Numbers" Man   177
"False Self" versus Transcendence   196
10. LENORE: RAGE AS A SCREEN FOR
OEDIPAL GUILT   **200**
Preliminaries: The Day's Work and the Night's
Dream   200
The Session: Too Close to Home   201
The Vital "Connection"   216
11. IN SEARCH OF A HOME FOR THE SOUL   **220**

A Farewell Note   237
Bibliography   241
Index   251

FOREWORD TO NEW EDITION

Eleven years have now passed since the publication of the first edition of *Between Therapists: The Processing of Transference and Countertransference Material*. During this relatively short time, we have become far more sophisticated in the creative use of transference and countertransference communications. Of equal importance, we have seen more acceptance of their use in the real relationship of the therapeutic dialogue, within the context of projections and introjections.

The field of mental health has continued its shift in emphasis which started in 1980. Currently, cognitive/behavior therapy and crisis intervention are often the treatment of choice both in institutional and private practice sectors. Psychoanalytic work, on the other hand, no longer holds out its seemingly magic hope for cure. Instead, a far greater emphasis is being placed on chemical interventions. Yet precisely because of this shift in interventions, it is now even more necessary to be therapeutically present, to be open to multiple levels of consciousness, so that we are able to make significant adjustments in treatment where needed. It is ever more pressing to understand out adaptations and maladaptations to projections and introjections. Despite the fact that we are concentrating more on strategic therapeutic planning, there lurks the potential for these newer interventions to create a defensive position when we are out of touch or dissociated from our patients.

Transference and countertransference cannot be separated from a broader sociological context. Even in these brief eleven years, we have become more aware of the trauma inflicted by a depersonalized society, in which patients feel more alone and unable to process the complex demands of life. It is symptomatic of today's living situation that many feel overburdened and completely exhausted from striving to meet its needs. At the same time, we have become even more attuned to the various emotional issues that impact our development, child-raising and family dynamics.

In light of the above changes in our awareness of society and its demands, trauma theory has become an important framework in our work with patients. The subtle but complex interweaving of abuse, addictive behavior, and alienation has compounded our work and made the use of transference and countertransference communications very cogent and meaningful. Our patients present to us work and life experiences where they report being overwhelmed, addicted, traumatized and out of control. In working directly with the process of transference and countertransference, we give increasing attention to bearing witness and testimony to our patients and honoring the reality that they have gone through. These issues were not as prominent in our first publication.

Since the publication of this first text, I have become far more mindful of the importance of systems theory as applied to group supervision. My son, Michael Robbins, who is also a therapist and trained in systems theory, has engaged me in many stimulating discussions about applying this theory to countertransference supervision. Some of the principles that I have applied intuitively to my supervision groups can now be articulated within this systems theory framework. Underlying this framework is a focus on the issues of working with the group as a whole. It is important to understand the positive and negative valences that ultimately impact upon group dynamics. I try to avoid making the presenter the scapegoat, but try to create an atmosphere within the group that stimulates subgrouping. Also, I struggle to keep the group balanced between the polarities of meaning and being. Consequently, I see each presentation as a statement as to where the group lives, how it is evolving and what problems it is facing. This type of learning continues to be a very vital and growing part of my professional work, where therapists are searching in a group setting for an integration of emotional and theoretical material that has not been accessible through individual supervision or through their personal treatment.

This short preface now leads me to restate the preface that was part of the first publication. While bearing in mind the shifts I have described in the intervening years. I believe the original preface will give the reader some insight into the genesis of this text.

FOREWORD

While I was attending classes at the Psychoanalytic Institute in the late 1950s I became completely immersed in the theory and technique of depth-oriented treatment. Transference, resistance, developmental theory and technique unfolded like a rich, complicated fabric. Yet, when countertransference involvement was noted, it was commonly met with the disjunctive refrain: Take it back to your analyst.

One course was different. The subject of the class was countertransference and it was conducted by Ruth Cohn, an old-timer in the Psychoanalytic Institute. We presented cases, as in other classes; but here the similarity with other courses ended, for we were invited to share our emotional reactions about the case presenter, patient, and group. What a strange class it was for this intellectual assortment of students. I was both moved and intrigued by the depth and complexity of the case material, but also threatened by the emotional character of the class. I rationalized to myself, does an instructor have a right to invite students into a class structure that felt like a group therapy situation without a contract? Yet I could not deny the power of this experience of combining the affective and cognitive reactions of both therapist and patient in case discussion.

Other students and faculty became equally intrigued by such an approach, and the education committee soon established a 1-year requirement that embodied these very same principles. After a very short trial period, complaints were heard through the entire Institute community, and the innovation was dropped from the curriculum. As far as I could discern, the institution felt too threatened in dealing with such emotional material in a setting that was basically educational. Students required a free choice to enter into such a relationship, and it was painfully obvious that an institute was not the best place to carry out such an arrangement. Exploring the personal and private nature of countertransference reactions demanded a good deal of trust and safety that was not always implicit in an academic setting.

Perhaps another factor underlying the failure of this innovation related to the array of new instructors assigned to this very provocative course. Certainly only a very seasoned and trained analyst with special competence in this area could tread the terra incognita of countertransference exploration, that were neither group therapy nor traditional supervision.

This short experience in countertransference learning left a profound impact on my understanding of what constitutes appropriate and meaningful learning in therapeutic education. The course stayed with me and ultimately played a very important role in my professional future. Upon graduation I became a supervisor and teacher and initiated private supervisory groups that were conducted along the same lines. Through trial and error I developed my own innovations and slowly acquired a theoretical understanding of both the assets and pitfalls of such a procedure. Much to my surprise, many of my students have remained in these groups, even though they have become teachers and supervisors in the Psychoanalytic Institute. The members of my oldest group, some of whom have been participating with me for over 15 years, still report it to be the highlight of their week.

I feel now is the time to pause and reflect on why this procedure has been such a powerful learning experience. The focus of this text, therefore, is on working and living with countertransference material. Much is written in the literature regarding the theory of countertransference; but little is reported of the actual working through of this material through an ongoing group process.

This book, however, illustrates something more than the working out of countertransference problems. It is a presentation of the everyday drama of life that surrounds the practice of therapy. In this drama, we can observe the stress and struggle of therapeutic practice that overwhelms even the most analyzed therapists. It is hoped that this text may offer a technique to process this ongoing stress that is so inherent in the fulfillment of our therapeutic duties.

This book equally addresses itself to the supervisors and teachers who seek a structure to impart transference/countertransference learning within the context of case management theory and technique. Most important, however, is the living character of the supervisory sessions that may offer encouragement and inspiration to the fledgling therapist. All too often the young therapist views countertransference as a formidable obstacle that at best should be expunged with dispatch. From the perspective of this author, the therapist's emotional connection to his or her case is, in fact, the basic tool of treatment. Throughout this text, an underlying premise constantly comes to the foreground in case discussions: Trust your unconscious, for it can offer creative solutions that bypass the world of linear logic. Observing matured therapists struggling with similar issues may ultimately become the source that can give strength and power to a very unique and creative style of professional expression. In its broadest context, this should be the goal of psychoanalytic and psychotherapeutic education.

ACKNOWLEDGMENTS

I owe a very special debt to all those professionals who have participated in my supervisory groups and have graciously consented to have their sessions recorded. This procedure was an intrusion into a very private process, and I am most appreciative of their spirit of cooperation. In particular, I want to give special recognition to those presenters who endured such a microscopic examination of their work by permitting the transcription of their work in printed form.

I want also to thank Trudy Loubet and Priscilla Rodgers who have assisted me in the formidable task of editing these group sessions. Their enthusiasm, suport, and help greatly lightened the load in making this work possible.

A very special place in this text belongs to Ruth Cohn, formerly on the faculty of the National Psychological Association for Psychoanalysis. Her inspiring teaching in the course on countertransference became the impetus for my own professional growth and development in this area.

Last, but not least, I want to thank my wife, Sandra, for her comfort, support, and constructive criticism in reviewing the chapters as they took shape.

Chapter 1

COUNTERTRANSFERENCE LEARNING AND THE ROLE OF THE PROFESSIONAL ANALYST

THE THERAPIST AS "CONTAINER"

Being a psychoanalytic therapist creates an ongoing and gruelling emotional balancing act. In order to be effective therapists, we must maintain an appropriate objective emotional distance from our patients while, at the same time, we transmit an essence of humanity as we touch our patients' raw emotional nerves. We also try to be openly receptive to our patients' communications, offering ourselves as "containers" for such intensely powerful affects as abandonment, rage, loss, and love. This state of containment requires an emotional centering of ourselves, and demands that we put aside the stresses of our personal daily lives when we enter the office and confine our patient's confidential struggle to a very private section of our psyche.

As we are not supermen or women, this ongoing balancing act takes its toll in spite of the years of training and personal therapy or analysis we may have undergone. At times our receptive apparati are overwhelmed and we experience our patients' affects as fierce invading marauders. When this happens, we open ourselves up to defensively acting out in order to master the trauma. Metaphorically, the container-therapist springs leaks and spills out in any number of directions. This hazard increases in working with more "primitive" patients in the borderline, severe character disorder, schizoid, or depressed categories—the very core of the clientele who often come to us for help.

THE GROUP: AN ALTERNATIVE MODE

For some therapists, returning to analysis from time to time is a solution. Others of us, however, have found the need for an alternative mode of self-exploration that serves as a shock absorber for the normal stresses of analytic work as well as a means to investigate methodology, to better understand the mix of cognitive and emotional factors involved in analysis, and to offer a community of peers for support in this lonely business. For us, forming supervisory/integration groups represents our belief that affective and cognitive synthesis of case management material is a continuous process that will go on for the rest of our lives.

In the following chapters, the author will present transcriptions of group supervision sessions that emphasize this mix of cognitive and affective organization. This complex form of learning is neither group therapy or supervision in the traditional sense of these words. Within this dynamic interactive process, the presenter is encouraged to investigate the affective and theoretical issues involved in a case, as well as to receive emotional and cognitive feedback from his peers. Countertransference reactions are viewed as important sources of information and understanding of the patient/therapist interactions. Little distinction is made between "induced reactions," often ascribed to the projective identifications of patients, and "countertransference reactions," usually referred to as those feelings originating in and generated by the therapist based on some resonance with his past. Clearly, the impact of any given patient's affective communications will vary from therapist to therapist, depending upon the permeability of the patient's and therapist's boundaries, the similarity of the therapist's personality to that of the patient, and the particular defensive organization involved in the interaction.

THE FOCUS ON COUNTERTRANSFERENCE MATERIAL

It is this emphasis upon countertransference material beyond the more traditional didactic work regarding theory and technique that sets these groups apart from the usual therapy supervision groups.

This mix of theoretical, technical, and emotional issues demands a continued openness to preconscious as well as conscious case material. Here, the therapeutic and creative processes merge in an atmosphere that is nonjudgmental, open, and resistant to premature closure. Through the group dynamics, the very problems that interfered with the therapeutic creative process are often recreated in the case presentations. We may observe how the members and/or leader will excessively interpret or support rather than allow the learning process to find its own path. Ideally, both members and the leader attempt to deal with the resistance toward learning through a variety of interventions.

Besides such traditional techniques as confrontation or interpretation, the group is encouraged to play with images that hook up with primary process material. Role-playing, image trips, fantasies are employed to open up new avenues in a particular case. However, none of these techniques substitute for an atmosphere that promotes a freedom of expression. Needless to say, the group can easily be a source of projective transferences that can be viewed as critical, attacking, or overwhelming. Along the same lines, the group or particular members can act out these prescribed roles as part of the introjective/projective influence of the presenter. In such instances, either leader or members of the group ultimately must have objective distance to interpret the externalizations in a manner that facilitates case processing.

The material that emerges in working this way may stem from very early life experiences of the therapist. In these instances, it is assumed that group members have already had a good deal of personal treatment and ego strength to facilitate their shifting between emotional and cognitive levels associated with the case presentation. For the presenter in particular, it is assumed that much of the emerging material has been worked through in personal analysis, so that he is basically returning to old material that needs further reorganization and digestion.

Having said that, I can see the question arising as to why this kind of important affective material relevant to case management hasn't already been worked through in personal analysis. While supervisors often do make recommendations for bringing material to analysis, these recommendations may be experienced as an intrusion in the analytic process, or at best as extrinsic to what is going on between patient and analyst. By the same token, even if the emotional material that comes up in therapy does ultimately have relevance for case management work, rarely is there sufficient working through of the emotional issues to ensure complete mastery of the transference/countertransference material.

There simply are limitations to what analysis can accomplish. It is hoped that at the end of treatment our characterological defenses will be more flexible and elastic in terms of our ability to handle stress. Yet this understanding does not preclude patient/therapist defenses mixing in such a way that from time to time difficult transference/countertransference issues will be created. Character structure can be modified in analysis; but we are still left with our adaptive character style, however integrated, that may not respond well to our patient's character structure, thus creating a lack of emotional resonance. Similarly, working in these supervisory/integration groups cannot "solve" whatever characterological issues remain for us; but they can help us better to understand our problems as they are recreated in our work with patients, thereby giving us greater mastery. Needless to say, the therapist undergoing this type of experience requires a fairly mature and flexible ego as well as an ability to maintain boundaries and not be unduly threatened by the freewheeling atmosphere.

THE ROLE OF GROUP MEMBERS

Counterbalancing this unstructured form of learning is a good deal of inner discipline and commitment on the part of the members to maintain the goal of case supervision rather than treatment. There is clearly the temptation for members to play therapist for one another. In order to avoid this resistance to learning, the leader must maintain a firm hand to keep the group on its essential mission for working with the case. Material felt to be too far removed to be relevant to the presentation is not reinforced in the discussion, although there is obviously a good deal of subjective range as to what constitutes relevant emotional material in any given case. Usually, the relative comfort of both the leader and group members to the affective material under discussion becomes an important criterion. Consequently, each group has its own particular tolerance level for shifting back and forth between experiencing and integrating the emotional/cognitive material. Generally, the tolerance level becomes more elastic as the group becomes more experienced in this form of group work.

Obviously, this very complex form of training is not suitable for all professionals. For many, however, this moving back and forth between different ego states becomes a very exciting form of learning experience. Insight and self-integration accrue from dipping into one's preconscious reactions to the group. Patient and presenter, as they are enacted in the group, produce a mix that frames and externalizes the subtle interplay of projective identifications, defensive operations, and the therapist's early emotional underpinnings in the countertransference/transference relationship.

For the group members, however, this group becomes more than an exciting learning experience. The *group* becomes a "container," as members support the presenter's attempts to expand his ability to project, externalize, and investigate the myriad of affects that arise in transference/countertransference reactions. This "holding" helps neutralize the anxiety associated with the enormous strain under which a therapist works in grappling with patients' primitive emotional states. In the course of working with one another in this fashion, members become a community where mutual identification with one another over common issues forge strong bonds. Therapists begin to share not only their internal worlds, but also the external reality stressors that subtly undermine their competence as therapists. Financial worries regarding loss of patient income, birth, death, illness are all common problems that therapists share in the group communication. The ethos of this type of group, therefore, is not based on a disciplined "professional demeanor," with an agenda to adhere to. Often, members of the group dine with one another before or after the meeting and receive particular support regarding these matters.

An Aesthetic View of Professional Training

As the reader now surmises, the author's position regarding training is fairly clear-cut: Emotional and cognitive learning ultimately must live together in one life space. This view may come in conflict with those who maintain that analysis is in the main a scientific profession. To be sure, there is a body of organized information that can be tested out and communicated from supervisor to supervisee. Yet, as long as emotional-subjective factors play a role for both therapeutic participants, the development of professional style can best be viewed along artistic and aesthetic lines. As therapeutic artists, then, trained within a framework of broad-based organized data, how we shape and form nonverbal and verbal communications will be an outgrowth of each participant's personal dynamics. Implicit in this notion is the assumption that different therapists approaching patients with a variety of aesthetic and emotional sensibilities, as well as techniques, can still end up with roughly similar results.

Related to this approach to therapy is the notion of *therapeutic truth*. Different analysts do in fact hear and respond differently to their patients, creating a variety and range of interpretations and interplay that accrues from the mix of different levels of consciousness. The perception and organization of this mix, though different for each therapist/patient dyad, has its own artistic truth and can potentially lead to self/object individuation. Implicit in this, then, is also the observation that the therapist struggles, to some extent, with his personal issues with each therapeutic experience, and consequently must be equally committed to continually grappling with his personality dynamics.

What the reader will encounter in this text, then, is a series of actual presentations from these groups that encapsulate some common therapeutic issues. Several of the chapters will deal with a therapist's struggle, first to define the particular kind of holding or mirroring an individual patient may require, and then to pull up pieces of themselves to be utilized therapeutically for this purpose. Some of these "pieces" include softness and toughness, "maleness" and "femaleness," and various forms of mothering and fathering. The difficulties that emerge reflect the therapist's experiences with these parts of himself and his level of comfort or acceptance regarding them. Clearly, as a more complete peace has been made with parents and past, more of the therapist is available to create a holding environment that will resonate with the patient's psychic problem.

The reader may wonder what the author refers to as the essence of male or female, mother or father. A good starting point may be linked to the investigation of the therapist's intrapsychic mixture of personal and affective representational states that are projected in one's adaptive mode of listening and responding. Consequently, there are a number of intrapsychic representations that can be tapped in responding to and resonating with our patients: the soft or pointed father, the round or firm mother, the playful sibling, or the good uncle on the sidelines. Ideally, in order for these nonverbal affective states to be available, a synthesis of our past psychic and physical experiences should be integrated into our identity style of communication. Herein lies another therapeutic assumption of this text: Different patients require a variety of therapists' affective states for interpretive work to be effective. When a particular style of communication is not available to a therapist, such as toughness, soft-ness, or playfulness, we have, then, the risk of a lack of therapeutic fit with a given patient.

For instance, the lost child lodged within an adult patient's psy-chic economy may require a soft maternal response from the thera-pist to mirror some of the early maternal losses. Here, this therapeutic ambience acts as an appropriate conduit for the interpretive work to go on. Likewise, the frightened vacillating young boy within the adult patient may be in particular need of a gentle but firm father who can impart interpretive material within this emotional context.

By experiencing the inner representational world of patients, a transitional space is created which becomes the conduit for interpre-tive work in analytic therapy. These representational states are often elusive and fleeting. By attending to the kinesthetic and nonverbal modes of communication of both patient and therapist, our aware-ness can be heightened to this subtle image dialogue. The image, then, becomes the organizer of the nonverbal cues and dimensions of the transitional space. Within this space, demarcated by such issues as closeness and distance, and a variety of sensory inflections, interpre-tive work can be imparted with both resonance and developmental appropriateness. The "rightness of fit" that fosters emotional reso-nance can be monitored by the flow or resistance within the unfolding therapeutic process.

One of the most significant themes underlying the learning pro-cess is the analyst's vulnerability to emotional splitting. Seemingly the-oretical issues mask or contaminate a tendency to polarize rather than to integrate diverse material that covers emotionally laden conflicts. the reader can observe how the preoccupation of self psychology ver-sus classical analysis, or preoedipal versus oedipal, can be colored by the variety of emotional predispositions and dynamics. On the more manifest level, the therapist's integration of a variety of psychic polarities within his mental structure, i.e., male or female elements, will create either adaptations and/or conflicts that will subtly influence the perception of a given case. A linear form of thinking masking a true integration of these polarities often interferes with a more com-plex understanding of a given problem. There are, in fact, theoretical and technical issues as to when to mirror, reflect, or interpret. These decisions, however, subtly interface with the therapist's style and the adaptive organization of both therapist and patient. Consequently, the decision as to how and when to intervene becomes a very subjec-tive/objective choice contingent on the above mentioned factors.

As will be seen in more than one presentation, the realm of sexual, gender, or paternal roles can slide over into loaded political, cultural, or sociological topics. Inflammatory terms like "castrating female" or "phallic woman" arise, as does one provocative discussion of the parallels and differences between being a prostitute and a therapist. Initially enraged by being treated as a "thing" to be used and discarded, one therapist eventually moves through the patient's manifest content to view the communications as indicators of pregenital and genital issues.

Sociological/cutural issues emerge in another presentation in the form of conflicting crosscultural currents. Born in Japan, but assimilated into American culture, Reiko faces sorting out personal intrapsychic issues and cultural style differences when she becomes "stuck" in the course of one patient's therapy.

Grandiosity on the part of the therapist can take any number of turns. The most obvious pitfall is that of playing the good mother or father, temporarily pleasing the patient and gratifying the therapist. On the other hand, from the position of heightened awareness necessary to move among the various currents in a session, the therapist may become subtly arrogant and self-impressed, confusing therapeutic power with power over another individual. Finally, it can be tempting for the therapist to feel omnipotent, as if he is the salvation of a particular patient. All of these issues appear in various guises in the presentations to follow.

One more subtle turn grandiosity can take is for a therapist to be so invested in the identity of helper or healer that he denies issues of spite, greed, and hunger. As one therapist comes to recognize, in dealing with the enormous hunger of a depressed patient, we, too, come up against these issues in such spheres as placing a value on our time with fees or in setting limits and boundaries.

One presenter will wrestle with the very real and concrete issues surrounding life-threatening illness and dying. These reflect both ever-present countertransference responses based on the therapists' life experiences, and technical questions pertaining to modifications in the therapist's role at this very difficult life-cycle stage.

The reflective presence of the analyst often comes into direct conflict with a culture that prizes action and results. In its pathological form, conflicts are acted out rather than repressed and this becomes a familiar solution to anxiety. Oftener than might be supposed, analysts encounter patients who have had sexual experiences with key authorities, such as therapists or ministers, which in turn places enormous pressure on one's capacity to understand the dynamics without judgment or condemnation. A very unique situation will be presented by one of our group members whose patient had slept with her minister, who was also her confidant and adviser. The rage, judgment, and anxiety that became a very understandable response to this issue, can very easily mask some very complex dynamics.

THE PARTICULARITY OF THE GROUPS

Weaving in and out of all the presentations are questions regarding the role of the therapist and the use of technique, the need for individuation, and the purpose of the group process itself. As one might expect, each presentation is subtle colored by the particular group in which it evolves, since each group has its own particular "flavor" based upon its makeup and level of experience. Let me briefly give you the flavor of the groups from which we will be sampling.

Group One consists of analytic therapists who have, for the most part, 10 to 15 years of therapeutic experience. Many are on the faculties of analytic institutes; yet the members continue to present live and vital cases that are constantly opening up new areas of theory and technique. This group was formed in 1975 with very few changes in membership alignment from the original group. The members demonstrate very clear autonomy in their styles; so there is a good deal of confrontation and interaction between members of the group and the leader. By and large, this is a very cohesive group, with much sharing and outside socialization and contact. Characteristically, the members of this group often march in together after lunch in high good humor and camaraderie. My private name for them is "The Gang."

Group Two consists of relatively young analysts and therapists who have been together for approximately 4 years. Members have approximately 5 to 10 years of experience behind them and have either recently graduated from an institute or are in their last phase of formal training. In contrast to the other groups, all the members are women, which may influence the particular issues that arise in case presentations. Each of these women is characteristically eager to present, and there is therefore much jockeying for position even as the group files into our meeting room. They are avid in their quest for knowledge and understanding, but at the same time are supportive and nurturant to one another, and so I think of them as the hungry group.

The above comparison, brief as it is, touches upon the underlying fact that each group has its own particular process, its own unique "life." Consequently, it seems that the issues in case presentations will cluster around some particular topic or facet of theory, technique, emotional development or individuation for a period of time before the group moves on to a new cluster of issues, all without conscious effort or directing on the part of the leader. Needless to say, it is a fascinating example of group process.

The reader can also observe the unique ambience and tone of each presentation. Different presenters, as with patients, require a variety of transitional opportunities that facilitate the learning process. Some ask for space; others for support; while a few need either playfulness or confrontation. The supervisory process, then, becomes a model for different interventions that occur not only through role-playing, but by the very live example of the supervisor and group working with the supervisee.

One last word is in order here. Due to the massive amounts of material in each recorded session, the sessions have been edited to make them more readable. Where necessary for clarity, and to help the reader better see and feel the atmosphere in groups, descriptions of nonverbal material have been added. The group presenters have read over these manuscripts to ensure that I have kept the essences of these very exciting and telling sessions.

These recordings contain the essence of this text. They represent the actual application of an approach that is neither traditional supervisory process or group therapy. By offering such detailed descriptions, the technical and theoretical considerations that are associated with countertransference learning become highlighted. All too often, colleagues report that supervisory sessions that are run along the same format often deteriorate into group therapy. It is hoped that, the following detailed descriptions can alert the reader to the pitfalls and problems in maintaining this most challenging and difficult course of learning that combines the affective and cognitive resources of the therapist within the context of the actual drama in being an analyst.

I appreciate the generosity of all of the group presenters in sharing their vulnerability and frailties as human beings. I hope the reader will receive a living sense of how we, as therapists, struggle with the raw affects of our innermost selves that are the stuff from which effective therapeutic empathy and communications stem. The mastery of these elements does not come easily. Delving into transference/countertransference interactions involves risk and patience. Yet, the rewards of such a learning experience cannot be underestimated, for, our emotional balancing act as analytic therapists requires attention, care, and healing.

Chapter 2

DON

Therapeutic Collusion

PROLOGUE: THE CHALLENGER

Omnipotence is a double-edged issue with which many of us grapple in our roles as therapists. On the positive side, it can provide a certain daring, independence of thinking, spirit, and energy that lead to therapeutic innovation and authentic human interaction. On the other hand, the fears associated with grandiosity taken too seriously can create such defensive positions as projection, introjection, and a patronizing form of support to patients. This support which the therapist gives out of seemingly grand humanity, can actually be a subtle evasion facing his boundaries as a therapist while discouraging the patient's individuation.

In the following presentation, Don provocatively parades his grandiosity as he comes close to daring his peers to attack him. Underneath this facade, we will observe someone who is frightened of his own competitive hostility, leading him subtly to interfere with the development of the transference by selectively attending to material on a preoedipal level. The therapist is far more comfortable taking on the protective maternal role, than in allowing the father/daughter relationship to develop. As Don presents, a complicated group dynamic evolves. Don takes on a rather controlled, defensive posture, protecting himself from having to see the underlying oedipal dynamic of

24

sexuality and competition that reside in both patient and therapist; while group members take on roles that point up the countertransferential issues that will be evident in the following group session. Throughout this session, as well as all the other chapters, I will interject parenthetical comments regarding some of the issues that are not overtly expressed in the supervisory process.

Don was a relatively new member of our group. Since at first Don was a laid-back, watchful observer, his initial reactions to the group were hard to discern. Slowly, however, a rather charming and winning personality emerged, and there developed between Don and the other members of the group a mutual fondness and respect for one another. After 6 months, something happened; he became far more provocative and challenging. Don took on the role of teacher of the group, instructing members in how they should behave as therapists. Most of his colleagues responded with good-natured kidding, but a few were affronted by his intrusiveness. I wondered to myself what had happened to this rather quiet and disarming man who now seemed to be challenging everyone to attack him.

Gradually, a few more members of the group became increasingly angry and countercombative. In the last meeting before the holidays, Don became particularly challenging and provocative, stating that the presentation was boring, then elaborating on how it should work. The group confronted him and attempted to explore some of the deeper dynamics of that session. I redirected the comments back to the case presentation at hand, but was concerned that Don was isolating himself, and putting himself in an untenable position.

THE SESSION: THE IDES OF JANUARY

Reconvening after the holidays, the mood of the group was marked by a good deal of nervous laughter and joking. Some members commented that it was pretty hard to get back to work, and one member in particular commented that during the vacation she attended a *Messiah* recital in which an entire audience of 3,000 people sang in unison. "It was such a joyous event!" she exclaimed. I thought of the group, where we sometimes allude to and even reach this level.

Don commented, "I guess there's not going to be any case presentation today." Again, there was nervous giggling and laughter. This giggling and laughing punctuated the entire session.

It is an unusual emotional atmosphere for this group and it signified neither gaiety nor playfulness. The underlying mood was tension, and the members were threatened by Don's challenging tone as they struggled to be supportive, while suppressing their increasing irritation with his combativeness.

One woman did query, "How did you feel about our last session? You seemed to be upset?" addressing herself to Don.

"I wasn't upset," he said. "In fact, I felt pretty good. How do *you* feel?" This stimulated a good deal of bantering back and forth. "My wife was worried that perhaps I was obnoxious to people, but that wasn't my concern," asserted Don. Again there was silence, and Don volunteered: "I guess I could present, although I really don't have a problem in this case. I'll do it if no one else wants to, but it seems to me that the best way to present a case is if a patient is giving you some trouble, and there's no trouble here."

The group laughed, and I commented that sometimes that's the best kind of case to present. He said, "Maybe I'll see that I should have been worried about this all along! In any event," he commented, rather defensively, "I don't have much of a caseload."

It was as though he was trying to disarm the group members and distract them from his display of self-confidence, if not arrogance. However, there was little to be gained in confronting this type of character defense. More important, interjecting a note of playful acceptance of Don's arrogance would, one hoped, further a supportive atmosphere in the room.

"The last time I presented," he said, "I was asked why I was presenting this case. I believe that's a valid question, and I'm open to the possibility that maybe I should be concerned about this case. I don't know why . . ." In response, one of the members again brought up the question of how Don felt about the last session. He reacted rather combatively and wondered why she was asking.

We were beginning to move away from our overall mission and enter into emotional areas between members that essentially create a resistance to learning theory and technique. While I recognized that a good deal of feeling needed to be processed between Don and the others, I decided to leave it alone, hoping that it would come out in the main fabric of the presentation. At times, the leader has no choice but to clear the air if too strong negative

emotional feelings are built up and interfere with the presentation of cases. A very precarious line must be maintained between
group therapy and group supervision. In this instance, the group
container was elastic enough to permit the processing of the
case in spite of the undercurrent tension that exists in the group
atmosphere.

I said, "Let's get into the case," and we all agreed.

"I'd like to talk to you about a forty-one year-old married woman,
Sara, who has two children and is a Baptist. She is a high school graduate with a liberal education. She lives on a farm and is a kind of a
superwoman: She tends the sheep, works part-time as a receptionist,
tries to be an excellent wife to her husband. Her husband is a corpo-
rate executive. He is very nonpsychological, has a German background, the stolid type. He is certainly not in touch with his own pain.
His first wife abandoned him, leaving him with a child. He and Sara
have three children now; one from his first marriage as well as two
children from his second.

"Sara came to me with symptoms of agoraphobia, and now has
been in treatment for two years. The symptoms are such that she feels
anxious in such situations as going over a bridge or being in strange
places. She started out treatment not very self-aware. Her expectation
of therapy was that it would do something for her.

"Sara is the third of four children, which is significant because
the two older children have remained highly connected to both parents, while she and her younger sister have been overwhelmingly rejected. They're a year apart in age and seem to have formed an alliance with one another. The mother has a particularly devaluing
attitude toward the patient, constantly trying to run Sara down. By
contrast, the patient strenuously attempts to win her mother's approval and be a good daughter.

"Early in treatment, the patient discussed a good deal of material
regarding her relationship to her husband. Like her mother, he demanded perfection, and Sara felt increasingly depressed about her inability to meet his demands. Slowly this problem lessened as she became more psychologically aware and gained more insight into her
own behavior."

Don went on in a somewhat flat, detached manner. "There was a
major revelation in therapy during her first year of treatment when
her oldest sister found herself in some emotional difficulty. Why, Sara
was not sure, but her mother sent her sister, then sixteen years old, to

live with Sara. During this period, she acted out promiscuously, became pregnant, and had an abortion. This deep dark secret came up almost by accident, and Sara was eager to dismiss this material and deny its impact on her life. As we discussed some of the issues, a good deal of anxiety was stimulated, with many dreams of going psychotic emerging.

"Now, during the latter part of the second year of treatment, the patient has become increasingly alienated from her mother. Along with this change, she is much more in touch with her anger, and the depression has lifted. During the holiday season, there seems to have been a major regression, as there was increased contact with the mother through phone and writing. I recognize that the core issue of treatment is that Sara needs internally to separate from the mother, since there is clearly still a good deal of connection on an unconscious level.

"I worry sometimes that I am trying to push her too hard to face this, but, really, transferentially there's not very much open material regarding this area. We have a friendly, warm relationship, in which most of the material seems to be that of working outside the transference. I know that during the beginning stages of treatment the patient was quite worried that I was a freethinker who could easily put her in the hands of the devil. This was connected with the moralistic, severe attitude of the mother.

> There is no such thing as working outside the transference. At times, a patient may present resistances that deny or cut off transference feelings, but then that, too, becomes part of the working with treatment process. However, I saw little to be gained in confronting the presenter about this issue, but waited to see how the members of the group would approach Don in his handling of this case.

"Lately, Sara's preoccupied with an intrusive image that occurs when she is getting up in the morning. She sees an image of God naked and sees his genitals." Nervous laughter ran through the group, and one of the members of the group wondered out loud: "Could this image be you, Don?" Don replied, "I hope so, but I can't get at it. She can't seem to do much with it in terms of how it relates to me." One of the members of the group retorts, "She has this image of this intrusion into her consciousness, and you say there's no transference!" Don was quick to respond: "No, I didn't say that; I said there was no *work-*

able transference. I don't know what to do about it. I try to let her know that this is important material, that it means something, but she talks about it being 'bad' to think this and she feels guilty. Then she reverts back to this talk being too freethinking and evil. I related this once again to the mother's attitude."

One of the members of the group commented, "Are you sure that this isn't an eroticized transference where she sees her impulses as part of the devil?" Don's response was simply, "Yes, I know that, but I can't work with it." One of the members of the group requested that we receive more material and we all agreed. As Don started to give more clinical data, one of the members of the group interrupted with, "Does she always call you Donald?" to which Don said, "Most of my patients don't call me Doctor, and most refer to me as Don."

> I was aware that Don was presenting a very tight package that was virtually impossible to break into. Perhaps we needed to wait outside until all of us felt that there was a more open invitation to participate in the case. Certainly the time was not yet right to confront the presenter, as I did not feel enough elasticity in the presenter's defenses to permit him to hear other possibilities and ideas that might be of help.

This line of inquiry didn't seem to open any doors for Don, and he resumed talking. "One of the central resistances is that she is frightened of going crazy. I don't feel that she is trying to play with me, I really think she means it, and I try to reassure her that she isn't going crazy." Next, one of the members requested information about the father, who hasn't been mentioned at all. "Well," Don said, "he's very much fused with the mother. Sara idealizes him as a warm, wonderful person, but complains that the mother seems to keep her away from him. It's very apparent to me," he said, "that her feelings regarding him are more fantasy than real, but she maintains a fairly positive, warm attitude towards him."

One of the members of the group returned to Don's reassurance of the patient. "You reassure her before you understand what this is all about. Why not investigate what going crazy is all about? She seems to tie your hands. You reassure her, then she seems to go through a superego position, talking about how this is antireligious, and you can't go anywhere. We don't really know what she's talking about when she's frightened of going crazy." Another member of the group added, "She seems to disarm you with her complaints about anxiety."

I was aware of the group's increasing irritability and challenge of Don. Some of the comments seemed combative. Could this be an externalization of some of Don's problems in the case? Was there some underlying guilt about his underlying countertransference feelings?

Don offered more material regarding her husband. "He's very negative to therapy. He originally opposed it, and is now concerned about the money. He wishes she would just drop it. Their relationship is much better, however. She tries to be the perfect wife, and this seems to suit the husband just fine."

Suddenly Don became aware that one of the members of the group was yawning. He turned to her and asked whether he was boring her.

"Oh no," she protested, "I just had a rough night with one hour of sleep. My baby was sick."

After this Don said, "You know I've learned something about this case. I recognize I have to explore more of the images. That in and of itself is quite helpful. I don't think we have to push this any more. I think we've gone far enough."

Margy, who was previously yawning, immediately popped up with, "*Now* you're waking me up!"

Was Don controlling his patient in the same way he was controlling the group with his soft, supportive demeanor? Obviously, Margy was offering a subtle message, and Don's response was one of feeling hurt and wounded.

Another member complained, "You're stopping exactly where the patient wants."

At this point I intervened: "How do you feel now? What's going on, Don?"

Don's response was, "I recognize I was pressing to get more material. I felt loosened up, but I don't see why we have to spend the whole session on this."

Giggling now erupted in the group, and another member retorted, "You know, Don, you're quite a controlling sonofabitch." It was said in a good-natured way, but at the same time Jim was quite clear in his intent. The member continued, "You know, it was my New Year's resolution to keep quiet, and that about ends *that* resolution! When I walked in today, I saw you stretched out in Art's chair and I thought, gee, I shouldn't wake him up. Then I suddenly recognized it was you. You know, you project such a strong, imposing image. You're trying to control this material, and particularly Sara's feelings about you. It seems to me that you really don't want to go much further. I remember your last presentation: You wanted to wrap everything up and control where the flow of material was going. Come off it, and let's get into what's really going on."

> Jim picks up a subtle projection of the presenter. Was Don having difficulty in getting in touch with his own Godlike image?

Margy then asked, "Did you feel bad when you saw me nodding off?"

"Well, you did catch my attention," Don replied.

"Did it make you stop your presentation?"

"Not really," Don said. "I did put some pressure on myself and then wondered why I had to speak under this kind of pressure. If anything, I *used* you. I felt guilty and bored while speaking, and frankly, I was just trying to fill up space. What we discussed here has freed me up, so now we can stop."

> What did Don mean by filling up space? Was he denying a pocket of emptiness that was being covered over by a Godlike defense?

Don went on, "You know, when this patient first started treatment, she really wasn't a patient. She missed a lot of sessions, and I wasn't really sure whether she was going to stay or not." At this point, I changed the tape to the other side, and Don immediately asked if I wanted him to stop and wait for me. I smiled without comment, and Don wanted to investigate my feelings further.

One of the members of the group confronted him with: "You always change things around. You are constantly trying to find out about other people's feelings and not really looking at yourself."

Another colleague added, "Isn't that what this patient is doing, also?"

Noting Don's expression, I asked, "What's happening with you right now?"

"I felt a little anxiety," he said. "Well," I suggested, "why don't you explore this anxiety, and find out where it is in your body?"

Don's defenses seemed more elastic and I now felt that he was uncomfortable enough to want something more from the presentation than simply filling up space. I decided therefore that we were
all ready to move to a new level of communication.

Don noted, "I feel it in my arms and trunk."
"Now see if you can imagine what's in your body," I offered.
Donald replied, "I see a tree trunk."
"Look a little closer," I said.
"I see swirling holes, like a vagina," he said.
"Why don't you tell me more about it?"
"Well," responded Don, "there's no person connected with it."
"Do you want anybody connected with it?" I asked.
"No. I'm beginning to feel some anxiety again, but I still don't
know what to do with this." The group remonstrated that every time
he got near to exploring the process, he wanted an answer.

Someone offered: "Isn't that exactly what this patient was doing—trying to find out what's next, rather than exploring?" Don
agreed.

I then decided to move the thrust of the discussion to a group
level. I asked the members for their reactions. Some felt far more
connected and saw Don as far more accessible than in the past.
There was also a good deal of admiration for his ability to dip into
his unconscious and explore this case in spite of his obvious discomfort. The material was fairly charged and I wasn't quite sure
how prepared Don was to explore these issues with any depth. I
suspected that the image of the tree with swirling holes like a vagina was referring to a very strong nurturing component associated with his identification as a therapist. Certainly this explains
his involvement in being a very supportive therapist, not only
with this case, but with a few others that he has presented in past
sessions. Did the holes have something to do with the feeling of
empty space that Don was trying to fill at the beginning of the session with his presentation? If so, perhaps the feminine nurturing
role was a response to compensate for some of his own deficien-
cies in this area.

Don returned to the image of the vagina. He saw himself touching it, but then it changed back into a tree, a warm, open, rich tree.
"But that's not the patient," he protested. "I think that's how I'm describing how *I* am, or how I would like to be." Then he added, "I see a

sexual issue in this case, and when I think of this woman sexually, I realize I'm constantly aware of her husband. I'm worried about seeing him as a rival, and I fear her playing the two of us off. I try to avoid this by trying to get her to understand him so that she will be more connected to him. I want the marriage to be solid. I can see the defensive quality in this and I guess I'm acting counter to where the transference is really going." He went on: "I can see how I'm sending a message, saying, 'Don't idealize me,' because I see her as being afraid." One of the members of the group piped up, "Who's afraid, she or you?" They laughed in unison.

> The group and Don are getting nearer to the heart of the countertransference issue. They offer both support and acceptance along with some very pointed interventions.

"Again, I don't know where to go with this," said Don. "I know I shouldn't be asking you the question—I'm really asking myself."

I attempted to get Don back into the process with, "Don't you see yourself as God in this room?" Everyone laughed, including Don.

"I can be God here," said Don, "because this group is strong, and everyone can take me."

> Again I saw the group impressed by Don's honesty and integrity. Here was the mix that all of us were struggling with in our feelings with Don. He was open, direct, and honest, as well as being provocative and arrogant. I also wondered to myself whether his arrogance was a subtle masochistic ploy to be attacked and punished by the group.

"Now, let's talk some more about your being God," I said. One of the members commented, looking at me, "I recall your supporting Don last session, but I see you, Don as being the only-child, who has trouble sharing his space with the group." Don retorted, "I think you have my dynamics wrong. I was raised by grandparents who unconsciously hated me. I was a scrounger to them. I fought them. I'm not a nice pussy-footing person; I create a lot of trouble!" We all laughed, for we recognized that Don was facing the heart of the struggle with his countertransference.

> Don was presenting the bad boy who needed punishment as a form of connection. No doubt, being the target of so much un-

conscious hate could create a form of reactive omnipotence serving as a substitute for an inner sense of male authority.

Once again, he didn't know where to go. I decided this time to bind the resistance and play along with his express wish for help.

I queried, "How does it feel to be God? What goes on inside of you? Look around the room."

"I can't get it out of my head," he said. "I keep on seeing her husband. He's not going to like this. He won't be sophisticated. She'll get anxious. The whole treatment is going to get screwed up. It's going to be too horrible for both of them."

One of the members went back to the case history: "The mother really did, in fact, keep the patient away from her father. Maybe you're worried that the same thing will happen here. Maybe both of you are anxious about this. You keep on talking about the mother and daughter, as if you are avoiding the triangular relationship."

"I think that's where she is," Don replied.

I then took Don back to the case. "Let's see," I said. "The husband is in the room and you're God. She doesn't want to look at you, does she, Don?" Don replied, "No, she's very frightened of seeing me as a sexual person. It's 'bad.' I guess we're in collusion. We're both worried about this . . . I've got to stop this. But how to do it?"

Don begs off being God, and now wants me to take over the role.

"Well," I retorted, "how do you?"

"I thought you were going to tell me!" he said.

One of the members threw in a suggestion. "Why not be a little more playful?"

Don replied, "I've got to get more data."

Another member now interceded. "You're really too protective. This woman talks about being crazy when she feels sexual impulses, but what does it really mean? I think you have to emphasize that feeling sexual is not feeling crazy—they're just powerful feelings for her to grapple with. Certainly, I'd be a little more playful and reassure her that sexuality and craziness are not the same."

I then decided to give Don a chance to take a little distance and be reflective. I felt he needed time to integrate this material.

"What are the diagnostic issues?" I asked. "Does she have the strength to look at these issues, or do we need to take a more supportive posture?" It didn't take long for the entire group, including Don, to agree that there were no indices of underlying psychosis. She was a *capable* woman, taking care of her husband's children as well as her own, caring for her farm, and working part-time. Her boundaries and ego seemed fairly strong. There were no current signs of acting out or breaks in reality-testing. Don mentioned that she took Valium every so often, and one of the members of the group replied, "So do I!"

"Well," I said, "We're pretty much agreed that she can take interpretation. How do we go about this? But first," I said, "How do you feel about competing with her husband, Don?"

"I'd win so easily, hands down," he said.

"Now you're talking," I said, with a grin.

Margy seemed very wide awake and was not intently following what was going on. "See what's happening, Don, Margy's not going to crash her car going home after all!" And then I added, "You really shouldn't be so frightened of your power. How does it feel to be the powerful person in the group?"

> I tried to offer Don a positive way of integratig his grandiosity so that it does not provoke punishment.

"What do you mean?" he said. Everyone gave a big laugh. "Well," he owned up, "I feel great." Once again, the group laughed.

"Do you think some of these feelings are dangerous?" I asked.

"No," he said, as he turned to Norma, who had remained quiet throughout the entire presentation. I asked if he had any thoughts or feelings about Norma, and Don said, "I'm aware that she seems hostile toward me."

"How *do* you feel?" I asked Norma.

She replied, "I feel distrustful of Don. I don't know when he is going to attack, or be warm. I don't like what he says."

> Norma takes on the suspicious, fearful, wary role that has been projected into the group by Don.

Don retorted, "It comes as no surprise to me. I knew it was something, and I'm both surprised and reassured, because really it reflects some more positive feelings underneath."

"Oh yeah," Norma shot back, "where do you get that?"

"At least you can go from one to the other," Don answered.

"Where do you hear that?" she asked. Don said, "Well, I thought you were kind of frightened of being angry at me."

"Perhaps," Norma countered, "*you* were frightened of being angry at *me*."

"Well," he said, "I thought you were feeling negative all along as an ongoing process in this group, and now feel that it's really more specific to what's going on here." Norma once again corrected Don and stated that her mistrust was a constant, ongoing thing. Again, the group laughed.

> In a group therapy format, we most likely would process this material more directly. In the present context, the dynamics between Norma and Don do not interfere with the supervisory process. If anything, she becomes the externalization of the competitive male who is overtly hostile and belligerent. Don now has an enemy in the room that is clear and comprehensible.

"Well, I always thought," he said, "that it could get worse." She responded that it certainly could.

Again, there was much giggling, and I wondered out loud what the anxiety was all about.

"Well, we all must be getting used to this," one of the members said.

I said, "You've got the person in the room who feels angry at you, now what are you going to do?"

> The drama of the case unfolds. The hostile competitive male authority is faced within a playful imaginative context.

Don then stated, "I don't have to be afraid of the husband, and I don't have to be afraid of talking about this case with Norma in the room."

A long pause ensued. I suggested doing some role-playing, with myself as therapist; Don, as patient. Don started assigning the Godlike image to me and requested reassurance.

"Can you tell me what is wrong with me?" he said, in his role as patient.

I said, "How do I know? I'm not God."

"But I *need* you," the patient/Don said.

I replied, "You're frightened of seeing me as God, that's why you are asking me for reassurance."

One of the members threw in, "Why not even say that you are the naked God?"

I said that I thought it might be better not to overwhelm this patient, but to go step by step. Then the patient/Don said, "I see you as God. I thought I was going to feel better, but I'm going to leave here today feeling even worse."

> Here we see how the patient controls the therapist through a masochistic ploy.

I told him, "That feeling bad is kind of easy, but I think down deeper there's a part of you that doesn't feel so awful about these feelings." We stopped the role-playing at this point.

"Well," Don said, "I thought you were enacting the transference."

> Don's notion of transference interpretation appears to deemphasize the playful bridge from the metaphorical to the linear mode of thinking.

"No," I said. "It was there all along. The real issue was how much you were prepared to play with the notion of being God. From there, I think you can go anywhere with her, but it's your own grandiosity that seems to be getting in the way, or rather your own guilt about it. Look what's happening here in the group. You provoke everybody to get angry at you. Are you trying to be the bad boy who everybody hates? What's behind all this?"

Don was very thoughtful at this point, and I knew that there was the beginning of a shift in his perception. At the same time, I suspected that this would be an ongoing process, and we would return to some of these issues in the near future.

> As supervision is an ongoing process, there is no need to pull all the emotional pieces together. For the time being, I felt that Don had digested a good deal of the material and required time on his own to do some further assimilation of the countertransference dynamics. In the meantime, I believe that there was considerable material for him to digest regarding the affective and cognitive areas of the case.

As the session drew to a close, I felt a growing sense of unity between Don and the members of the group. As the members walked out of my office, I listened to the sounds of laughter mixed in with sighs of relief. All of us felt less isolated and cut off from one another, particularly in our relationship to the presenter, as Don's provocative challenge was perceived and understood: Hear my wish for support and connection.

RECIPROCAL EXPLORATION

Let's step back now and observe the dynamics of balancing group learning within the context of investigating countertransference issues.

With the defensive posture of the presenter so evident, a deadlock through a combat/control dialogue became a very real possibility. Initially, the leader decided to sidestep Don's provocative hostility that was leaking out in all directions. Our focus was maintained on the case itself, and the subsequent group dynamics stimulated, framed, and organized the exploration of transference/countertransference material.

A pivotal point in the unfolding of countertransference material was initially precipitated by Don's irritation with Margy. In spite of her protest that her dozing off had nothing to do with the case presentation, both, at a preconscious level, heard the unconscious message: Don was taking too much distance in the presentation and most likely from his patient.

I took my cue from this interchange and broadened the interpersonal drama by calling Don's attention to Norma. I was aware of her hostile silence and suspected that the presenter was equally uncomfortable by a subliminal awareness of her presence. The ensuing dialogue was charged and negative; yet something inexplicable was released. The entire mood of the group became energized and alert. Perhaps Don's inner enemy now found an external figure to attend. Neither party was destroyed by the interchange; but I suspect that Don's underlying fear of punishment was somewhat lessened now that the enemy was in clear focus. Here, I worked on the assumption that Don's provocative behavior was basically *counterphobic* in nature: Attack before you are attacked.

The roles of Margy and Norma illustrate how different members of the group become external screens for the playing out of different facets of the case material. Margy was unwittingly carrying a message to Don: You are colluding with the patient and not moving into the heart of the therapeutic communication. On some level, Don equally knew this piece of information. Norma, on the other hand, would have none of Don's disarming overtures. She felt his hostility and responded accordingly. The group, at this point, shifted to a far more involved stance and the giggling subsided as the competitive tone moved into a central position for group discussion. Perhaps this encounter released to some extent the underlying competitive combative impulses of all the members.

The genesis of Don's vulnerability soon emerged. He was the target of a good deal of hostility from both parental surrogates: a fertile breeding ground for the development of a grandiose self. On an unconscious level, a child may well conclude that he deserves such a negative response from the world, since he is inherently bad and capable of heinous sins.

Don's presentation of this piece of personal history afforded the group a new opportunity to move into the family mythos. This challenge, then, slowly emerged in the group interaction as the group started to see through his provocativeness and recognize his need for support.

Much of Don's competitive challenge was most likely directed toward the leader. In response to this challenge, my interventions were basically good-humored rather than confrontational. I hoped I was still making my point that he was neither bad nor dangerous.

Let's now take a cursory look at the role of the presenter. In general, a group can easily overwhelm the presenter with interpretations, confrontations, and recommendations. It is the job of the leader constantly to protect the presenter from being bombarded. In Don's case, his defensive posture, marked by control, arrogance, and provocation, indicated that he needed both distance and protection, as well as some format to become more emotionally involved with the material. At times, therefore, he was given the opportunity to move into a more intellectual or didactic level. The experiential mode of working, however, was invaluable in helping him to drop some of his defenses and gain a more emotional assimilation of the material. The decision as to how and when to alternate to a more cognitive style is based on an assessment of the presenter's ability to tolerate stress and still maintain enough control to process the unfolding case material.

Thus, throughout the presentation, there was an attempt to help Don move into a playful position with his patient. The notion of "playful" has little to do with acting playful. If anything, playfulness can be a screen to act out the therapist's unconscious sadistic impulses towards the patient. By "playful," I refer to the shift into an imaginative, nonverbal mode of relatedness. The visual exploration of Don's body image, then, became a critical juncture in deepening his level of awareness of the countertransference involvement. Some very deep and profound material was stimulated by this exploration. The symbolic meaning of the holes in the tree was never fully elaborated and perhaps needed to be saved for his personal analysis.

Don clearly exhibited difficulties in maintaining an open stance to the flow of preconscious material. During the presentation, members constantly confronted his resistances that were manifested by his requests for direction, or premature end to the investigation. The callibration of different cognitive modes of thinking then becomes another function that can be carried out by the leader. In Don's case, he was much more at home with a linear form of thinking, but struggled with a good deal of courage and integrity in his shift to an image form of exploration.

Near the end of the presentation, Don found himself in the heart of the oedipal competitive battle. First with the group members, and finally with the patient's husband, we slowly entered dangerous territory. The fear of exploding the case through an investigation of erotic material came to the foreground. Here, on one level, the therapist saw himself as superior and more powerful as the patient's husband; but in the end feared that he would lose the case and upset the applecart by taking a more interpretive stance.

The message from the group to the presenter slowly crystallized. Accept your defense of playing God, but also take it with a grain of salt. Don't duck the interpretive mode of investigating the transference and face up to your unconscious fears of punishment as you become the container of an erotic transference. Herein lies another notion of container. The male authority accepts the erotic communications of his daughter without becoming unduly threatened or counterseductive.

Looking back at the session, a number of signals of countertransference involvement come to mind. All of us should be wary when we "decide" that there is no evidence of transference, or that it is unworkable. We can also suspect that countertransference anxiety is in operation when we are overly helpful or friendly to our patients. Other signals of countertransference involvement include such statements as that our hands are tied as therapists, referring to Sara's use of a religious barrier to avoid explorations; the use of support to reassure a patient when we have not investigated what we are supporting; or the need to "collect more data," which may well represent our reluctance to listen to our inner therapeutic voice.

Two weeks later, Don requested permission to take the tape home and proceeded also to read my comments regarding the material. He felt embarrassed and chagrined as he listened to the presentation, but he felt my comments were fair and to the point. This session became the impetus for a slow but perceptible shift in Don's relationship to both the group and the leader. In sessions to come, Don became far more comfortable and trusting of this process and truly became a member of the group. In many respects this session was a rite of passage.

Before concluding this chapter, a few key principles of countertransference investigation require elaboration: 1. Therapists tend to be overly sensitive to either the preoedipal or oedipal dynamics of their caseloads. An overemphasis of one area at the cost of another should be a signal of some type of countertransference involvement. Rarely are dynamics so neatly organized and reduced to such simple dimensions. 2. When there is a paucity of image or symbolic material in a case presentation, one can raise the possibility of collusion between the therapist and patient. In instances where there exists a high degree of patient defensiveness and, as a result, cut-off of the direct transmission of symbolic language, the therapist's inner psychic world becomes an important agent in the exploration of the patient's symbolic material. Defended patients transmit nonverbally their symbolic material and the therapist becomes a receptacle for this material which will in turn demand some type of inner exploration. The closing off of this area raises the possibility of countertransference resistance. 3. A good starting point for an investigation of countertransference problems can be the therapist's kinesthetic visceral response to the patient. In Don's presentation, visualizing his bodily response within the context of the presentation opened up new psychic territory.

Chapter 3

JULIE

Cast in the Role of the Healer

DEATH GUIDANCE

Among the joys, fears, wishes, sorrows, and conflicts of developmental crises that we as therapists share with our patients, facing untimely death can be one of the most excruciatingly difficult. In the presentation to follow, Julie, as therapist, goes through a second round of treatment with a patient in the throes of a life-and-death struggle with breast cancer. The helplessness and despair connected with death hangs over their sessions even as the patient affirms and fights for life.

SIMONTON: PROS AND CONS

Having been asked to read Simonton's book and incorporate his techniques in therapy, Julie is thrown into a crisis. On one level, she isn't at all sure she wants the burden of responsibility inherent in working with this patient; but also present is some degree of confusion over the role of healing in insight-oriented therapy. While she comes to recognize that there are therapists who, as "natural healers," transmit to their patients a climate that promotes a mending of the self, Julie is also well aware of the traps and pitfalls of such an orientation. Rescue fantasies, loss of boundaries between therapist and patient, underlying manipulation of power are but a few of the complications that can emerge. The following represents a very sensitive portrayal of this dilemma.

Julie hesitantly moved into the role of presenter. Originally from Australia, she spoke with a mild English accent. There was a power and force in her precisely articulated words but, at the same time, warm emotional tones filtered through her speech. She conveyed a presence and a sense of integrity in her manner that occasionally gave way to a little childlike giggle. Projected, then, was a woman who was both very mature, yet young inside.

"I guess I don't really want to present, but I have this case that's very much on my mind. I spent a good part of my supervisory session this morning speaking about this patient whom I have seen for three years. Actually, she stopped treatment two years ago and came back last week. She has breast cancer . . . I find it very hard, emotionally, to handle the situation.

"She did something very interesting. She heard about Simonton's book and talked about it. Then when she came to the session, she brought the book. It's about the whole imaging process and fighting the illness with imaging and a positive attitude. So, she brought the book with her, and said that was the way she would like to work if I would be willing to do it. She left the book with me, and I read it. It's very interesting. I felt a lot of fear as I read it, because it focuses on what people do emotionally to make themselves available to that disease in the first place. Apart from life circumstances, he cites things like divorce, middle age, and losses being significant in women prone to breast cancer. He believes that some personality types respond to loss in such a way that the body breaks down and develops cancer. So, the focus is upon what people do unconsciously to make themselves available to cancer. He also maintains that it also means you could make yourself unavailable to it and get rid of it by understanding what your mental attitude is and then fighting it. Well, I like the second part, but I don't like the first part."

> Julie rightfully was upset by the overinvestment in the power of the unconscious. This seems a rather peculiar statement in light of the particular orientation of this text. However, even the unconscious can be invested with an aura of tyranny and primitive magic that gives it awesome proportions.

Julie continued in a controlled voice, but the group sensed the fear behind her words. "There are a lot of possible losses, but this one is very high statistically. I think what is happening is that people are so afraid of cancer and know so little about it, that they are finding every possible avenue to fight it. The problem I have with the book is that if a person doesn't get well, the implication is that he or she failed *psychologically*."

I enthusiastically supported Julie's concern and criticism: "In the *New England Journal of Medicine*, a similar critical position was taken. The author discussed people feeling that they caused their disease and can cure it. The evidence for such a position is, to say the least, controversial.

> The investment of the healer with a magical power that can cure disease seems to lack any sense of humility and wisdom in terms of man's limitations to do anything and everything.

Julie, with a sigh of relief, responded, "Okay, it's interesting that you say that, because when I read the book, I remembered your reporting to us your work with imagery with a cancer patient. I thought that it fit in with Simonton's hypothesis, though I couldn't remember what else you said."

"My assumption is a fairly straightforward one," I said. "The more a person can employ his inner emotional resources as an adjunct to treatment, the better equipped he will be to utilize the available medical treatment. By no means am I stating that emotional problems bring on the disease. There may be some mild interrelationship between the two, but the disease is so multidetermined, including genetic and environmental influences. It is very destructive for patients to believe, 'My God, I caused the cancer. I must emotionally image the cancer out of existence to cure myself'."

Julie tried to be fair and evenhanded. "It's not that blatant."

"No, it's not," I agreed.

Julie went on, "They say if you handle stress in a certain way, you will be *prone* to having it go to your body."

I said rather pointedly, "That's exactly the controversial issue."

> Obviously not all tension becomes somaticized.

Julie went on, "Some people thrive on stress."

"So the thesis is too *simple*," I said.

Julie now spoke in elegant, measured tones. "It takes quite an effort to really feel that we can control this, too. I think it is a bit unrealistic and omnipotent. The danger lies not only in feeling at fault for falling ill in the first place, failure if the imaging does not work, but also denial of one's lack of control. I think it is important for people to accept that this happened, that they don't know why, and then they take some course of action. At the same time, they should be able to say, I can't control everything'."

> On a subliminal level, I felt Julie's need for support and continued along the same vein. I knew that a supportive atmosphere could only serve to open up the presenter in terms of further investigation.

"There is a whole movement going on in this area," I noted. "There is obviously some relationship between body and mind, but it's a big jump to go from an interrelationship between body and mind to direct *causality,* or one curing the other."

Julie continued, "I told my patient that I would be willing to work with her toward having a positive attitude in fighting it and also in getting better in touch with repressed feelings that might be inhibiting her sense of well-being, but I've stressed my concern about her blaming herself a couple of times."

George offered his support: "That also puts pressure on *you.*"

Julie went on, "It even says in the book that therapists ought to be aware that unless they have the most positive attitudes, they may not choose to work with the cancer patient. I immediately thought, 'Oh, good! I don't have to work with this patient!' And then I saw *that* as my negative impulse."

Mary sarcastically interjected: "Can you imagine thinking of a four-year-old kid magically thinking she has caused her mother's disease?"

"It's complex," I added, "because a positive attitude can be very useful in combating disease. We can even talk about a healing environment over and above the analytic structure. There are definitely some therapists who are 'healers'."

> I refer to a therapeutic attitude that implies a profound acceptance from one individual to another within the context of very clear therapeutic boundaries.

George posed the hypothesis: "Maybe one has to differentiate between healing and doing therapy."

I was somewhat perplexed. "I don't know if you can differentiate there. Do you have any ideas, George?"

"Well, there are people who have been in teatment two or three times. Maybe they didn't get the right emotional connection from the therapist."

I continued, "There's a whole bunch of research that indicates that the medical doctors' attitudes toward patients' illnesses will have an important prognostic influence on recovery rates. Even patients under anesthesia hear the doctors' comments during the operation and their recovery after surgery can be affected by these communications."

> The group then went off on a tangent, discussing research in this area, the concept of energy, and finally returned to the case presentation at hand. Many of us needed distance from this charged topic.

Julie continued in her measured, quiet voice: "There is a whole part in the book about patients hypnotizing themselves with step-by-step instructions through specific types of suggestions. Then there's a whole section about energy, with cancer cells depicted as weak and hopeless, and the white cells as very powerful. You're supposed to see a war and then draw them. I'm willing to do that. I have even made a tape for her that she's supposed to listen to every day. She said she finds that very helpful and likes the sound of my voice."

Don now attempted to bring some focus to the case discussion: "What it's like to have this patient back?"

"I Don't Need This"

Julie spoke in muted tones: "If she had come back with some other issue, that would have been fine, because she did really good work in three years and could have done some more. She's gone ahead in lots of ways! What's hard for me is that she got divorced because of therapy. At least, it certainly enabled her not to repress her feelings, to be more in touch with herself. I found myself saying 'What was my part in it? Did I fail her?' I found myself . . . only for a little bit . . . but doing that."

> The subtle countertransference dilemma occurs with any number
> of patients who return to treatment. Did we really help them, or
> was there some type of transference cure?

"I also felt the fury in her voice on the telephone answering tape that said the reason she wanted to come back was that she just wanted me to know that she had a lumpectomy and she wanted to work on her recovery. Then I walked around the house filled with rage myself. If she had come back for almost anything else, it would have been fine; it might have been exciting. I am better than I was then in my work. It felt unfair, like she spent three years really struggling with herself, did some neat work, and really coped with a lot of things . . . But I mean, what's 'fair'?"

Don looked confused and asked, "Fair to you or fair to her?"

Julie responded in an empathic, clear tone. "Not fair to *her*. I was angry for *her*. But in terms of myself, I thought, 'I don't need this in my life right now.' I haven't seen my current AIDS patient, and the other one dropped out, too. I really don't know what happened there. I thought, 'I don't need *this!*' and yet I also didn't feel I could refuse her."

> Julie starts to open up the areas associated with her countertrans-
> ference problems. Where does responsibility to her patient end
> and living out one's unconscious guilt begin? I suspect that more
> of this issue will come out as the case unfolds.

Julie continued to speak in a forthright manner: "I have problems with physical illness. You could bring me the muddiest person and I'm okay, but with someone who is physically ill, especially if there's the possibility of death, I feel helpless, hopeless, and . . . frightened. It frightens me. Breast cancer is even worse."

"Why?" someone asked.

Julie continued, lost in her own thoughts. "It's in her nodes as well."

"It's what?" a member asked.

"It's in the lymph nodes as well. She had the lumpectomy, and nine nodes are cancerous, so her chances are greatly reduced . . . it's already spread . . ."

Jim echoed Julie's hushed tone, "So, she's on chemotherapy."

Julie nodded and continued: "She started the chemotherapy Thursday. It's really astonishing. She has this really upbeat attitude about it, and she's not denying it. She was told that she would feel pretty sick, but all that happened was that the night after the treatment, she woke up in the middle of the night and vomited. Apart from that she feels okay. In fact, she's playing tennis on Saturday. She really didn't feel bad at all."

The group was listening very intently, faces taut and pained.

"She is devastated at the prospect of losing her hair. She's already ordered wigs. But that's the thing she can't cope with at all. So why . . ." Julie seemingly posed the question to herself, then continued, "Physical illness is hard for me, and death's not so neat for anyone. I mean, I think you can understand why I'm not so thrilled about that . . . But because it's breast cancer, because she is about my age, because she is divorced, it feels scary to me."

"But why is the divorce so central to you?" Ava asked.

Julie answered quickly: "Because you can't believe the statistics on this."

> I believe the entire group as well as the leader were in collusion with the presenter. Julie's recent divorce was an extremely painful experience. None of us wanted to get into this area, either consciously or unconsciously. Perhaps what is being raised here is that separation, even if it is for a very positive affirmative step, can be associated with punishment.

"Clinical studies state that some cancer patients have in their history an early loss followed by a later loss," Julie went on. She added, "Her mother died when she was eight."

Ava tried to console Julie. "Maybe the divorce was something good and positive for your patient. Maybe it *wasn't* a loss."

I offered a bit more information: "Usually this type of patient has had a lot of early deprivation and loss. Finally they've made a very important reparative connection with a significant figure, or even activity, and when that connection dissolves, it's a loss that shocks the whole system."

"Well, that fits her," Julie said, "even though the divorce was positive."

Mary pointed out: "*You're* the reparative connection and she's come back to you."

Julie asked, looking tormented: "She wants to *beat* this, and I'm supposed to *help* her beat it . . . but what if she doesn't . . ."

Mary wouldn't let her finish the sentence. "Chemotherapy is

wonderful, does wonderful things. I have a friend who just had some radio implants."

Julie was not sidetracked. "Her chances aren't very good statistically because of the spread."

Jim took the discussion to safer grounds, "The statistics reflect no advancement in chemotherapy in twelve years. The drugs make you a little less sick now, they are a little more selective, but the survival rate depends more upon the initial spread than the impact of the drugs themselves. And if there has been a spread from the primary site before it was detected . . . that's probably why they did a mastectomy."

"No, she *chose* the lumpectomy." Julie took a deep breath and plunged into the emotional material. "Eight years ago my best friend died of liver cancer. Her first cancer was in her colon. She had surgery and survived it. Then she had some chemotherapy, but obviously it had already spread and they did not know . . . Six months later they discovered the liver cancer . . . she didn't even feel sick. When she had had chemotherapy she became so sick . . . I've never seen anyone so sick in my life . . ."

Jim broke in with more objective clinical information. "Breast cancer has a better cure rate. I know five women right now who have breast cancer. It's the most amazing thing, it's all around us. The woman across the street got breast cancer. I often talk to her, and she says she was a high-risk candidate to begin with, ovarian cysts and miscarriages, then they discovered cancer. She's had chemo. It's a year and a half since her symptoms reerupted. Then about six months ago her younger sister got breast cancer. It's that kind of family. This woman/neighbor is a very nice woman, but she is the kind of woman who seems to take out her anger on herself, and if there is any type who does have a readiness for cancer, she would."

> Jim brings in research information regarding cancer. The line of emotional inquiry gets abruptly interrupted. I wondered to myself why this was happening, as this was very unlike his posture in past group sessions.

Jim continues, "Anyway, then the woman next door to us, her mother got breast cancer, and when she went and got an exam, she had a lump she had to have looked at. I don't know the results yet, she just had this done about three days ago. It's like, all around us, there's all that breast cancer. These three women are very restricted, tight, a lot of anger is not discharged . . ."

George added: "You will find that cancer patients are usually nice people."

Julie spoke quickly: "That's what this book said . . ."

Mary took sharp exception to the general tone of the discussion. "When I think of the people I have known in my life who have had cancer, they all have totally different kinds of personalities."

> I believed we had enough distance from the material and were ready to go back to the emotional context of the presentation.

"In any event," I said, trying to get us back on track, "I think it's important to have the frame of mind that we're not going to cure our patients and that our patients haven't created their problems, even if there is some interrelationship. You want to give your patient the best fighting chance to use all her resources."

Don added: "This patient wants that clearly. She wants therapy and is pursuing medical treatment as well."

Julie's voice went up an octave. "As a matter of fact, I've only seen her three or four times. It's fascinating how quickly she's picking things up, getting insights, and wanting to work on them. Of course, it's all based on the foundation that we had before. You know, it's a weird experience when a patient comes back. It's like you have them on a computer, and once they start talking, all the stuff comes back. It's really strange. Some exciting things are happening already, and that's nice. I think what's happening, though, is that in order for me do that, I'm paying some kind of hidden price.

"The first day she came, when I saw her and then read the material, I felt *so depressed,* very depressed and anxious. By the time I saw her again, I felt pretty good and I was sort of going along punching with her." Julie's voice dropped. "I'm still feeling that way when I'm with her, but when I'm not with her, it doesn't last . . ."

Risa, who has been very quiet, empathized in a very low voice. And you're worried that you will lose some of this spark when she gets sick with chemotherapy. At this point maybe she'll miss a session and won't quite function so well."

> Observing a patient literally deteriorate before your eyes creates an enormous sense of unconscious guilt within the therapist. We often feel that we are not doing enough, and become increasingly obsessed with our own helplessness, as we face the inevitability of death with our patients.

Julie mustered up her gutsy Australian self and responded: "I haven't visualized it too much. I try not to think too much about what is going to happen. I know I don't want to watch her die. I know I'm not ready for that, that's what happens."

Ava asked: "Do you feel you have to work extra hard?"

"Yes," Julie replied, "because I have to fight myself at the same time."

George asked for clarification. "Is it to keep her alive, in some sense?"

Julie struggled to find the truth. "I think that if she had not come in with this book, I wouldn't have felt so much. I think that book may have thrown me a little bit." Julie's mind seemed to wander and she said, "The first time she burst into tears, I didn't know how I was going to hold it."

"Your tears?" George asked.

"Yes . . . I did it, but . . ."

Ava asked in a high-pitched voice: "Do you think there's a potential loss for you or her?"

Julie shrugged her shoulders: "Not really, because she has essentially been gone out of my life."

Reiko cautiously raised her point: "I guess that's what I'm having trouble with."

"What?" Julie asked.

"That you're so close to her still."

Julie hesitated. "I don't know if it's that . . ."

"Well, that's what I'm saying. What was she for you originally?"

Julie pondered. "I think I did good work then. She became very alive after she left therapy. She had some relationships, she became sexually free, she got *alive* . . ." Her voice rose. "And *that* really sucks!" After a long pause, Julie went on. "She joined a study at the Pittsburgh University where there are three groups of women. Her cancer is estrogen-dependent. In that way, that's very positive because they can give her drugs to suppress the hormone, so the cancer won't get fed. That's very positive, but she got assigned to the heavy chemotherapy section. She says that she wishes that she had been in hormone therapy only . . . I would too . . . but really, I have a lot of powerful issues with this disease myself, so . . ."

As painful as it is for all of us, we have to get down to the emotional material.

"What are they?" I asked in a low, flat voice.

"What are they?" Julie echoed back. "Well, my father died of it
. . . He got sick and died after I left Australia." Julie continued to talk
with her voice choked up. Her words came out in short, tight spurts.
"And my mother told me . . . that I broke his heart by coming to
America . . . Okay, that's all stupid and irrational, but I somehow
think that I will die from it because I might have an identification with
him . . . and it's really weird, I don't know if this is just coincidence,
but I have had cystic breasts all my life with no particular problems.
In menopause, they very gradually subsided. In the last two weeks,
they've become all cystic again . . . I don't know if it's just part of the
menopausal cycle, or if there's a weird type of identification going on
with my patients . . . I'm on top of it all in my analysis, I've been talking about it, but that doesn't make it go away . . . So, I guess in a way I
don't even want to have anything to do with her. I want to save her, I
want to protect myself."

> We are getting nearer the core of the countertransference prob-
> lem. In the work with any given patient, I believe there is always
> some form of an identification process going on. How to be sepa-
> rate and yet empathically related becomes a very formidable task,
> particularly when a patient is dying.

"It's really weird because I am going away tomorrow. I'm going
to Sydney. I feel a bit guilty going away this time because of her. I realize the guilt's on two levels. On one, it's because I'm not supposed to
leave, because of what happened to my father, but I also identify with
the person who is left behind because of my own problem. When I
was small, my mother abandoned me so much that I identified with
both the "leaver" and the "leavee . . ." It's very loaded for me to go
away . . . Every time I go away, I get so depressed before I go, I get so
upset. Once I'm on the plane, it's fine, I don't ruin things, but I remember my son . . ."

> We see a very specific connection between autonomous moves
> that invariably promote separation and individuation, and fears
> of punishment that are associated with induced feelings of guilt
> and omnipotence.

Ava asked in a gentle soothing voice, "What about your son?"
Julie continued with obvious difficulty: "Well, once when I went

away, my son got into absolutely nightmare messes. Things were very bad. I felt something was wrong when I was away, and I called . . . that's very strange. I'm entitled to go away, and I want to go away, but I guess that's why it's so loaded."

"I don't think, though, that it's that strange, being a woman of my age in my situation, to have a hard time dealing with another woman with breast cancer. I don't see my breasts as just another part of my body. They are especially symbolic to me. I think most women feel that way. There may be some women who are lucky enough to think a breast is just a part of their body, no different than any other, so what's the big deal? But I am not one of them . . ." Julie's voice trailed off.

> Julie fears that she will be punished for deserting her first love: her father. But on a deeper level, the real punishment relates to the mother, for her job in life is to be supportive and caring to the child in her mother.

A long pause followed. Finally, feeling Julie pressed by the enormity of her case, I said, "You don't have to carry the burden all by yourself."

Julie flashed back, "I don't intend to!"

In spite of this, Risa inquired: "Art, who are you refering to when you say there are other professionals who can help?"

I proceeded to clarify my point. "Find out the kind of support your patients can utilize, what makes sense for them. With a particular patient I was working with, I did use some of the Simonton techniques. The cancer had spread from the primary base, and she needed all kinds of support other than what I offered. She attended a cancer support group, worked with different types of healers, and was fortunate to receive a lot of help from her family. It was a wrenching experience for all parties.

"It's difficult to watch somebody undergo chemical treatment because of what happens after each battle of chemical treatment: Their resistance is lowered. You can become identified with this. I, too, had a father who died of cancer, and a grandfather who died of cancer, and an uncle, who was my teacher, who also died of cancer. The battles and the emotional identifications are very painful . . . especially grappling with your rescue fantasies . . ."

"I know," Julie mumbled. "If only she weren't alone, too," she plaintively added.

"In spite of everything," I said, "in terms of why somebody undergoes treatment, my patient wanted very much to live, and yet, both of us had to face the inevitability of death."

Jeff broke in: What I want to say is that she doesn't have to be alone, because there *are* a lot of support systems."

"But there's something different about being married or just living with someone," said Julie.

> I believe that Julie is referring to the price associated with independence and autonomy. Can her patient receive the support she needs in spite of the fact that she's divorced and living alone? Is Julie referring to her own dilemma as well?

I added: "Sisters, brothers, relatives, friends, all fill this vacuum."

Julie now spoke somberly: "It's interesting. In some of the papers I've read, it says that it's very important to foster the cathecting of objects, old and new, on the patient's part. She is doing that all over the place. In fact, tonight a man is coming to see her with whom she had an affair all summer. She is wildly anxious about him, but she is going ahead anyway."

I continued on this somber note: "Patients who work within this kind of situation need a part of you to reach out to them, but at the same time you must maintain your boundaries."

Julie, now more composed, went on. "It's interesting, one of the strongest features in her work is her hungry eyes. Now she's really lost that look in her eyes. It's not back yet, but I picture that coming back, that very alarming kind of look. People have problems with it; her family, her sister, and her friends, because when she looks at you, you feel like saying, 'What do you want?' You know, she actually has people say that to her. I was very gradually able to tolerate that look, but I guess I don't want to see it again for physical reasons rather than just some intrapsychic stuff. It was intolerable then . . ."

"What does it mean, those eyes?" I asked, with interest.

Julie responded quickly: "Well, at first it was sort of draining, exhausting, and then gradually, it became almost annoying because I couldn't fill the well up. It didn't matter what I did. She used to cry all the time . . . It was almost how she communicated . . . then she stopped doing that. I guess after being irritated, I took a much more direct approach instead of being afraid of it. It's haunted me."

> We see the connection between the patient and Julie's mother. Was there a parallel between Julie's mother and the patient?

"It haunted you?" Jim asked, with a question in his voice.

"Yeah."

Jim, ignoring Julie's comments that the hungry eyes were present before the cancer offered more information: "I used to do cancer research years ago," [referring to his clinical internship] "and that haunted look is very much a part of the battle with cancer. People look haunted, it's like seeing a ghost. I could imagine that the treatment is even haunting, it's so intrusive, puncturing. I used to see patients on all floors of the hospital. Some had made peace with it as part of the process . . . I don't know how I would describe it; it's like a malevolent presence."

Julie added in confirmation: "Look at the AIDS victims. You see them walking around the city and can spot them right away by the way they look."

Jim's voice softened: "I imagine that whatever feeling of wellness your patient has, whatever internalization of you that she has, may become depleted very quickly, even if she defeats this. I remember my own reaction in dealing with a tumor that we brought to the lab to study. Until we got to the point where people made jokes, nobody wanted to look at it, and the tumor wasn't catching."

I was aware that some closure was needed, so, with some reluctance, I started to move into an intellectual area. "What you want to do with cancer patients is to get them to work on and into their bodies. Often, they can be very resistant and many prefer the pain of the illness rather than the psychic pain. One of my cancer patients who is now with me in his sixth year, walks into my office and calls it the "Gloom Room." As soon as he sits down, he starts to cry, but it has taken us a long time to get to that level. The nearer you can get your patients to the use of symbols and images, the more they can master the pain.

"Sometimes, I invite patients to draw their cancers. I ask them to depict what their cancers look like, what the medicines are like, how the medicines are applied to their bodies, etcetera. Many patients don't think in image symbols or form, but want factual practical solutions. Here, we can see how inner processing of material is just too threatening."

These exercises are offered within the following therapeutic context: I take the position of viewing the cancer and the body organs *as if* they symbolized various inner representational forms of the patient's life.

Julie broke in, having followed the discussion with a look of taut-
ness: "How is the ability to image connected with the suppression of
feelings and verbalizing affective states? That's what my patient cuts
out, the anger . . ."

I considered a moment, then responded: "The two work together. The image form usually contains representations of important people. The feelings about these people have been buried
in bodily form. We find enormous hate as well as love. Also fear of de-
stroying the love object. The "object" in the body therefore becomes
the prisoner and we can either kill it or find some means to make
peace or reparation with it."

A New Therapeutic Alliance

The group walked out with somber expressions on their faces,
talking quietly to one another. Julie called me the next day, ostensibly
to thank me for the presentation. She felt much more "up," she said,
abler to face whatever was coming down the pike. Then, in a somber,
tight voice, she commented that when she returned home, she found
her cat ill, lying on the sofa. The vet reported that her cat had cancer.
With the ordeal of the presentation behind her, she felt far better prepared to deal with the impending loss of her cat. Most importantly,
she felt stronger in facing whatever fate had in store for her patient.

We observe from the presentation that Julie's history interfaced
with the patient's problem. Separation and death were very much associated with one another. Leaving always hurts the people who are
left behind, and Julie's sense of obligation and responsibility weighed
heavily on her conscience. Her job in life was one of mothering her
mother. On a countertransference level, this very same issue was
raised by a dying patient. Julie wanted no part in rescuing her patient, as she suspected that she was very vulnerable to feelings of guilt
in this area. When we are faced with the possibility of death with our
patients, and there are similarities in background, a countertransference identification is an inevitable outcome.

The patient's hungry eyes haunt Julie and remind her that she is
there to fill in the patient's emptiness. Julie does not want to comply
with this deathlike hungry plea, but her identification with her own
hunger makes the struggle a particularly difficult one. Often, we, as
therapists, are all too aware of these empty pools of loneliness within
our patients' lives. Yet we cannot comply with this covert call to fill

their emptiness. For our job is one of retrieving a patient's lost sense of *self*, which may, in time, be regained, but only through a good deal of work that will invariably be accompanied by rage, hurt, and depression.

During the presentation, we clarified the healing approach and emphasized the positive, constructive side of such a method. We came to the conclusion that we want to give the patient every possible chance to utilize his or her emotional resources in fighting a disease, including viewing the physical illness "as if" there is an emotional causality that is connected with it. We can then give symbol and form to the respresentation of the cancer, the medicine, and the hidden objects associated with the cancer. We want to look at the hate and love that are associated with these objects, so that the patient can focus as much energy as possible *outwards*, rather than trap it inside the body. Through such an approach, we give the patient every chance to utilize constructive forces inside and become an ally of the medical doctor.

In spite of our therapeutic efforts, we must also face, with our patients, the inevitability of death. We can work with them to address their rage, despair, helplessness, resignation, and such issues as the meaning of life. Their helplessness often taps into our own rescue fantasies that invariably interfere with our ability to hear our patients going through the various stages of preparing themselves for death.

The group attempted to give as much support as possible to Julie by neutralizing some of her overwhelming sense of responsibility and guilt. A soft, empathic tone filtered into the group process. Inside all of us there was a need to cull nurturance and support from one another as we all took a secret glimpse of our own frailty and the inevitability of death. All of us project our own particular fears and conflicts onto a patient's struggle with life and death. Though not explicitly stated, Julie's concern about her patient's recent divorce may well touch upon some of her own issues. This area was never directly handled either by the group or the leader.

I suspect that there was considerable countertransference identification with the presenter by all parties concerned. The leader had lost both his father and uncle through cancer. The moving back and forth into cognitive areas, rather than staying on the highly emotional charged area was undoubtedly connected to these issues. Nevertheless, we were able to move in to some very important dynamics regarding countertransference issues. Julie was able to explore her fears of becoming autonomous and leaving the past behind. There was a seriousness and somberness that characterized the group as we observed Julie's conflicts in dealing with her cancer patient. She knew for herself that breast cancer strikes at a very vulnerable part of a woman's sense of identity. We all came away with the hope that the sharing with one another of the love, hate, fear, and revulsion associated in working with cancer patients would help us face these feelings and expand our ability to tolerate some of the conflicts that cancer engenders. Herein lies the hope that we, as therapists, can develop the strength to work with our patients in facing these problems.

Major countertransference issues that are dealt with in this poignant presentation are:

1. Modified analytic work can go on with patients who have major illnesses; but the material must be viewed within the context of their illness. The therapist's fear of contamination and/or identification can create any number of defensive maneuvers, producing a lack of emotional resonance.

2. In contrast to the above, we may fear the omnipotent magical role that can be cast upon us by a patient in a crisis state. Defensively, we can either play out the role or ultimately master the anxiety that is associated with feelings of magic and power.

3. Fears of death are often associated with an objectless state of existence. This dread can create again a defensive countertransferential reaction that has a most primitive hold on both parties.

4. Because of our patients' very real need for outside help, as well as their emotional vulnerability, we may, as therapists, shy away from conflicts that create too much anxiety. Paradoxically, the opening up of difficult issues may at times strengthen the patient's ego to face and combat illness.

5. Because of the emergent nature of a life-threatening illness, the analyst may at times step out of a more traditional role. Fears of losing an analytic perspective may interfere with one's ability to offer emotional support of a nonanalytic nature. The decision as to where the line can be drawn between concrete help and the analytic discipline is full of shadows and emotional states of subjectivity. In the end, we, as therapists, must make our own individual decisions as to how we can be most available to our patients.

One final tragic note: Throughout the presentation, Jim constantly refers to cancer living around him. Three months after this presentation, he reports that his wife has terminal cancer. With despair and sadness he wonders if somewhere at the edge of consciousness he knew that his wife was already ill.

Though Jim's patients have yet to be informed of his personal tragedy, their recurrent dreams of people dying of cancer indicate that we hold no secrets from those with whom we have such an intimate relationship. Yet none question, as they do not wish to intrude. He rarely attends group sessions. Nevertheless his presence is felt. The members offer help in any way they know how. They exchange any new word. But most of the exchanges are wordless.

I cannot call this group "The Gang" anymore. They are closer than ever, but it is a tacit kind of closeness. Their presentations often take on a very heavy quality. Occasionally one breaks down in tears, though the work seems to have very little to do with Jim. Yet, the themes of the presentations have much to do with pain and depression, and have an uncanny effect on the themes of the group. Jim must deal with his personal life along with transference/countertransference problems that invariably arise within the reality context of his work. The therapists in this group now often walk out with heads bowed, as if to the frailty of human existence.

In spite of our pain and despair, the group members and leader continue to work. None of us want to be swept away by our sadness, yet there is guilt about going on and presenting cases. The spirit of the group collective is all around us, as each one of us now struggles to regain separateness.

Chapter 4

GEORGE

Homosexual Anxiety

CREATING THE "HOLDING ENVIRONMENT"

We all know, as therapists, how important attending to our countertransference and induced feelings can be in creating an appropriate holding environment for or responding to our patients. The group session discussed in the first part of this chapter is an excellent example both of what happens when these valuable clues are not heard and how group members can play out the various facets of a patient's underlying fears using their own characteristic defenses. Even the supervisor becomes embroiled in his own countertransference issues, and here wanders off the mark with his supervisees.

There are many signs that something is amiss in the group dialogue. At the end of the session the material appears to be without any true cohesion, and one easily discerns a good deal of defensiveness on the part of the leader as well as some dramatic acting out by the members of the group. Fortunately, the presenter recognizes that something is missing after the first presentation and brings the material back for a second review.

The initial supervisory session presents a number of formidable obstacles for the group. George tends to become intellectualized and controlled, draining the life and energy out of the case presentation. Consequently, the verbal dialogue does not flow and, in fact, becomes punctuated by tight questions and answers from members to presenter.

Supervising an obsessional therapist can present special problems in overcoming these barriers to effective communication. First, there is a tendency to become bored, or equally intellectualized in response to the flatness of the presentation. Secondly, as a response to lack of affect, the supervisor can equally fall into the trap of being provocative in order to evoke an emotional reaction from his supervisee. This type of interaction can easily reduce itself to a power/control battle where both parties become enmeshed in a resistance to learning. In the past, the supervisor and the group members have been caught up with these issues when George presents.

A few comments about the initial supervisory session: Shirley presents a dream that sets the stage for the case presentation. As is so often the case, a seemingly unrelated piece of information shaped the group interaction. Shirley's dream became the group dream, although we formally spent very little time in attending to the material. Through the metaphor of the dream, Shirley voiced her wish to become an authority in her own right. In the course of the session we allowed her to become an authority, of sorts, on Joe, the presenter's patient. In the past, Shirley had shared her problems with her own father, a high school principal, whom she experienced as pedantic and rigid in his relationship with her. In the dream, Shirley wanted the job of principal, but found that she didn't have the qualifications. Though I was aware of the unconscious message to me, I completely disconnected from this material as the group evolved within George's presentation.

George felt cut off by his patient, yet even as he lamented his sense of isolation and perplexity, his own overpreparation sapped the juice and life from his material, leaving the group disconnected. After George had droned on for a short while, Shirley moved in, as she had in other sessions, and wondered out loud if George needed a father to help him out. The unconscious message that all of us picked up was quite clear. If you can't get it up, perhaps you need help. George, in turn, felt attacked and responded to her with a benign, patronizing attitude. Shirley contained herself for a while, but in the middle of the session got up to leave for the ladies' room. Later on in the presentation, she shared her identification with the patient and complained of feeling wounded, bleeding, and unrecognized. George, meanwhile, felt equally unrecognized by the patient. Having each felt like a nonexistent entity, Shirley, George, and the patient seemed to be interchanging projective identifications.

In this session, Shirley found the blurred boundaries particularly difficult as she experienced an inner press to work though some personal material with George. I found myself irritated with her demand and, in spite of myself, responded to her with a somewhat attacking, judgmental stance. I pointed out how, to George, she too was "attacking," and was partially responsible for his response. I even referred her to the tape and only belatedly realized that something was amiss in my countertransference attitude to Shirley. On a deeper level, I suspected that my sense of maleness was being threatened. Only at a later point during the next session did these issues become further clarified.

In retrospect, the telltale signs of countertransference were reeking throughout the group process. My rather passive attitude toward the competitive stances of the two male members of the group was undoubtedly covering some part of my own castration anxiety. I opted to let the group go its way rather than integrate the opposing treatment approaches of mirroring versus confrontation. By allowing the splitting to remain unanalyzed, the group's progress was temporarily halted in further understanding the dynamics of the case. The fact that no one picked up on George's initial comment, "I cannot penetrate this case," was, in and of itself, suggestive. Was there some homosexual anxiety being stimulated in the presenter and acted out by the leader? I knew that I had breached an axiom of case supervision by not paying enough attention to the initial comments of the supervisee in case discussion.

I found myself trying to summarize the presentation when, in fact, no real closure was evident. Again, I was artificially attempting to play out the role of supervisor without getting to the deeper layers of material in evidence. To be sure, some of the issues I summarized had germs of truth; however, the lack of real cohesion in the group process was an indication that none of us were really getting to the heart of the problem. I suspect that my identification with the presenter and the wish to be the "nice guy" leader ultimately had its roots in latent homosexual issues. As it turned out, all was not lost. The presenter returned to the group with a strong desire to discuss the material further.

THE CASE OF "ARCADE JOE"

Let us turn, now, to the second supervisory session. The group came in together 10 minutes late. I complained that I was being deserted and wondered why. I suspected that it related to some underlying discontent with the previous session. Nevertheless, I was summarily passed over and told that lunch took longer than expected. I decided not to explore this resistance, but to wait and see what would follow. George then spoke. "I don't think we really talked about all the different aspects of this case. The first time I presented Joe, I said he was acting out his oedipal problem, and last week I talked a little about narcissistic injury, but something is missing from the picture.

"As you recall, he was born in the South; he moved every two years. His father was a minister; his mother, a teacher who sent to school and worked. One of the things Joe kept asking for was continuity. Remember, I mentioned the business about his distress at my vacations. He didn't say anything about missing *me*, just the session. *That* was important to him. This most recent vacation, two things happened. First he came in and said he wanted to take the whole month off, from Thanksgiving to Christmas, to save money, and then the week before I left for vacation he didn't come at all. He simply said he couldn't make it, he had to go to work."

> The material was presented in a rather flat monotone. I wanted to bring life into the presentation and waited for the opportunity to find some opening to bring drama into the material.

George continued, "Something else that strikes me is that he has no friends; he's really quite isolated. Once in a while he'll go to Forty-Second Street. Usually he goes to the peep shows or talks to women across the window or whatever. His other form of socialization is to hang out in this bar near work, though it's lonely, very isolated. He's talked about playing some kind of spider game where you shoot down whatever."

A member broke in to ask, "You mean on the machine?"

"Yes. He'll go there during work. He'll take a long lunch hour, or after work, he'll stay there instead of going home. He just hangs out." George turned to Jim to say, "You look puzzled."

Jim responded, "I'm not sure why you're presenting. I heard what you said about thinking Joe's not oedipal, but narcissistic. I never thought he was oedipal, so I'm curious what you felt you missed."

"Well, what I felt I didn't present was this material about his going to the bar and Forty-Second Street."

"Not so," I responded, "but maybe we weren't helpful to you last time."

George doggedly went on. "I want to understand something about his behavior and his acting out."

> I was aware that George was sidestepping any direct confrontation with his dissatisfaction regarding last week's presentation. I knew that the time was near to bring drama and aliveness to the group. I was also aware that Shirley was still angry from last week and needed some vehicle to express her feelings. I decided, therefore, to return to some of the loose ends of last week's presentation by bringing Shirley immediately into the picture.

"So why don't you ask Shirley?" I responded.

"Yeah, I'll tell you how it feels to be that guy," Shirley quickly responded.

In a somewhat sarcastic tone, George said, "Okay, Shirley, you're going to be helpful this time?"

"Shirley, give it to him!" I encouraged her, but then George apologized before Shirley could respond.

"I meant to be helpful the first time. It's unfortunate that a couple of men need to see me as attacking. That isn't the way that I intended to be." At this there was a good deal of laughter in the room. Don grinned and pointed his finger at me as one of the attackers.

Shirley went on. "Let me tell you what happened. I felt like I was doing my own psychodrama experience as I was sitting out there. I felt like I was living through an episode of Twilight Zone; that I really was experiencing what it felt like to be this patient, Joe. It was the weirdest experience I've ever had. When Art asked what I wanted from the group I was too confused to really know, but I thought about it when I went home. I wasn't focused on myself, I was thinking about your patient. When you started out presenting, you said you were presenting this man who couldn't verbalize what he felt and acted out a lot. As things started to progress in the group, I started to feel a lot of the pain, with no way to communicate it. I was feeling powerless and in increasing pain, and the more I tried to communicate, the more I was misunderstood. My pain and sense of loss were misunderstood as anger, and the harder I tried to be heard, the more I was put down and misunderstood. It was a no-win situation."

> Shirley presents herself as being misunderstood, and in pain. I heard the unconscious message that we were to feel guilt ridden and punished for our behavior. I knew that a masochistic defense

was in operation and was most likely covering over some of her own competitive drives. Yet it didn't seem quite appropriate to go into this issue, for it would only serve to interfere with the flow of case material.

"I started to feel like I needed to get out, and then I started having those images of this guy being attacked: There was blood dripping, and no one could even see that the guy was in pain. I kept thinking that if my coat was available, I would get up and go home. I have never felt so terribly trapped and hopeless in my life. The best I could do was to escape and act out by going to the ladies' room. I hoped that people would hear what I had to say. I kept thinking this is the way to act out, to act like Joe."

I became further aware of Shirley's exhibitionistic use of pain. What part of the case material was Shirley living out? Was she expressing the underlying masochistic core of this patient?

"So the point is, I wonder if you're not relating to the feelings that this man is having, but then not responding on a feeling level. You're saying that he's narcissistically wounded, but you are not hearing him. Here's a man who's feeling powerless and in as much pain as I was feeling last week. I can understand why you want to distance yourself and not be in touch with him; it hurts like hell."

If essentially we were observing someone who was narcissistically wounded, I suspect that the more typical reaction would be one of withdrawal. Here the feeling of being wounded is in the service of power and control.

A member retorts, "I think I'd respond to hurt and pain, but somehow I didn't feel like that towards you. I usually *would* respond to somebody who was very sad. I'd want to address that, but I didn't feel it."

The members also don't buy Shirley's use of pain and are aware that it can be used as a distraction to avoid competitive and power motives.

"Well, I did want to talk about what was going on in me," Shirley said. "This is a man who does not have the means to communicate his feelings; that's why he acts out. I felt that pain, and it was the worst pain I've felt in my life, but I had no way to communicate it. I kept wondering what it all had to do with this case. All I wanted to say, when I kept on breaking in, was that I wanted to bring it up to see if it would be of any help . . . It was so hard to describe what it felt like to be a nonentity, and the more upset I got, the more I wanted to break in and say something about that, but there was no way in. Then it struck me that we were doing the same thing in this group: We had recreated *Joe's* experience in a session."

"You mean *you* felt like a nonentity?" I asked Shirley.

"I felt like I was in a psychodrama with the man. I was the patient. I could have been doing this whole number, for whatever it's worth. George, you come in here saying you're missing something. Well, I think Joe's really wounded. Obviously he counts on you. It matters to him when you're there, and he has no power to influence whether you come or go. He doesn't have a way to communicate how important you are."

> Obviously Shirley has a very effective mechanism in attempting to influence the group. This is equally true of the patient, but is demonstrated through a much subtler mechanism of cold, guarded impenetrability.

George looked thoughtful as he said, "I guess I do see him as a nonentity, with his mother giving birth to his brother about eleven months after Joe was born. Once a woman is pregnant, she often turns inward to concentrate on her own body. That really is a kind of abandonment."

Jim now added, "But what happened with Shirley did not provoke understanding or empathy, but a sadistic verbal attack, so I think it's more than just a narcissistic wound. This guy, as he was played out here, provoked sadism."

> Jim moves in to another aspect of masochistic behavior. He is absolutely correct in his observation that she provokes sadism rather than empathy. Here the provocation becomes one of control and power through guilt.

Shirley now responded, "Yes, but I remember some other incident in the group, where there was an amazing dichotomy between what one person was experiencing inside and what the rest of us were seeing outside. There was an enormous gulf . . ."

George broke in: "Okay, relating to this patient, I said to him last week, 'You're really cool and distant. That might be a part of you, but there is this other part of you which enjoys the closeness, really wants to be at home with your wife.' He's talked about their good times together when they were just cuddling. He calls it the spoon or fork, whatever, at night—a way of holding, a way of sleeping close. There are these two parts of him: the cold, aloof part, and the other side he wants or needs a great deal of. I said this to him and he said, 'Well, no one ever sees me like that.'"

> We are beginning to see a clue to some of the dynamics of the case. What does it mean that he is warm and dependent with his wife, while being cold and aloof with his therapist?

A group member asked, "Is he ashamed of it?"

"Very ashamed, very frightened of it."

The member went on: "It could have to do with the big discrepancy between the way his mother used to see him as a miniature adult while he felt like a baby inside."

George commented: "It's pretty strange the way he responds when I say something to him. In the last session when he talked about moving around and changing jobs, and feeling indifferent, I brought it back to him, saying, 'It seems that's the way you feel here.' He said he felt indifferent and it was just like his work or any job he'd had; after a while he'd feel indifferent. Again I tried to make some connections for him and said: 'That's what happened when your mother was pregnant. She was indifferent to how you felt.'"

A member interjected here, "I don't think he was indifferent, but enraged, at how his mother felt indifferent to him."

I decided at this point to bring it back to the here and now by addressing myself to George: "Can you picture what Shirley was feeling as the patient, or would you rather back off?"

> My intent was to bring the drama into the room as George demonstrated difficulty in being empathically connected to his patient. Perhaps by meeting his patient in a dialogue, a clearer picture could emerge.

George said, "Some of the things I was able to experience . . ."

"Well, I was aware that you couldn't look at her too much," I noted.

". . . that I couldn't look at her . . . that's interesting . . ." George mused.

I started to continue, "You felt that you had let her know that you had hurt her . . ." but George broke in with: "No, no. I don't think so. Well, just a little. Maybe, not too much. Not very much. I guess what I did was to play out the nonentity part, the not being seen. That's something I could relate to."

Shirley rejoined the discussion, gently saying, "Considering that you've gone through a lot of pain in your own life, it would be only natural to keep some distance from this patient. I'll tell you. It was difficult for me to come back here. I didn't want to deal with that patient again. I wouldn't feel that again if I could help it."

"Yeah," said George, "It's painful to feel like a nonentity."

> George's seemingly empathic remark to Shirley did not ring true. Was George really placating Shirley, or just playing along with her?

A member added, "And what about the panic of not having words . . ."

I was a bit puzzled at this point and said, "I'm not quite sure what you want."

> My attempt to introduce a more active interplay with the material wasn't working. I expressed my puzzlement and waited to see what would happen.

"Maybe I just want to talk about what's going on," responded George. "I think in certain ways I'm not touching him; I'm not reaching him. I said that he did not feel appreciated. Something happens and he loses interest. Everything's superficial, I don't seem to be able to get into the inner world of this patient. I guess that's his defense against feeling that whatever he wants the mother can't give him."

A member asked, "Would you give him that interpretation?"

"I started to tell him that," responded George, "but it was all staying on the outside with him. I started to translate it to his job. I suggested that his starting to lose interest in his job was like his mother losing interest in him, that he was defending himself against possible loss by losing interest in his job."

A member brought up a different angle, reminding George, "He doesn't speak very much, so you have to touch him on a nonverbal level," and another member added, "You have to touch him through the transference."

George took up this theme. "Touching is a good point. That reminds me of something. When Joe came to the session on Tuesday and we discussed his coming only once or twice a week, I reminded him that he knew where I stood on this. Joe's response was, 'Well, I was expecting to use this money to go to a chiropractor,' and he went on to list all the places that hurt. So I said, 'Well, I guess you really want to be touched.' This was as he was leaving. He was almost out the door. Then he said: 'And also, I will be able to go to the gym.' So I responded, 'I guess I'm really taking something away from you.'"

> Attempting to reach out to someone who is cold and aloof implies that the diagnosis is schizoid. I am not quite sure that this is so, for we have no indication that this dynamic exists in the transference/countertransferential relationship. Schizoid patients usually provoke a wish to be touched in spite of their ostensible obstacles to contact. With persistence, the therapist usually succeeds in making contact. In this interaction, we see a good deal of control and invulnerability manifested by the patient's interactions with the therapist. This does not reflect a schizoid pattern.

Before George could continue, a member challenged him. "I feel like you see it with your head, but you don't identify or empathize with him. When you're feeling his craving for contact, you might put it into language that will be relating specifically to what he's experiencing."

> Will talking about contact threaten this individual, especially because he needs so much control?

Another member continued the challenge: "Does this guy crave contact, or is he frightened of abandonment and doesn't want to let himself feel it?"

George reflected, "Perhaps these are the issues I'm not feeling, and that's why I'm staying on the outside . . . In fact, I'm pretty sure of that."

> This has a very phony ring. I decided to mockingly mirror his defenses.

"So I guess you have the whole thing wrapped up," I said, "and we're ready to go into the next presentation . . . I'm not quite sure what we can do at this point."

A group member interjected, "I have a feeling that this patient is craving contact, but this may be an issue related to you. I think underneath, he's very frightened of contact. In fact, he's probably more fearful, and I think that's one of the reasons he's hiding under a narcissistic cover."

> The question is an open one as to whether this patient has a narcissistic cover. More accurately, I suspect that we are seeing a character structure that emphasizes a feeling of invulnerability.

I reiterated what I'd started to say. "We're at an impasse because I'm not quite sure where we can go in this presentation. I understand that we don't need to go into the emotional area, here, but I'm not sure if all this understanding can accomplish anything. We need you to get into this patient's world, George, so you can be in contact with him. Why don't you be the patient and take over Shirley's role."

> I decided that I was going to go past this very intellectual tightly controlled discussion and get into the grist of the material.

Shirley added, "But it's not only the issue of abandonment. It's also what it feels like to be acting out."

"Okay," I said. "Suppose we invited this man into the room here, what would he think about this discussion?"

"I don't think he'd really hear what was going on," George responded.

"Now, come on, speak as the patient," I pushed.

"I'm not giving you my insides," said our patient, George, stonily.

A member piped in, "He'd actually use that language? Why?"

"It's to cover up everything. It's my experience."

A long silence follows before Shirley said, "What's your body feeling in the chair?"

George replied, "My knees are tense, and my shoulders are a little bit tense."

A member retorted, "You don't look tense. You look kind of relaxed. Did you know that?"

George replied, "Well, my knees certainly felt tense."

One of the members now played therapist. "What makes you feel good? I hear you like to go to bars."

George the patient, replied, "I don't *like* to go to bars, it's just something to do."

"It must feel like being back in the family," a member said.

Sidestepping the emotional content, George/the patient replied, "You know, I had my grandmother and my aunts around. It was a big family and my grandmother and my aunts used to watch me."

A therapist queried, "Does it feel overwhelming . . . what we're doing here?"

A long silence followed. The presenter/patient replied, "I'm just doing the same things I've been doing for the last two or three years. I don't know if I've expressed this, but I don't know if you're really helping me. Somehow I need a push, a pull, something. I just don't feel any better. I feel like I'm in the same place as always."

A therapist replied, "Something overwhelms you. What overwhelms you?"

"I don't know that. All I know is that I'm feeling in the same place. You know, I went to church and I thought that might help. I even spoke to the minister. I talked to him about marriage counseling, maybe I'll see him."

(A long silence)

We can observe through role-playing the therapist attempting to make contact with his patient. Yet all of us are not quite sure why there is such an impenetrable wall that surrounds this patient.

Another therapist responded, "I'm a little confused. You said it was overwhelming, and that you really don't feel this is really helpful. How can I be helpful? You must have some thoughts on it."

"You're not *doing* something about it," said the patient.

"I need some help from you about what I might be doing right," persisted the therapist. "Do you have some thoughts, any ideas?"

"You're not pushing me enough."

"Did I upset you by going away?" asked the therapist.

"I don't know, I feel indifferent," said the patient, as he shrugged his shoulders.

"Did you always feel indifferent? When did it change?" began the therapist, but a member of the group now stopped the dialogue with, "These words feel empty. Maybe you can go only so far with words.

He isn't getting it. He's saying all the right things, but it doesn't go anywhere."

"Well, when I say things to him," said George, "he looks at me and I don't really know what he's taken in, or if he's taken in anything."

A member now reflected, "How can he take in anything? If he takes you in, then you become meaningful, and when you become meaningful, then if you disappear, he's going to be in tremendous pain. So it's not a question of words, it's part of the process of getting through to him."

> The group appears to be following the abandonment hypothesis. Very few are aware of this patient's fear of being attacked. If the patient felt abandoned, I suspected that there would be many more possible bridges and connections into this patient's inner life. The patient's nonchalant watchfulness indicates that there are more complex dynamics afoot.

Another member added, "Making contact with that inner self is important. You are assuming that he can't make contact. We are saying that maybe he can't take anything in."

Jim jumped in here. "When I asked you what might be meaningful, however I put it, you shot me a look that was incredibly suspicious. At least, that was my reading of it. So I see a really paranoid side to this guy. Remember, he gets his jollies by looking through windows . . ."

George considered this comment. "I think he *is* very suspicious, very cautious with people. It's like he's casing the joint. At first he's very cautious, very distant, and eventually there's some warming up. He doesn't really get that close to anyone. One day I asked him what it felt like to work in this white-collar job, how he dealt with it. He replied that at first he was very cautious, but eventually he felt accepted by the people."

> The heart of the countertranference material starts to open up. Why did the presenter dissociate from the patient's cold, aloof, suspicious demeanor? What this too painful a perception?

A member now asked, "Is he always like this? When you ask questions, he answers you with questions?"

"Yes, except when he talks about jobs and money . . ."

There is now more confirmation of this patient's basic paranoid
orientation.

A member broke in here, sounding somewhat disgruntled.
"There sure is a flat quality going on here. Do you think he is like that
outside the office?"

Jim responds, "He's not schizoid, but disorganized inside. You've
got to remember that he was a star in high school."

Thinking of the star with no family in attendance, I now asked,
"What do you think was going on in that family structure?"

George replied, "I see his father as almost a caricature with a lot
of sadistic traits. He reminds me of Lou Gossett in that film where he
played the role of sergeant, the hard, sadistic officer. Joe's dad was
very severe. He'd come home at night, have dinner or watch televi-
sion, perhaps interact with the mother, but not deal with the kids."

We begin to see historical material that solidifies the impression
of a paranoid orientation. The fear of an attacking father creates
a tightly controlled invulnerable individual who guards himself
from attack.

A member asked, "How was that severe?"

"He wanted to have the kids seen and not heard. Joe's quite
frightened of his father, and I've gotten the feeling that his dad was
abusive."

A member added, "Some ministers play with this enormous
power that is backed up by the church. There's a whole package
around sin. You know, you don't have to be abused physically to be
abused."

George picked up on that. "In fact, when Joe first came into
treatment, he was very much into that: what's good, what's bad, sin
and sinning . . . anything that he wanted meant sin. It was so bad that
if he took a vacation it was a sin. Anything for himself was a sin.

We are now seeing further amplification of a very powerful
superego.

"What is being brought in focus is an extremely important diagnostic problem," I said. "Is the issue one of abandonment, or are we
dealing with an underlying hatred of the father with accompanying
paranoid defenses? It's interesting that the paranoid part only came

through when we observed the nonverbal communications of how the patient looked and held himself." I turned to George: "You put emphasis on the narcissism, but this may be a defensive protective cover that looks like invulnerability."

> We see how a therapist's selective perception can influence the emergence of the transference/countertransference material. Many of the participants in the group were all too ready to see problems around abandonment as the central issue.

A member now added, "He's so frozen with hatred and sadism that he's holding everything still. He's terrified that he's going to get killed."

I continued. "If the paranoid issue is paramount, then you're going to take a different treatment approach than if we encountered narcissistic damage. No wonder you feel shut out in the transference/-countertransference!"

A member now added, "You know, for all this talk we've done about his not making contact and the narcissistic damage, he does *not* come across as a guy who is needy or craving . . ."

Responding to this observation, I commented, "If George had been playing a schizoid individual, we would have experienced a different affect in the transference/countertransference. We'd most likely feel both a wish to touch the patient, as well as a removed distance. In this case, we never felt sympathy for Shirley when she was acting out Joe, and in sessions, George has felt shut out. I suspect there is even a mutual fear of violence. If you get any closer to this guy, George, watch out."

A member agreed, and then George added, "You know what else? Often I have fantasies about patients, and I don't have them about *him* . . .""So that he doesn't let you in his life so easily," I said.

"No," said George. "If anything, he shuts me off with his eyes. One day when he looked at me in this way he has, I really wondered what he was hearing, what was going on inside."

A member noted: "Theoretically, you're talking about some very early stuff, here."

"Not necessarily," I contradicted. "If you have abandonment by the mother, the father then becomes an important force in the organization of the personality structure. Here, on the oedipal level, there are fears of retaliation interfaced with feelings of abandonment. The underlying rage and fears of retaliation become the mix of a paranoid approach."

The importance of a powerful and important father in the family constellation also sets the stage for homosexual issues. Contact and fear of penetration become merged into a central personality constellation.

George picked up on this. "That's a possible reconstruction of Joe's early life. If he was abandoned by his mother, the normal expectation would be that the father would be available for him to move on . . ."

". . . But here the father was available, but only in a very frightening form," I concluded.

George noted, "He's severe. That's a good word, the father is very, very severe."

"Then Joe will have to organize himself around that fear," I said.

"In some ways his father gave him more in his severe way than his mother did," George added. "At least he gave him something to identify with."

A member now asked, "Have you been too intrusive?" inasmuch as he's been skipping sessions? You may have been giving him all the correct reconstructions, but perhaps you've also been giving him too much contact."

"That's a good point," I said. "If you place the focus on the paranoid issue, you would be trying to reduce the superego pressures. Let's go back to the previous dialogue where Joe requested cutting down sessions. He said to you he'd rather go work out at the gym . . ."

". . . Or the chiropractor," added George.

". . . and you responded, 'You need a lot of touching, a lot of contact.' Now that could be very threatening to somebody who's paranoid."

And another member chimed in, "or homosexual . . ."

I continued, "Offering a good deal of contact makes sense where the diagnosis is narcissistic injury, but if this man is paranoid, that's looking for trouble."

Suddenly George remembered something and blurted out, "You know, he did have one or two homosexual contacts when he came to New York . . ."

This "slip of the mind" reflects a piece of the countertransference issue. We need to explore some of the therapists' attitudes and feelings regarding homosexuality.

"What is interesting is how everything is starting to come into focus," I noted. "When you started to act like him, George, and we became aware of those interminable silences, your coolness and reserve was not compatible with a patient who was narcissistic. Your patient is watching you and insulating himself from you. So now the question is, how do you handle him?"

"I want to express the conflict," began George. "He needs distance, he needs to be cautious, and at the same time he wants contact."

A member asked, "Why do you think he wants contact?"

"I just think he does," responded George.

"You know, George, you are much more receptive to a warmth, contact level of relatedness," I pointed out, and the entire group nodded in unison. "This patient has tremendous fears of homosexual submission. When you see him cool and watchful, you should suspect that he's frightened of closeness. I might add that he has to keep on the move with bosses because they are potential dangers."

A member now asked, "What if he *is* afraid of the homosexual submission. What do you imagine this would mean; that he was afraid he could have been killed by his father?"

"No," I responded, "it's more like, 'If you want contact with me, you better submit, give up your penis and show me your ass so I can fuck it.'"

A member now stated, "I've never quite understood what the body was denying in a person in this state."

I explained, "First, the patient feels a tremendous fear of assault to his body integrity. Then there's a feeling of placation followed by a fear of that means of warding off danger." I turned back to George. "Now your contact and warmth needs are getting in the way of perceiving where Joe is. It's not that he doesn't have some close contact needs, but they are confused with other problems."

A member broke in with, "I had a woman whose father and mother were really brutal people, alcoholic. What would panic my patient was that after a session with me she would actually have vaginal sensations of warmth and orgasm. She would feel her body move. It was so frightening to her, that she'd have to hold her body still and not think. Your patient may be fighting his body sensations the way my patient did."

George responded, "What is interesting about this patient, though, is that he was a football player and an actor. You have to have access to your body to do those things."

"Perhaps in certain protected roles, he could be free," I said. "Here the role helps him to hide. I imagine he moves from job to job to protect himself from exploding."

A member added, "He's not only afraid of the bosses' rage, but of those softer sensations."

"So where's the direction of the therapeutic intervention?" I asked.

"I want to make him feel less frightened," responded George.

"I would start raising the whole general area of his rights and his ability to make choices." I said. "And when he starts talking about wanting to leave, you might reply, 'You know, you're trying to express your rights to spend your money the way you want, and I would hope that you have these rights with me as well.'"

George said, "It's that he did not have those rights with his father . . ."

". . . Right. Exploring the underlying dynamics of homosexuality is not the question. Find a metaphor for his search for freedom and his fear about being pinned down. What you want to express is that he's searching for something on the outside that he can find on the inside; that he has freedom to differ with you, to question, to challenge. He even has the right to say, 'This relationship is difficult.'"

George added, "He would have the right to say, 'I want to cut down to once a week.'"

"No," I countered.

Another member pointed out, "That's acting out."

"That only creates more anxiety for him when you don't differentiate between action and feeling," I added.

George went on, "I also feel that this patient needs verbalization to understand his internal world; that he needs to have it translated for him. I'm thinking of such aspects as his being sadistic and his fear of countering his attacking quality by saying in essence, 'Well, maybe I'll go away.'"

"Given that he's paranoid, I wouldn't emphasize his attacking quality," I suggested. "Go on the other side and stress the underlying fear of being attacked, and you'll be on safer ground. The thrust of treatment is to give support to his impulses. If you want to help him, clarify his inner world, then you don't stay at the outer defensive level. You don't even talk about his being attacked, as that undermines his sense of invulnerability and mobilizes anxiety. You don't want to threaten his defenses. Try not to show that you're onto him, because that will scare him. This man does not know that he has a right to have feelings and to make choices."

"Like he can say no to his wife," interjected George.

"That he can say no to his wife, even yes to his wife."

A member added, "It's the whole separation/individuation period with a narcissistic father."

"I assume you'd want to tell him that," George stated.

"No!" I responded emphatically. "You would try to find the metaphor that he is acting out on the outside and translate it to his inside life. You've got to remember that a paranoid person doesn't give you too much to hold on to. They want to keep you on the outside and are certainly worried about your being too empathic. He's not going to give you any sense that you're making headway with him, because that will just make you more powerful. You just have to expect that a good deal of the time you will be in the dark."

I then turned to Shirley and said to her, "Last week when you brought in the whole issue of your wanting to feel better with authorities, there was a lot of anxiety about the closeness you felt with me and with others. Then everything got converted into a sense of being attacked and misunderstood."

"But I hope you will remember the interpersonal issues," Shirley countered. "You started with me in a certain way. I came and gave you a compliment at the beginning of the session and what you did was to attack me."

"Yes, I started all that," I admitted, "and I hope I can listen better."

Shirley continued: "You made it dangerous for me once again. You attacked me."

"I'll try to reform!" I protested, with a grin. I was being playful and going along with the defense and also illustrating how to make contact with issues around paranoid masochistic operations without getting embroiled in a fight.

"That's on *tape*!" parried Shirley. The session ended on a light note of resolution.

THE PROBLEM OF THE PARANOID PATIENT

I thought a good deal about this session. I wondered why such important clinical material only emerged near the tail end of the second session. It was obvious that George's role-playing of the patient gave all of us dramatic insight into the nonverbal communication. Here, the paranoid suspiciousness became very evident. Yet, as was previously mentioned, there were a number of indications throughout the presentation pointing to a paranoid orientation. One critical dynamic was the therapist's wish for a warm positive male contact with this patient. For the therapist, being seen as a threatening and frightening father was at odds with George's wish to find gratification in playing the good father. The therapist seemed to be searching for some type of theoretical format to justify his wish to repair his own narcissistic damage via the patient, but the entire flow of material in the group went contrary to the therapist's premise and underlying desire. The sessions were marked by a good deal of competition and challenge, and there was a lack of the softness and support which usually permeates a group when a narcissistically damaged patient is presented.

There's no question that this patient has suffered narcissistic damage, along with patients whose diagnosis ranges from psychosis and depression to masochism. It is the unique combination of this narcissistic damage with other historical forces in the patient's life that requires a different holding environment within the transference/-countertransference relationship. The therapist does need to offer support; but at the same time must provide a *container* for a violent father who is ready to attack the patient. Furthermore, the therapist's role of being the good father at times seemed more of a caricature masking sadomasochistic undertones than offering a vehicle for the patient to test out some of his own aggression. On an unconscious level, the patient may well have received the message of weakness rather than strength from the therapist, creating a conversion of the aggression into a sado-masochistic style of communication. In the case presentation under discussion, this violent father was dissociated from awareness and consequently floated around in the group discussion. Quite clearly, Shirley was one of the messengers for the patient; however, even in this instance, her message was one of an identification with the damaged, nonentity part which was but one facet of the picture.

Shirley played out some of the masochistic fears that I suspect are hidden underneath the paranoid structure of this patient. She felt wounded and in pain, as well as unrecognized. What was hidden and never fully worked through were some of her own fears surrounding her competitive drives and wishes for power. Here, once again, we see a mirror of some of the patient's issues. Joe's wish to be seen comes into direct conflict with his fears of vulnerability and retaliation. It well depicted how as patients move nearer to the center of power, enormous fears of retaliation may become mobilized. I do want to point out here, that whereas Shirley and I managed to get past the combative dialogue in the course of two sessions, with a patient it would be considerably more difficult to discern the needs for support and for power. To put emphasis on the outer defensive layer of a paranoid patient only serves to create and maintain this combative dialogue. Much more is gained by supporting the inner impulses of competition or power.

As I forewarned George, however, paranoid patients usually do not give the therapist an opportunity to see very clearly their needs for support. As therapists, when we work with paranoid mechanisms, we must be able to deal with our feelings of being isolated and inadequate, and not defensively try "to make our point." It is all too easy to respond to the induction and to reconfirm the terrifying conviction this patient feels that exposure opens one up to sexual assault. Thus, if the therapist is to make an empathic jump into the patient's inner world, the countertransference feelings, as well as the inductions, must be very much under control.

In this case presentation we saw a particular type of paranoid organization that combined both preoedipal and oedipal issues. Mobilized were enormous amounts of unconscious anxiety and guilt overlaid by feelings of vulnerability, fears of submission, conflicts around warmth, and a generalized ego restriction in the areas of choice, mobility, and frustration tolerance. As is so often the case in working with patients like this, our group fell prey to countertransference and induced feelings. We saw how all the members of the group, including the leader, became parties to the underlying paranoid fear of attack and submission. Each member presented his or her own particular defense, be it of compliance, attack, dissociation, or denial. Yet, in spite of these confusing complications, we ultimately arrived at a consensus of the diagnostic and therapeutic issues at hand. Having grappled with the paranoid mechanism in the peer group, I have hopes that in the future, when group members become inundated with feelings of isolation and vulnerability, that their therapeutic antennae will shoot up, and they will investigate the genesis of these telltale feelings.

A number of principles can be distilled from the above discussion:

1. The transitional therapeutic space that marks the territory of the paranoid patient can be blocked by a number of defensive layers. On the surface, one can discern a guarded distance emanating from this patient's presence, creating a therapeutic unrelatedness and a reactive wish by the therapist to penetrate the defenses. Sharp, pointed interventions, however, increase the paranoid's fear of anal penetration, and consequently should be blunted with supportive, but clear, interventions.

2. Feeling attached to, or not trusting the patient can also color the transitional space of both parties. In these instances, the therapist's overidentification with the patient's defenses can interfere with responding to the underlying fears and wishes of the patient.

3. This paranoid space can blend into a masochistic picture where the patient feels wounded and misunderstood and the therapist feels guilt ridden or manipulated. The therapist can either pull back with a degree of suspiciousness, or become oversolicitous. Shirley's interaction with George and the group is a case in point. George was wary of being "pulled into something" by Shirley, and ultimately found himself at the paranoid end of the spectrum. Thus, we can see an interplay between masochistic and paranoid positions for both parties. Consequently, both members can either fear or attack, or feel an attack in the encounter.

4. Placation of the paranoid patient may be a response to the therapist's unconscious perception that rage is a very frightening business. Here, the therapist's fear of his own rage becomes merged with that of the patient. A soothing response to alleviate these fears inadvertently only increases the fears of attack.

5. The defensive hostility of a paranoid patient can provoke a combative therapeutic dialogue. In the short run, this may clear some of the tension, as the internal enemy has become externalized. This defensive anger covers over the reactive rage that resides on an omnipotent psychic level. Not responding to the provocative defensive level then becomes an important countertransferential understanding.

In conclusion, we observe a fascinating interlocking of transference/countertransference hostility that emanates from different levels of consciousness. The patient, fearing attack from the bad father, becomes cool, detached, and impenetrable. His actions are also full of devaluation. Yet, also projected is the hope of finding a good father. The therapist, on the other hand, requiring control of the situation, and experiencing a loss of contact, subtly acts out his own sadism. From the patient's perspective, control is a necessity in order to protect oneself from being overly vulnerable. Control, on the other hand, for the therapist, is a defense against object loss and separation anxiety. Paradoxically, both long for a good father, but each deals with his anxiety through his own particular characterological defenses. Therapists and presenters, then, must cross the boundaries of their own defensive anxiety to create a space where two minds can meet rather than collide.

Chapter 5

REIKO

A Mirroring Stance Flows into Fusion

As would be true of anyone moving from one culture to another, Reiko's very sense of identity was challenged in her relocating to the United States from Japan. In her struggle to forge a modified conception of the self from a blending of old and new mores and attitudes, Reiko's ego resources were strained to the utmost. Under this pressure she dissociated or repressed various ego states and attitudes from her past world. As Reiko presented her work with Ruth to the group, it gradually emerged that this patient stirred up conflicts close to Reiko's heart. The crosscultural issues, along with Reiko's personal intrapsychic areas of conflict, became the basis of the group's investigation.

Reiko began the session in her usual lyrical fashion. Her words flowed out with liquid ease as she lamented her confusion and her sense that she had lost her analytic stance with this patient. She complained that she felt disconnected, at times even bored, and that she'd find herself being very active, as if to prove to herself that she was doing *something*. In the end she complained that it all felt wrong.

TWINSHIP AND SEPARATION

The history emerged: Ruth had a twin brother with whom she had had a long-standing problem of envy. Her father, a dentist, and mother, a competent owner of a large dress store, were legally separated and divorced when Ruth was six. At ten, after years of fighting, Ruth and her brother were separated; the twin went to live with the father; Ruth, with the mother.

As she reached adulthood, Ruth became overweight and promiscuous, having very little real relationship with the men she saw. She told Reiko that she thought she had an identity problem in being attracted to the gay world, although she was not homosexual. She was also actively involved with drugs. Ruth's only area of success was in the world of work. At the onset of treatment, she was twenty-one, but acted like a worldly-wise thirty. In spite of knowing her way around, she was a baby when it came to relationships.

Ruth's mother was seen as quite narcissistic, being mainly responsive to her daughter when she was successful in school or at work. As a means of making contact, Ruth spent many hours listening to her mother's problems. Ruth's envy for her brother would come in up such contexts as her complaining that while her mother generally maintained an empty refrigerator, she would have it full when the brother came to visit. Ruth inferred that it was all right for men to gain weight but not for women. Reiko further saw this story as one of many examples of Ruth's placing emphasis on the outside rather than on the inside.

The brother, it seemed, could get away with murder. He would hit Ruth, and the mother would remain completely oblivious. In other ways, she was quite intrusive, leaving her contraceptive in view, and exposing to Ruth her ongoing relationships with a variety of lovers.

When Ruth first came to treatment, the mother was seen as someone who could do no wrong. The father, on the other hand, was seen through the mother's eyes, as a withholding wimp. In the course of treatment the father came to be seen in somewhat more positive terms, with a genuine good feeling gradually forming between him and Ruth. In fact, Ruth now reported that during her adolescence, she spent a good deal of time visiting her father during weekends, describing her contact with him as like going on a date.

Ruth spent an enormous amount of time struggling with her weight, but as was true with so many of Ruth's communications, the therapist felt uninvolved with the material. Reiko complained that she felt "heavy" in the sessions, her eyes droopy. She toyed with several possibilities: Was she carrying the burden of her patient, this being how the daughter felt with her mother? Was there a lack of identification with the mother? Were there oedipal or preoedipal problems?

She saw a good deal of deprivation, but at the same time she saw sexual identity problems and a masculine protest. To top it all off, the patient was very frightened that she would be forced into the role of the breadwinner.

> When the therapist's eyes droop, we can explore any number of different possibilities. At times, the patient is not emotionally engaged with the discussion. In this particular instance, we must wait to see what will happen as the material unfolds.

Amid this somewhat disjointed presentation, Reiko pointed out that while the patient complained a good deal about somatic symptoms like pain and weight gain, she rarely could get into identity problems. Ruth was considerably more receptive to the issues of feeling psychologically deprived and empty than to concrete complaints about body size and physical discomfort.

The supervisory session wore on in a not quite satisfying manner marked by a variety of different interpretations and approaches. Some members placed emphasis on the oedipal issues, others on the preoedipal. Some spoke of the importance of twinship. As the session progressed, the presenter confessed that she not only accepted her role of being nonanalytic, but occasionally even found herself thinking that the therapy session was like a break. Here she could enjoy herself, she could be nice to look at and live out the role of the mother who demanded that her daughter be cheerful and vivacious while failing to make any deeply related contact. In the last minutes of the presentation, Reiko offhandedly remarked that there were twins in her own family. The group broke out in laughter, as members queried how such an important factor could fail to come up until the very end of the presentation. We all agreed there was more to learn about this case and that the countertransferential factors required more investigation. We go now to the following week.

Reiko picks up the threads of last week's presentation and speaks in a very soft, languid, delicate voice: "I have twin sisters. They were the youngest children in the family, eight years younger than I, and they were not raised together. One was adopted by my aunt. Unlike my patient, they are identical. I don't know why I didn't say that. The sister who lived with us was my baby. We are still very close. I was also close to my other twin sister, who was very much part of our family, even though she was raised separately."

A member immediately asked the obvious question: "What were the reasons for the separation?"

"Oh, it's a very dramatic story," said Reiko in her enchanting voice. "Do you want to hear it?"

Reiko cast a spell over the entire group. Her voice is melodious and soothing. I wonder what this has to do with the countertransference problem.

"Of course we want to hear it!"

Reiko began to spin her tale: "It was my mother's sixth pregnancy. Before the twins, there had been two other pregnancies when her very good friend, who was so like her sister that we called her 'Aunt,' came to my mother to say: 'Look, you have so many healthy children, why don't you give me one of yours? You know I'll raise the child well. Why don't you give me one?'

My mother said: 'No, nothing doing, each child is an individual,' and she meant it. Every time my mother would get pregnant, my aunt would pester my mother to give her the child. Finally, when my mother had the twins, my aunt arrived at the hospital and said: 'These are identical twins and God sent one for me. [A giggle broke out in the background.] You have to give one to me.' And my mother did. I don't know, I never used to think that it was such an amazing thing until I talked to other people, especially in this country. It surprised me that people were so amazed and said things like, 'You don't do that; a mother doesn't give a baby away.' It was not common practice, but ownership in my country is not such a big thing. What's yours is also someone else's."

The group was now very involved with the story. Someone asked: "How did your mother choose which one to give her?"

Reiko continued to speak softly: "I feel some anxiety when I talk about it, there must be something else going on. This aunt used to come in and spend a lot of time in our house courting the baby she wanted to take. Actually, the baby who went with my aunt was not the one my mother and father originally decided that they would give away. This is a very special aunt. She is very lovely; a wonderful woman, not a witch at all. Anyway, she would take the baby out, and do lovely things with her. She spent months, six months, getting to know her, taking her to her house and spending a lot of time with her. Sachiko, the one my aunt wanted to take, got suspicious of her and did not like her. It got so that she would cry every time my aunt would come near. By this time, the twins were about ten, eleven months old. The other baby, Hiroko, was easier and got close to my aunt. In the end, my aunt took her, and to this day I think that Sachiko, who ended up staying with us, does not like my aunt much.

"I don't know, I grew up idealizing and admiring Hiroko. We were six children and shared everything. This sister of ours who went with my aunt was really the princess and had everything she wanted, including her own room. I suppose that underneath there was a lot of fear and sadness, too, but outwardly she was the princess who had everything. Now that I think about it, maybe Ruth is that rich sister, the one who has everything, who makes a lot of money."

This seems to be too easy an insight. I don't trust it.

"I enjoyed Sachiko. I think I could go on and on talking about my twin sister, but I don't know where to go . . ." Reiko's voice trailed off.

"Why don't you go on and see," I said in a soft voice, responding to the tone in the room.

Reiko now spoke in a quiet, intent voice. We all heard the pain and sadness just below the surface as she continued her story.

"I guess I don't want to talk about what comes to my mind, because it's not easy to look at my mother as someone who could do this. Whenever people have said anything, I've defended her and talked about how wonderful my aunt and uncle were. I never really looked at the fact that my mother was unusual in that she could give away a child. I know there are a lot of loose boundaries regarding ownership, but still, that my mother could do that . . . I never wanted to think about that . . ." Her eyes filled up with tears, and continued, and she quietly sobbed. Reiko's voice became almost inaudible until she visibly pulled herself upright and took on a more intellectual, detached tone.

"Ruth and her mother's defensive styles are very similar to mine: we seem to cut off and deny painful feelings. I was feeling that I wasn't connected; but there are a lot of unconscious connections that I can make. I think I am acting out something with her, because I don't want to see the underlying pain in her life, or maybe her mother's which resonates with mine, maybe in the realm of abandonment. It's much easier to get the happy side of things, the smiling silent side. That's what was happening last week: We were manic, laughing."

After a long pause I asked: "What's going on?"

"I'm thinking about what I should do now," responded Reiko, thoughtfully. "I have a lot of things I could say about my patient."

I knew that Reiko needed plenty of room. She was a very autonomous person, and her associations would lead her to the heart of the issue, if we but offered a supportive holding environment.

"What comes next to mind?" I asked.

"How I had to be for my mother. Like my patient, my mother dealt with me better when I was successful, talented, extroverted, friendly, and social. My mother could not deal with me when I was . . ." Reiko couldn't find the words but finally went on with: "She would get very upset. She'd feel that part of her was insulted and injured if I wasn't doing what she wanted. Even now, if I tell her I am depressed, she can't deal with that at all. She's there, but only when I give her what she wants to get.

"I think there's a lot of matching my patient. I never thought of it like that before, but my patient's life is so similar to mine that I guess I don't even question some things with her."

After a pause Reiko continued: "I don't think my mother intruded on my body and on me the way my patient's mother intruded on hers. If anything, my mother was too absent. She was very busy with a lot of stuff."

The atmosphere was very quiet, gentle, and supportive, mirroring the image of Reiko flowing through all of us like a melodious echo.

This atmosphere often occurs when we present narcissistically wounded patients.

"My patient has constant dreams about her body being taken out and cut up, of things being taken out. A lot of references are to the mother. I told you how the mother took my patient to the gynecologist when Ruth was twelve supposedly because Ruth had too much hair all over her body. There was something wrong with her.

Reiko's voice continued the melody: "Until Ruth started treatment she never thought of getting her own doctors. She never had separate doctors from her mother. I do not intrude at all. I don't even interpret. I think you're all feeling that . . ."

The musical chimes continued, "You're not using your authority in the relationship."

". . . Not at all. I'm kind of, I'm her twin . . ."

". . . That's what I was wondering, do you resonate more to her than to your twin sister who moved with the aunt?"

Reiko did not answer the question directly, but referred back to the patient: "The more I think about Ruth, the more I see her as a sister of some sort."

Another soft voice entered the dialogue: "What was the difference in temperament between the twins?"

"Very different, dramatic difference."

"How?"

In a soft but controlled voice Reiko described the two. "The sister who was adopted is extremely extroverted and happy; a person of the world. She is into music and art, and is very successful. She's married, has one child, and is pregnant with another. The sister who stayed with us is also an artist, actually they are both artists, but she's very shy. She's very competent, not at all needy but withdrawn and shy. It's amazing. They look identical, but their temperaments and dress are so different."

"How?"

"My sister, the one who stayed with us, is a subtle, conservative dresser. The one who was adopted is in Japan. She is very fashionable, very into clothes and makeup. My family always compares me to her."

> I wondered to myself whether there was some splitting going on in Reiko's life regarding good and bad self. The sister who was left behind was conservative, quiet, and certainly not flamboyant. The other appeared to be the opposite. Were these the opposing forces struggling within Reiko's personality?

"To the one who was adopted?" someone asked.

"Yes."

"How so? What type of comparison?" the speaker pressed.

"In terms of being, maybe, at ease with people: with social style, clothing, makeup, fashion and stuff. Having a preoccupation with stuff like that that my sister who stayed with us does not have. My mother has a tendency to group people: 'You and Yuko, this one and that one, are alike.'"

"So you're the twin of the sister who was outside of the family," a voice floated in.

"Yes," responded Reiko. "I am more like her than her twin."

A group member spoke in a low supportive voice: "You've talked about visiting Japan, about how great it is to go there, and I remember your telling me one day at lunch that you're treated like a princess. You've said that your mother tells you, 'Sit, Reiko, everybody else can do the work.' So you're the princess in *your* family, and the twin is the princess in her family."

"Yes."

Jim spoke, sustaining the supportive tone: "I keep trying to find the envy in Ruth because it is certainly in your relationship with the twin who lived with your aunt. What I heard last time was your struggle with the issue of why this patient isn't happier and more satisfied, particularly with her work situation. She is earning a high salary, and you feel impatient with her for not being more satisfied with her life, or at least some aspects of her life . . ."

"Yes," said Reiko in a wistful tone.

"That feels similar to the issues between you and the adopted twin."

Now Shirley continues the soft dialogue. "It's as though you feel Ruth's neediness is a kind of greed and not appropriate. She wants too much. Maybe the needier side of you has that same experience and it's not acceptable."

> I noticed that Reiko changed her body posture to a more objective stance. As we moved from a mirroring approach to interventions that approached an interpretive style, were we now beginning to facilitate some type of differentiation between Reiko and her patient?

Reiko pulled herself up straight and became more objective in her manner: "My sister who was adopted has everything materially, but when she visited and stayed with me, she took a lot of my stuff, she wanted something of mine. When she went to my other sister's house, she wanted some of hers. She took things like jewelry, clothing, from us."

A flurry of comments now came from the members.

George suggested, "I think she wants to be a part of the family."

Joan added, "She is maybe pissed too. I think quite unconsciously she is angry."

Again, Reiko spoke in a soft, lilting tone.

> I am beginning to wonder whether her tone is in part defensive in manner. Does the presenter bind her audience into a supportive role so that both parties never really look at the darker, evil side of things?

"I think I have had a lot of envy for my sister's life-style, and in terms of abandonment issues, my patient was the one who physically lived with her mother. Her brother was the one who was given to the father . . . but you're right, there was a lot of abandonment. He was still the favorite one." The voice became really muted until finally the group lapsed into silence.

"Where do you want to take this?" I asked, rather matter-of-factly.

Reiko now spoke with more open feeling. Her voice quivered as she said; "I guess I feel confused because he goes somewhere, then she regresses. Now she seems to have regressed back to overeating and wanting to mess up in her job. Suddenly the job isn't working out. I guess my problem is in understanding the dynamics when she gets into that state. And then, of course, there's the transference and what happens between us where we sort of merge. . . . I don't see clearly. Nothing I say feels like the right thing to say."

George's curiosity was piqued. "Is there any difference in a Japanese family that might be useful in understanding the situation?"

"Yes, it is different."

George pressed for more information. "What's the difference? Is there more identification with the total family unit than one individual?"

"Yes, and the *belonging* is different. There is much more of a 'what's mine can be yours' attitude. The sense of possessiveness and belonging is much less."

I tried to offer some clarification: "So that the whole issue around autonomy is not a big thing there."

"Autonomy? What's that?" said Reiko, with a grin, as empathic laughter rippled through the room. She continued: "Autonomy is nothing. There's a general sense of belonging to a large family unit."

I continued on a clarifying objective tack. "Well, maybe we need to know more about the psychology of a Japanese family. There is a different cultural framework, and we may have to understand developmental issues within that context."

Jim, irritated by this approach, challenged me. "I don't know. I think we are pushing the cultural issue. Someone who has to take care of a baby at eight years old is not going to be generous and loving about her family. It may be that the feelings are different because of the cultural setting, the difference in socialization; however, I can't imagine any human being not reacting negatively to the loss of some aspect of themselves, no matter how transpersonal their culture is."

Addressing myself to Reiko, I asked, "Is there a difference between the two cultures? You know better than anyone else."

Jim cut right in. "Whatever the answer is, Art, what Reiko has been saying is that she and her next sister were mothering these children, and no matter how you slice it, she got cheated out of one of the children, and I don't hear the reaction. But I'll hold my position till I hear from Reiko. Reiko is the one who could tell us what she remembers. But I am curious about one thing: Did you have a preference as to which twin left? Did that come up for you at all? Do you remember that?"

"No," said Reiko. "I don't remember that. All I remember is that they were so identical that we had to put a black thread around one of their wrists."

Joan joined in to ask, "Do you remember anything when they were young?"

I was aware that the tone of the group had changed. The quiet reflection was broken up and the members seemed to be pushing too hard.

"Something's happened," I said. "We are asking too many questions."

Was the competitive challenge from Jim creating tension in the room? What did this have to do with the flow of material?

"Do you remember the aunt?" a member pressed on, ignoring my comment.

"Yes, I remember her coming with tons of toys to seduce the little baby."

"There's perversion here!" Shirley blurted, with much feeling.

The group members all started talking excitedly at once. "They were one, they were one egg! . . . ." "Sure, so to take away part of it. . . ." "It's too much . . ."

Reiko seemed perplexed and spoke with a questioning voice. "I am very cut off, obviously, if you people think that I should be feeling things . . ."

The group broke into good-natured supportive laughter. Again, I tried to focus the direction of the discussion. Reiko looked baffled and needed distance.

I decided to turn the discussion toward the patient. "How cut off is your patient from her rage at her mother? There are a lot of feelings that you're not in touch with. Maybe your patient has the same kind of defense system."

A member rushed to Reiko's defense. "What a minute, we are *assuming* that Reiko is not in touch with certain feelings."

> My suspicions as to what is going on are reinforced by what is happening. Reiko induces everyone to protect her even when she has openly admitted her vulnerability to certain issues.

Reiko tried to clarify what did happen as she spoke in an eloquent open voice. "As I grew up, we went on with life and did not ask any questions. I love my sister, [referring to the one who was adopted] I love all my sisters, but she I really love because she is so bright, so creative, so talented, and sweet. Sometimes I feel like shaking her up and saying, 'Don't you see' . . . She has a lot of stuff that she does not want to look at, but when I am with her, I just want to give her everything. I don't know why, but I just want to do that.

"I give her a lot of presents and I give her child a lot of presents. I do that with all my sisters, but more so with her. She is my baby. Maybe I feel that part of her was given away, but she is still with me . . . something of that nature. There's no rage, no anger."

> We are starting to move into the heart of the countertransference problem. Does Reiko identify with her twin sister, and is she unable to separate and maintain her own autonomy?

Jim then attempted to clarify what had been said. "So she is still with you and you continue to like her today. And you want to shake her—this must have something to do with the case."

"And I am not like her at all, actually, but I'm being like her now—I can feel how you're all wanting to shake me and make me see . . . Maybe my patient is in me as my sister baby, and I become that cheerful extroverted person talking to her, I don't know."

"WE DON'T DO THAT TO PEOPLE"

> At this point I felt Reiko needed to contact some of her feelings and I suggested a more experiential mode. "Let's make believe your patient is your sister. How would you act with your sister/-patient? Would you want to give to her, be generous towards her, care for her, or would you want to shake her up?"

"I can't," Reiko replied.
"What stops you?" I asked.
"Because we don't do that."
"Tell us more about your 'not doing that.'"

The group was very quiet and involved as Reiko spoke. "You don't do that to people. You don't challenge them that much. You don't separate, that's what it is. In a western sense, you're separating each time you do that. In Japan, in a Japanese family, when you're close to someone you don't hurt their feelings. You don't tell them something that might hurt them. You don't confront their defenses." Reiko was very thoughtful and clear. I realized that in our gentle, nonconfronting approach, all of us had joined the Japanese family.

"That's right, you don't individuate, you don't confront."

"You assume that you would hurt her if you shook her up," I said.

"Sure."

"But also, you might help her."

"Yes, but . . ."

I now launched into a rather active dialogue with Reiko: "So, we understand a little bit of what is going on with this patient. Your Japanese self is being brought into this case. You don't individuate or separate."

"Right, right! Yes, I am so giving to her."

"But you can't see what she is suffering, what's really involved."

"I do, intellectually I see it," Reiko protested.

"I know, but with your twin you couldn't see what was wrong, it was too painful to see what was really going on."

"It would hurt her."

"Was it that it would hurt her, or was it simply not *done*?" I asked.

"Not done." Reiko looked pensive.

We are now ready to connect the Japanese and American world of Reiko. I decided to give her plenty of room to explore the matter.

"Now, where do you want to go with this?" I asked, gently. All of us heard a deep sigh, and joined Reiko with sympathetic laughter. Reiko began to speak again in her soft, lyrical way.

"I wanted to tell you a dream Ruth had. I think it is pertinent here. The dream is not recent. Ruth told it to me a year and a half ago. At that time she was losing weight, that was the main thing that was happening to her. She also was beginning to feel that she could challenge her mother and be assertive without being totally aggressive and cutting off. Before, she could not talk to her mother for months. That was the only way she could separate from her mother. She could not be assertive for fear that her mother wouldn't be able to take it. Ruth's mother turns out to be—even though she is not Japanese—a little bit like my mother. Anyway, this was how Ruth told me the dream." Reiko got out her notes and read.

"'I was in a hospital with another woman, visiting. We were trying to get to the third floor to see a little girl who was ill, but the elevator would not go there. Finally someone told us that the clinic for children was on the tenth floor. So we went up there. Throughout the whole dream there was this fear that I would contract what this little girl had, but I stayed, even after her parents and her friends had left. The girl had a very high fever and she kept switching back and forth between feeling fine and talking to me and feeling very sick. When she was feeling very sick it felt good to be able to make her feel better. The girl was about nine years old.'"

"Okay," I said, "what do you think of this dream? Why did you bring it up at this moment?"

"Now, as I am reading," said Reiko, I am thinking about the nine-year-old little girl and how I was nine when my sister was adopted. I feel the sad part in me and I think Ruth has that too. My patient is very comfortable taking care of other children, other babies. In that dream she is taking care of the little girl who was really her. I guess the woman and she represent the two of us. It's interesting, because I took care of my twin sister a lot, but I don't think I liked it. No, I know I did not like it. I wasn't such a natural mother at eight as my second sister was. She was very nurturing and loving. I was much more interested in fun, so I wonder if I felt bad about that. My patient is like a little baby with an overlay of a mother. She is very motherly and is very nurturing to people and animals. Anyway, I guess I felt guilty about the child in me that wanted to play and just have fun and not help my mother with babies. And since I was the oldest one, I was supposed to take care of children. I was supposed to be there on my mother's side."

> We see how a family pattern can be reinforced by societal pressures. The child must be mother's helper, and this is seen as good behavior by the culture.

"Oh! another important fact," Reiko said, with a giggle. "During this time when all this was happening—guess I don't want to talk about it—my father was not in Japan. When my twin sisters were born, my father was in South America and I was with my mother."

A long silence followed. "I was supposed to be very responsible with my mother because I was the oldest. My mother did not know that she was going to have twins until the week before she gave birth. I remember how big she was. There was no room in that environment for any kind of feelings such as 'I don't want to have,' or 'I am angry,' or 'I don't want to be loving.' There was no room for any kind of aggression or any kind of assertiveness. My patient was also supposed to always be the giving, nurturing little girl for her mother and brother and father, wife and mother to everyone. She could not be the playful little girl that I was in spite of it all. But then I was considered selfish."

A reflective silence followed until I asked, "How long were you separated from your father?"

> I recognized that her lack of a father during this crucial stage of developmenht would have an important bearing on Reiko's attitude towards men. The family balance is out of whack as the father leaves the family. Her job was to take over the role of the father. I suspect that there is an underlying wish for a very strong male who will save her from this onerous past.

"One year."

Someone else picked it up. "Do you remember any of the content of that session with the dream?"

"I have no idea, I wish I did—that was a while back."

I decided to bring the material into the room. "If she were here right now and she gave you that dream, what do you think she would be doing with that dream?"

"She would say that the two women are you and me taking care of the little girl that's her," Reiko easily responded.

"Okay. Now, what would you do with that response?" I gently pushed.

"I don't know. I might ask 'What does this little girl have?'"

> The group gently started to interpret what was going on in a supportive way.

"What are you protecting this patient from?" Joan asked, gently. "Do you hold back from going after certain issues because you are protecting her?"

Reiko answered, "Maybe I'm afraid she can't take it. I don't know. It's true that I'm not going after a lot, and I'm certainly not going after her aggressively. Somehow I keep thinking of her as this baby, this little crippled helpless baby. On some level she may be that, but she is also more than that."

> Now we are approaching some of the issues regarding the split in Reiko's perceptions of the twins. She identifies with the fun-loving and outgoing twin and is left with the one who must take protection and nurturance while the real mother is involved with other duties. Is Reiko's protectiveness covering over a good deal of hostility that cannot be permitted in a Japanese family?

"Is it possible that being the sick baby has been the only way she has gotten nurturance?" I asked.

Joan quickly added, "It seems like you're trying to compensate for her not having been cared for earlier."

Reiko enthusiastically agreed, "Yes, and that's not always the right thing to do. I am being the good mother, and I don't think that she necessarily needs that."

Frances took a slightly different tack. "I'm just curious if you didn't want to be taking care of those babies, would you have been relieved that the burden was reduced?"

In a barely audible, defensive voice Reiko replied, "I might have . . . oh, I'm spoiling her," she added, with a gentle moan.

". . . Now you're mothering this patient of yours. I'm wondering if you confront her like a daughter whether your own guilt might be mobilized," Frances gently prodded.

Jim now brought in a new perspective. "You know, I see how important my baby daughter's relationship is with me . . ." ". . . And my father was away," interjected Reiko. Jim went on, "The point is that your patient is also obsessed with her father."

"No, no, the divorce was at five, he left then, but her brother was given to the father," protested Reiko.

"But her father deserted her," Jim emphasized.

"But she did go to them on weekends and, she would take care of both of them; cook for them," Reiko maintained. "She's always taken care of her brother, even though they were the same age. She has strong defenses against all the other feelings but those nurturing ones—the hate and envy of her brother or the anger for her father's having left her and taken her brother."

"So there's a lot of material to digest," I put in, "the oedipal and preoedipal mixed up together. Any thought on how you want to proceed?" I wanted to see what Reiko would do with all this material. I wasn't quite sure what was being assimilated.

"You mean with my patient?"

The tension in the group was relieved by laughter. I continued, "Is it too much? Do you need some pressure taken from you so you have room to digest some of this?"

"No, I am hanging on."

Again the group broke out in laughter as though to protect the little girl in Reiko.

Reiko continued the story about her father. "You see, his plane crashed and the pilot landed the aircraft into the ocean. It was in the Atlantic and he almost drowned. He was finally rescued by a little boat off Colombia."

"And he went home?" a member asked.

"Yes, and meanwhile we went to the airport having no idea this had happened."

"Oh my God!" Shirley exclaimed.

"The decision about the twins had already been made?" Joan asked.

"No, the decision was not made about the twins."

Again I thought some synthesis was called for. George quickly interjected, "Could I just make an observation? I think you said the twin who stayed home, who stayed with you, was the one you spoiled and made a lot of fuss over and really took care of. But then you describe yourself as identifying with the one who went to your aunt. I find it interesting that you overcompensated for the one who stayed home as if she were the suffering one. It fascinates me that you saw her as the one who needed all the care, *not* the one who was sent away."

An intense dialogue broke out between George and Reiko. "Yes, it's true. Because the one who was sent away had all the luxuries."

"But it's probably a bit more complex than that," protested George.

"It seemed a better thing to go away than to stay."

"I think you wished you had been taken."

"Yes, there was a part of me that wanted to do that . . ."

"What's the advantage of being adopted? What would the advantage be?"

"A lot."

"*What?*" said George, somewhat exasperated. The tension of the group temporarily broke with laughter.

Here I am encouraging her to differentiate from mother. Perhaps some of Reiko's little-girl wistfulness will diminish as she separates from the family.

"Reiko's mother has a headache," I quipped, which brought on more laughter.

Reiko answered, "There's a lot she did from a very early age. For instance, she travelled with her parents. They went all over the world."

"Were there fewer pressures on her?" someone asked.

"She had no responsibilities," responded Reiko. "She never had to share anything."

I stepped in to start summing up, since our time was running out. "So there's a lot of pressure to share and be responsible, as well as a prohibition against complaining or becoming angry in your family."

"Yes."

"How does this relate to the years three and ten of your patient? The envy she's related here? The wish for the father? The sickness? How does this enter?

I am pushing the therapist to take a much more analytic differentiated perspective.

Reiko spoke rather forcefully now, "Her father was much softer and more accepting of who she was. With her mother, it was more conditional. My sense is that she was completely swallowed up by the mother, given some things, but also swallowed up and intruded upon. Then she would go to the father who, in his quiet, passive way, would give her some things in return. There was also a lot of sexualized stuff for my patient and it all got mixed up, so she looks for men who are somewhat effeminate, but giving."

"When she starts moving, something happens to create a regression. What do you think occurs at these times?" I asked.

Reiko thought a moment. "Maybe when she has a boyfriend who is really going to be in her life and could be a marriage partner, it frightens her."

"What is she frightened of?" I prodded.

"I think she is frightened of . . . she keeps saying, 'I don't want to be running the household and be this ambitious woman while he is a house-husband.' That's the manifest content." Reiko went on, "I see the underlying feelingis that she doesn't want to be an aggressive, phallic woman."

I noticed that the tone of the group had now shifted to become cooler and more analytic as we tried to put together the pieces. I continued, "If she did become the aggressive phallic woman, then what?"

"Then she'd step on him like her mothers does, which she rejects . . . Ruth isn't very comfortable with either side of the identity."

"You say she rejects. *What* does she reject?" Jim asked.

"As she gets near a man, she moves closer to the identity of her mother, and this scares her," someone clarified.

Reiko readily agreed. "She's frightened of the identity of her mother, but is attracted to soft men who give her contact." Reiko added, "She is with a soft man," referring to her fiancé. "At the same time this is something she does not want. She does not want to repeat her mother's history, but she does not know what else to do. That's where she is. She is very happy when her boyfriend says: 'Cut it out! Stop it!' and is dominant and controlling. She likes that."

> I suspect that there is some confusion on Reiko's part regarding the difference between dominant and controlling, as contrasted with aggressive and assertive. I decide to leave this alone, for it is a side issue in terms of the major theme of the case presentation.

"Then she feels she is taken care of," Joan added, filling in the picture.

I now tried to give a few organizing comments:

"When she becomes like her mother, she feels that there is no one to take care of her. She separates from the male part of herself, the father, and feels abandoned and anxious. Complicating the picture are envious feelings toward males her own age who are like her brother and in turn get more mothering."

"That's right." Reiko nodded in agreement. "That's exactly what her conflict is, so you can imagine how glad she was when she became pregnant, because she wanted to test her boyfriend. He said: 'Look, what are you worried about? We'll get married.'"

I was aware of having become very active, but it did seem to help, so I went on. "Now, just to throw some more feelings into the pot, she put more pressure on you to take care of her, to take over the burden. You did not want that, perhaps because it felt similar to when your father was away and your mother wanted you to take over. At that point, you wanted to have your childhood. You wanted your father there, and you could not tell your mother to lay off."

"Oh, no," blurted Reiko, vehemently.

"You could not deal with that kind of resentment or loss," I said, "so it was all glossed over. Your patient is getting nearer this man, but at the same time that she deals with her boyfriend, she also has to deal with a new perception of herself as a woman. Inside of her, women are either destructive toward men and basically do not get nurtured, or, if anything, they get abandoned."

"I hadn't thought of it like that . . . with the abandonment—"

"—So that she is struggling with sexual identity, as well as some very early pregenital issues about mothering and what mothering is, as well as what femininity is. Also whether a man can take care of her and respond to her without abandoning her."

". . . or being the passive father," Reiko added.

"That's right," I concurred.

"Because I think my father was like that, too."

A thoughtful silence pervaded the room. I finally asked Reiko, "Do you have any last feelings, or have you had enough?"

"This has been very powerful. It will take me a while to take it all in."

"Do you want to take home the tape?"

"Sure, I'll bring it back."

TRANSCULTURAL RECOGNITION

The session ended on the gentle lyrical tone in which it had begun. The group, for its part, mirrored the quiet, lonely, sad part of Reiko that alternated with the playful girl in her who wanted support and protection from a very demanding mother. We can see how the cultural attitudes interfaced with intrapsychic issues. The cooperative atmosphere of Reiko's early culture worked to blunt her striving for autonomy. She thought she had eluded these pressures and separated from the pull to remain fuzzy and merged in the family matrix when she left Japan to adopt the American culture as her own. In fact, the old attitudes did not entirely dissolve, but lived on below the surface, only to return in Reiko's work with Ruth.

Reiko's identification with the twin role became an important dimension in understanding the countertransference. Reiko unveiled the role of the fun-loving sister who played center stage for her adopted family. This self, though enacted, also was seen as the "bad," selfish part of her identification, for Reiko's role in the family was to be the helper, the support for Mom while Father was away. A good Japanese girl was expected to live up to her familial obligations.

Reiko complained that the case was both burdensome and tiresome. She lost touch with her western self, the part of her that must confront her patient. Perhaps what she had done was to regress, along with her patient, to the good, self-effacing little girl who could not deal with her own aggression.

Sexual identity issues combined with strong abandonment issues serve as major forces for regression in Reiko's patient. The delicate balance of offering true support and connectedness through mirroring the patient's loneliness, while simulatenously offering a firm structure, was the initial challenge for the therapist. Unfortunately, the very mirroring transference that was so necessary, drew Reiko like a magnet to an early fused identification with her patient. The need to *confront* further complicated the picture, since it meant that Reiko must leave the psychological nexus of her Japanese family. As noted before, one simply did not do this in her native society.

The group gently supported, interpreted, and organized some of these important issues for Reiko. To her credit, Reiko did recognize that behind her boredom lurked feelings of envy and aggression that had been prohibited in her own background. She also came to see complicating problems that had to do with her own ambivalent feelings around sexual issues. Her own father was somewhat passive and abandoning, similar to the patient's. Thus both therapeutic parties must ultimately be drawn to men who are somewhat less than powerful fathers but who may also be men. Finally, both therapeutic parties may some day examine the patient's fear of the therapist, masked by the role of the fun-loving, seductive girl. This fear of the female authority's aggression may be a necessary link for the patient fully to work out her feminine identification.

The group became an important model as it mirrored, as well as interpreted, protected and cared, all the time maintaining a focus on the organization of the case. As leader, I often found myself in the role of protective father, perhaps hearing on some level the unconscious needs of the presenter. I did find myself wondering if I was organizing a bit too much at the end of the session. Yet, upon further reflection, perhaps this was exactly what Reiko wanted from the presentation.

A few points regarding this presentation bear special emphasis:

1. A mirroring role can create a regressive pull towards fusion with a given patient. In the preceding presentation, Reiko's dissociated early background, both in its conflictual and cultural contexts, seems to be a fertile field to support such a countertransference regression. As we become close and holding with our patients, the loss of analytic distance becomes an increasingly important issue that bears attention.

2. A mirroring stances does not preclude the use of interpretation. When there is a good deal of the former at the cost of an interpretive role, the possibility of a countertransference issue requires some investigation.

3. An empathic mirroring role can be very gratifying for both therapeutic paticipants. A seemingly theoretical technical stance that provided this type of closeness can cover such issues as aggression, hostility, and autonomy strivings.

Chapter 6

DAISY

Greed in the Therapist

No Perfect "Parent," No Powerless Patient

The issues surrounding greed and a hungering for nurturance that emerge from Daisy's case presentation reflect problems with which the group had been struggling for at least 3 months. Through the guise of looking at such questions as how much to charge a patient, whether to charge for cancellations, when and how much to raise fees, group members anxiously touched or avoided touching the hungry children within themselves.

While all of us must struggle in one way or another with our needs for nurturance versus societal bounds on greed, the therapist who sees himself as a giver and helper may have a particularly difficult time coming to terms with that part of himself that remains a hungry child. This conflict may become reflected in the therapy situation, particularly if the patient comes from a psychologically deprived background. With this kind of patient, an immense hunger is projected into the treatment relationship, and just as we, as therapists, may avoid looking at and coming to terms with our hunger and our revulsion at our greed, so too, we may deny that important process to our patients. We may fall into playing the good mother while dissociating ourselves from the bad one, thereby undercutting the necessary evolution of the negative transference. Ultimately, both patient and therapist must face a bitter piece of reality: There are no perfect "breasts" nor powerless patients.

Daisy and her patient struggle with these issues as their respective defenses mirror one another and muddy the treatment process. They each get trapped along the circular path of depression. The rules of this road are that one must be lovable and undemanding to get "fed," yet no one could possibly tolerate such a greedy "child," so a devaluation of what is given occurs, reinforcing the sense of deprivation and hunger.

As we look at the presentation, notice how the dynamics of the depressive cycle are recreated in the group from the very beginning, then proceed to weave in and out of the discussion as the focus moves back and forth between the case material and group considerations.

THE SESSION: GIVING AND GETTING

Daisy began: "Has anybody said he or she is going to present a case?"

The group laughed, and Dorothy jumped in to complain, "I was thinking that we have to *talk* about this, because it is really starting to drive me crazy. If I'm not exactly on time, someone has already volunteered to present."

Another member took a conciliatory position. "Well, we can talk about how to deal with this better . . ." Someone else chimed in, "You people have a way of wanting to figure out a method, and it just doesn't work. I don't like any system."

Dorothy now retorted, "I don't like the method system either, but before I left to come here I was sitting in the house thinking that I wanted to present a case, I started extra early, since I've got farther to come than the rest of you. And I still end up standing out in the foyer because I don't want to fuck up the floor—it's crazy." The group laughed and Dorothy continued, "I don't want to go through this every time. I realize, of course, that some of that is my problem, but not all of it . . ."

Daisy defensively responded, "I may not use the whole hour."

Dorothy cut back in, "I mean, it's not an emergency, by any means. We shouldn't even be having this conversation. You have a right to take the whole hour . . ."

"And you have the right to take it for yourself," responded Daisy.

I realized that we were getting into group dynamics, but the build up of feelings required a clearing of the air. Occasionally there is a need for this in supervisory groups, but one has to be very judicious in making this decision to let the group take this direction. In this instance, the underlying feelings were getting into the way of presenting the cases.

I decided to take the role of referee and asked, "How would you people like to approach this problem?"

A member took this up. "We could probably have a schedule, and if somebody didn't want to take their turn it could be given up to someone else."

"I have resistance towards taking turns," another member objected. "As you were talking, I was thinking that everybody knows that next week Dorothy wants to present, so that means that now I have to wait two weeks before it's my turn."

Daisy, again trying to be conciliatory, remarked, "Maybe she won't feel like presenting next week."

"She will," another member adds.

For the next 15 minutes, the group continues to struggle with feelings of greed, guilt, and efforts at conciliation. Finally we arrive at an interim solution: No system can take the place of taking, giving, negotiation, and ultimately accepting partials. Finally, Daisy moves into the substance of her presentation.

Daisy started to speak. "I'm the only one who works mostly with children. Even though I've been in this group a long time, I'm realizing I don't have enough experience with adults.

"The patient I'm concerned about is a twenty-eight-year-old woman. I think she's neurotic. I started working with her at the end of December, and we had a honeymoon period at the beginning. She felt very good about coming, even thanking me at the end of each session. She reported that she had been feeling better than she had previously, but then just recently, in the last two or three weeks, things have changed.

"I want to understand my anxiety over this case, and perhaps reassess the diagnosis as well. Maybe I should go right into what makes me uncomfortable.

"The session before last, she started questioning if I could help her and wondering if I'm a good enough therapist for her. I responded that I would not be here if that wasn't the case. I could see by her reaction that she did not like when her questions were not answered. Somewhere in the session I answered more directly by saying, 'I think I can.' That session stayed very much in my mind.

"In the next session she asked if I was angry with her. Some of it was her issue about being assertive, but more importantly, I felt that I was defensive. Part of me felt, 'Right, I'm not sure I can do it.' It really hit a nerve that I wasn't quite in touch with. So in the following session I apologized à la Art Robbins. I admitted to a failure."

> Here we see a misuse of a previous supervisory session. Being open with a patient regarding one's errors should not be confused with a form of confession to one's patients. Note, we see a patient who is frightened of her hostility and may only become more threatened as the therapist apologizes for her defensiveness.

"Failure to what?" a member asked.

"Not really a failure, but that I was somewhat defensive when I answered with, 'I wouldn't be here if I didn't think I could handle it,'" replied Daisy. "I wanted for something in the material that would relate to what happened last week. She talked about a wonderful teacher and worried about being a good enough student. I brought in her concern about being a good enough patient, so we could explore the connection to last week. First she denied it, but then she said that a friend of hers had asked how old I was, and she started thinking that I was in my early or mid-thirties; pretty young, she thought. That led her to wonder what kind of experience and training I'd had. I commented that I had been defensive in answering her challenging question of the week before, and we explored her wish that her therapist could make her better in a very short time on the one hand, and on the other hand, her feeling I was more human now that I made mistakes. She liked that I was more human, yet at the same time it took away the magic that she wanted to establish in our relationship. My feeling, however, was that something changed. I seemed to lose distance in the case. I felt vulnerable. I admitted to being defensive, to not being the all-knowing, on-top-of-everything therapist. It reinforced my general feeling that I'm not sure that I can really do it. That feeling is uncomfortable."

> The self-attacking attitude of the therapist appears to undermine the confidence of both participants. Humanness should not be

confused with being apologetic nor serve as a screen to control a patient's hostility.

A member broke in to ask, "When you say, 'do it' what do you mean?"

"Work with this woman, have enough knowledge and therapeutic distance to be able to help her," responded Daisy, quietly.

Another member inquired, "How does this woman make you insecure?"

"She's bright, she has insight into herself, and a lot of her issues come close to *my* issues."

"What are the similarities of issues?" the member pursued.

"She says that she has a hard time feeling feelings; that she can understand what is going on intellectually, but has a hard time staying with her feelings. Also, when she first started, she told me she didn't want a quiet, passive therapist; she wanted an active therapist. So from the start I asked questions and I tried not to let her go off on her own."

> Instead of exploring the patient's need for activity, the therapist complies with the request. Again we see evidence of the therapist's fear of frustrating her patient and provoking hostility.

A member observed, "She sounds like she's pretty aggressive and controlling. She calls the shots and tells you, 'I want you to be this way.'"

I commented, "When your patient said she didn't want a passive therapist, you immediately became active, rather than exploring why she didn't want a passive therapist."

"I tried," said Daisy, "but we really didn't get very far with that." She went into a long, labored explanation of what went on in the session.

Another member complained, "I'm lost. Maybe I just don't have a sense of what went on in the beginning, of what you wanted to deal with." Many heads nodded in agreement.

Delores tried to be helpful. "The last thing you said kind of struck a chord. She was telling you on the one hand that she wanted you to take charge, and in the meantime she was running all over the place. You were trying to hold on to her, when maybe the issue is her *running*."

Daisy continued to express self-doubts. "She is ambivalent about coming to a therapist. I was feeling that I didn't have much experience."

> The therapist continues to attack herself and feels inadequate.
> The competitive challenge of the patient seems to reinforce the
> therapist's masochistic defenses.

Delores continued: "I know how you have experienced your past therapists. When you were talking about your patient, I thought about you and your difficulty with the therapists you went to up to your current one. You've often asked, 'Is she doing the right thing for me? Am I getting the right thing?' It sounds similar to what you are saying to your patient—'Am I giving her what she needs? Am I good enough?'"

I turned to Daisy and gently said, "You look sad and anxious . . ."

> I tried to emphasize the tone of Daisy's voice and explore the underlying affects.

There was a long silence before Daisy started to speak. "I don't know if this is something to work on in my own therapy. I really haven't had a good therapeutic experience in treatment for . . . seven years now. That makes me question how I can do therapy without having had a good experience. It's a very basic question of adequacy. If I have a patient who challenges me on that score, it's very hard for me. It feels loaded, and I'm not sure if it's an issue for supervision, or if it should be kept in my personal therapy. That confusion is part of my ambivalence about bringing it here. I was trying to stick to something that I could work with here. I wanted to stay with the patient and with how to work with her. I could talk more about her and . . ." Daisy's voice trails off.

Daisy requests soothing and support from the group.

> I wondered to myself whether the group will buy her masochistic
> maneuver.

Delores reiterated: "It seems to me that the issue is your experience with therapy and how it's touched you or hasn't."

Daisy became virtually inaudible at this point.

I encouraged her with, "You can take it anywhere you want to go."

Delores coaxed her with, "Why do you feel that it's not relevant here? We *do* get into things like being stuck or what's standing in the way or interfering with being a therapist. We could talk about it."

> Delores takes a very supportive position. I wasn't quite sure whether we were being punished by Daisy for putting her on the spot.

Another silence followed before Daisy could muster something within and speak up. "It's starting to come out as the issue that I mentioned earlier when we were talking: my issue about being able to really put some trust in another person . . ." Her voiced trailed off once again.

Dorothy must have been quietly seething, because she suddenly broke out with: "Were you the one who said that some people were presenting more than others, and that maybe the ones who present more should let others take turns? I'm furious, because my feeling is that it's a real guilt trip, although I don't know if you meant it that way. I don't think I'm pulling the issue away from you. I think that if we can work something out it will be helpful in terms of this case. I've presented a lot, and I'm certain I'll continue to present a lot, but in some way I feel it reflects real anger on your part for you to say something like what you did. The implication is that now the people who have presented a lot should just take a back seat."

> Dorothy picks up the silent accusation and attempts to deal with some of her own guilt regarding this issue.

Daisy made a vehement denial. "I *didn't* say that! What I said was that if you come in and want to present, and someone else comes in and wants to present, that in some way it would make sense . . ." she trailed off . . . "there are eight siblings . . ." Again she became inaudible.

"That's not fair," protested Dorothy. "That's asking me, or whoever I'm representing, to take responsibility for you, or your *reluctance*, or whatever."

> Dorothy goes after Daisy and refuses to be controlled or punished by Daisy's humble demeanor.

Daisy flashed back, "I'm not asking you to take *responsibility*; I'm just asking you to accept the fact that other people have space here. I don't take a *lot* of space, but when I do take it, I expect you to accept it."

> One should be rewarded for suffering and be paid back for receiving pain.

"I don't hear that," responded Dorothy. "I hear . . ." but before she could continue, Daisy came back with, "Well, that's how I felt I was presenting it to you. I have no resentment that you are presenting more. I take responsibility when I don't, and I'm not asking you . . . If I come into the room and you say you are going to present today, even if I haven't presented for six months (I'm exaggerating) I wouldn't say, 'Hey, since I haven't presented in six months, you should step down and I'll do it.' I've never said that; I'm not planning to."

> Daisy pulls back and alters her position.

"That's not what I'm suggesting," said Dorothy. "Of course I know that you wouldn't do it that way, but I think that there's something in your statement that suggests that people who have taken a lot should take into consideration the fact that other people haven't presented that much. I think there's something else in that statement."

> I am aware that we are getting into fairly heavy group dynamics, but I suspect that it will be ultimately relevant to the case. For the time being, I've decided to let the material follow its natural course.

I interrupted the two of them to address Dorothy: "Do you have some guilt about that?"

Dorothy thought for a moment and said, "It's hard for me . . . It's always been, I guess. I do feel guilty, even though I know that it's not rational and I don't feel that what Daisy said was a fair statement."

I turned to Daisy: "Do you have any response?"

"Maybe part of it is that I want you to see that I'm not presenting a lot, but you seem to hear that I'm asking for some acknowledgment. Maybe on some level I'm taking responsibility through the back door . . ."

I turned away from Daisy to address the group at large. "I'd like to raise a more basic issue. What's wrong with getting as much time as you want and fighting and *plotting* to get it?"

The group members laughed anxiously.

Delores was the first to speak. "*I* do that, but there is some guilt. When I came in last week I felt that there was no way I was going to present, but when I saw no one was going to present, boy, I wanted to get in there."

I turned to Dorothy and asked, "How do you feel about her attitude?"

"I don't like it . . . Well, I plot too . . ."

I continued, "How do you feel about these people who want time and plot for it? How about seeing a vacuum and Delores saying, 'I'm going for it.'"

"I wonder how it is for her," Daisy mused, "because I can't be that way. It's amazing. I wish I felt entitled, or was able to use the time."

"Me, too," Dorothy spoke up. "I want to feel entitled, too, while I'm doing it."

Daisy continued, "It's not even feeling entitled, it's having the ability to *take*."

I added, "It's not just the ability to take, it's the ability to take without *guilt*. Apparently," I said, turning to Delores, "your mother didn't induce too much guilt about this."

"Oh, yes she did!" retorted Delores, emphatically. "Most certainly she did, and I don't do what I do without trepidation. I'm fearful every time I feel like I'm taking, because I'm afraid I'm going to be knocked down every time I do it. But I think that over the years I've gradually been able to get my courage up and just do it. That's *therapy*, that's not *me*. It doesn't come easily."

The group giggled in appreciation.

I took issue with this. "Even when I knew you as a student at Pratt, you were like that."

"That's when I was coming out."

"That's when you were coming out?" I asked.

"Yeah, Pratt really fed that."

"Okay," I said, "now we are getting at the heart of the issue. Is hunger dangerous? Is there really too much of it inside each of us for anyone to take? Is it so repulsive that we must sit on it and watch it so it won't get out of hand? Is it really such a terrible part of ourselves?"

> I am trying to broaden the issue to give Daisy an opportunity to observe others explore their particular issues and adaptations around greed. The hope is that distance will give Daisy permission to see various alternatives to handling oral aggression.

A member commented: "I was lectured that if you felt 'hungry' or needy, it was very bad, and if you acted on those feelings you had to do it in a way that people didn't see it."

I turned back to Delores. "But Delores waves it out there. She's provocative . . ."

Delores interrupted me to say, "I may be provocative to the point of self-destruction."

I turned to Rachel: "What's your position on taking as much as you can get?"

"Well, I go through periods when I get very greedy and it's okay, but then I think I get guilty and hold back for quite a while . . ." The group laughed in unison, and one member piped up, "And then you're good! You've had your gorge and then . . ."

"But when I'm in there, I don't feel the guilt at all. I love it. Then later I feel the backlash that says, 'let others have *their* turn.'"

I commented, "So hunger is the bad part of lots of people, not just you. Maybe it's a 'universal anxiety.' There are very few people comfortable with their hunger."

Daisy rejoined the discussion with, "I think. . . . I think also my mother felt my needs were disgusting."

"Disgusting?" I asked.

"Yeah," said Daisy. "There is a part of my father that is greedy, and my mother is very critical, always putting him down."

"So when you need something immediately, there's the bad part saying that you are not worth very much. Perhaps you say, 'I'll do it myself,' or suffer silently with it. Other people get counterphobic. There are different ways of handling the hunger, but it's very, very tricky. Now, when Dorothy said to you, 'I don't like you accusing me, making me feel guilty about my hunger,' in so many words, what was your response?"

Daisy said, "Dorothy started questioning, maybe she had a point that I was overlooking, so I took it back and tried to take responsibility."

I continued, "What if Dorothy said, 'I want to be Miss Piggy of the group.'

Everyone laughed.

Dorothy popped up with, "You didn't call me that by accident." More laughter erupted.

I went on. "Now, what if Dorothy announced in every session, 'I am going to try to get in any time I want and you people better be on guard. I want as much as I can get from this group'?"

"It's close to the truth," interjected Dorothy.

"And if it is close to the truth . . ."

"Wait a minute! Stop it! What do you mean?" Dorothy countered, becoming visibly uncomfortable.

Daisy asked, "You don't want to get as much as you can from this group?"

A long silence ensued before Dorothy, acutely distressed, responded. "I guess this issue is really hitting me where I live and I don't want to joke about it. I'm not capable of laughing about it . . ."

"I'm not joking," said Daisy.

"What's the big deal with wanting as much as you can get?" I asked.

Dorothy responded, "I guess this is the disgusting part of me."

"Well, I wish I had some of it," said Daisy. "Mostly I'm envious that you're able to do it. When I try to picture myself doing it, a part of me feels too *loud* . . . It's hard for me to put this in words . . . maybe the critical mother in me, or whoever put it on me or prevented me from going towards that position . . ."

> Daisy is starting to make connections regarding some of her own internal representations and the expression of need.

"So, Daisy," I said, "what if you now become Miss Piggy of the group and you announced to people, 'Every session, you people be on guard. I'm going to get in there and get as much as I can and watch out. You better all be on time, because as soon as that door opens, I'm running in and saying, I'm presenting.'"

"I'll present even if I'm late!" Daisy joined in with relish.

Through the laughter one member chimed in, "Maybe you could set up a system so that people would pay more money if they presented more."

As the laughter died down, Daisy picked up her thread of thought. "A lot of times when I'm thinking about presenting, I get scared, so then I convince myself that I don't really need to present the case. I tell myself I can resolve it myself, that I'll wait to see what happens in the next session with this patient and what I do about it. To imagine myself as Miss Piggy is not even possible in fantasy."

Delores commented: "Last week I knew that Daisy wanted to present. We see each other outside of here. So when I was getting ready to present I asked if she had decided not to do it. I immediately said to myself, 'All right, I'm going to do it!' But I felt really guilty because I knew Daisy wanted that time . . ."

"But not quite guilty *enough*," I pointed out.

"No, not guilty enough to *stop* me."

I went on, "Not guilty enough to say, 'Daisy, I know you really want to present and I'll give you my time because you need it.' You couldn't do that."

"No."

"Thank God," said Daisy emphatically. "If Delores had to take care of me so I would be able to present, it would be horrible."

"Ah . . . so you are going to have to have the courage enough to say, 'I want,'" I gently goaded. Daisy nodded affirmatively.

Dorothy didn't feel quite settled about the whole issue, however. "I guess I want a fair system set up so that I don't have to get in there and scramble and *show* that bad part of me."

> We see how a system can cover up the "bad" part of a therapist's individual psyche. I thought that this group needed a cognitive breathing space and started to shift the level of discussion.

By the looks on the faces around the room, it was clear that Dorothy was not alone in these feelings. I remarked, "People who have a deprived background constantly feel that their hunger is the destructive part of themselves. In fact, they're convinced that it is their hunger that created the punishing atmosphere of their families in the first place, and if they were at all able to control their hunger, maybe they would have received love or support. All this is concluded unconsciously of course. This hunger is powerful as well as dangerous. We get this circular kind of business which says, 'If I weren't so needy, I'd be loved, so I deserve to be punished in my deprivation,' which intensifies the neediness." I turned to Daisy: "Now Daisy, where do you want to go with this? Do you want to give yourself limits as to what is appropriate to bring to this group in terms of the help you need? I'm going to give you permission to be greedy. So what can we tell you to do . . . Take a little morsel? You wouldn't want to take too much after starving yourself for so long."

> Again I was mirroring one particular facet of the masochistic character. Set your own limits before someone takes the prize away from you.

Silence followed. Finally Daisy spoke up. "Okay, I appreciate it. I'll take a crumb."

A member adds with much laughter: "I keep thinking, 'Good, we'll give her five minutes, and give Dorothy half an hour, and then I'll get it next time. They shared this week, they're finished." I returned to Daisy. "Are you sure you've reached the saturation point of what you can take, or do you want a little more?"

"My presentation is not over," said Daisy emphatically. The group laughed.

"Good," I replied with a grin.

> We had come to the end of our group process and it was quite apparent that all of us were ready to go back to the case. This is an excellent example of how the selected working through of group dynamics does not interfere with the overall goal of case supervision.

Daisy picked up her presentation. "I want to talk about this patient. This is a woman who was in therapy first as a teenager, then again late in adolescence. She states that she went to therapy because her parents sent her; that she was never really engaged in it. She describes herself in her adolescence as quite withdrawn and depressed; not making much contact with people. She bought a lot of drugs. Her parents divorced when she was fourteen.

"Then when she was eighteen she started working. Her mother worked for a dentist, and she started working at the same place. During that period she suffered from hives, while her mother entered into an affair with a distant relative. My patient was obese until age twenty-two, when she lost one hundred pounds. At twenty-four she met her present boyfriend. She lives with him at her mother's house. Now twenty-eight, she also has three younger brothers. The twenty-one year-old, the youngest, is considered the successful one because he's married. The twenty-three year-old is in therapy. Then there's a grandmother the patient was close to when growing up, a warm, maternal figure who became gradually senile and subsequently died, causing a lot of upset for the patient."

Someone asked, "Is she still obese?"

"No."

"She kept the weight off?"

"Yes. But lately she is complaining that she isn't doing any exercise."

"Is this the same woman who had sexual problems with the boy-friend?" Delores asked.

"Right, that's part of why she came to me. About a year and a half ago she started having problems with her boyfriend. She's not inter-ested in sex at all and thinks this is a major thing about her. She doesn't understand it and wants help with that. Also, she gets panic at-tacks about eating, over fear of overeating and what might happen."

A group member asked, "How does this woman express anger?"

"When she gets upset about things she becomes demanding."

> We see a regression to an oral demanding level when the patient
> approaches anger. I suspect that the therapist does not pick this
> up because it comes too close to her own issues.

Rachel asked, "What do you think is behind her not being inter-ested in sex with her boyfriend? Was she interested at one point, and then it stopped?"

Daisy responded: "I'm trying to get a more extensive history about her sexual relationships. It's loaded. Her grandmother was raped, and she was in the house tied up while it was happening. The grandmother called for her and she went, but wasn't able to do any-thing. Her first sexual encounter was not pleasant. It was with some-one she met at a party. She's hazy about what exactly happened."

"She describes her relationship with her mother as very sym-biotic; the same way she describes this boyfriend. For a year they haven't had sexual contact, but they are still close. She feels there's something wrong with him, yet he is the only one who really under-stands her. She offered an example of a family party when she made a toast. No one understood what she was trying to say, but her boyfriend did.

"My experience of it is that they are so in tune with each other on a very early level and that sexuality is not really necessary for the rela-tionship. I'm not sure what else this signifies."

I stepped in here, wanting to get some material we could really sink our teeth into. "Could we get into the case now in terms of the interaction?"

"Ours?" Daisy asked. "Me and her?"

"Yes. Give us your last session, or any session that sticks out in your mind."

"One more important detail," said Daisy. "In the beginning, when she first came and gave me a lot of history, I took notes during the session. She was giving me a lot of information, and I knew I wouldn't retain all the material. It seemed like information I'd like to have written down in case I wanted to go back to it. So I took notes, and when I brought it up with her to see how she felt about it, she thought it was very important. She wanted me to preserve everything she was giving me. She felt that I should have a record to go back over. It seemed that she was even more obsessive than me. She even describes herself as such a person. My reaction to her comments was to stop taking notes. The way we started seemed significant in terms of our working relationship; she talked from the beginning about obsessive features."

> Both patient and therapist seem to have obsessive features that mirror each other.

"Okay," I said. "Let's get into a session; on with the two of you talking." When a long silence followed, I suggested, "Try the last session."

Daisy began, "She had started school so she couldn't come at the usual time. I had prepared her for being in a different room where there would be toys from the previous session. She looked at the toys and asked if that's what I did, then asked, 'You don't have Uno? You don't have Parcheesi?' I didn't have certain toys she expected me to have, games that she has. She said she bought the games for a kid in the neighborhood. It seems the kids in the neighborhood like to come to their house, but actually, she bought them for herself—she likes to play board games."

"Okay, now what did you say?" I asked.

"First I listened more to what she said about it, and then I asked her if she would like to play some of the games here. Wait a minute—no, at first I reacted to the toys I didn't have."

"What did you say?" I asked, trying to get more of a feel for the tenor of the interaction.

"I asked her if I didn't have the right toys. She said that they seemed pretty good and I didn't say anything else."

I interjected, "Just in terms of technique, you might say, 'Yes, I don't have as much as I should have.'"

"I see, elaborate on the fear," said Daisy, then continued. "Then she talked about toys and made some more positive statements about my toys, and I said that if she wanted to use them she could. She said she might, later, which made me wonder if she would regress in the room. I started to worry about it, too; like she might start playing with the doll house or something. What's going to go on here in the future?"

"What if she did?" I asked.

> This is an extremely critical point in the session. Daisy implies that regression is destructive. Are we talking about the therapist's fear?

"I think it would be good," said Daisy, "although I don't know why, but I have the feeling that that *amount* of regression could be bad."

A member added: "Although you had invited it, in a way."

"Yes, and I think I liked the idea of that part. I usually work better with regressed patients. Then she started telling me about the anxiety of trying to do really well in school."

> We quickly shifted from a fun to an achievement orientation. I suspected that the therapist did not see this shift, as it came too close to some of her own problems.

A member stopped her with, "How did she share this with you? What did she say? Can you be her?"

Daisy went on describing. "In this part of the session she was more distant. In the earlier part of the session she would even sit like me, and I would try to change the way my arm was to see if she would change too. We were much more in tune with each other. That's disappeared."

I tried to get her into real dialogue. "Tell us more of the interaction between you two."

"I had an agenda from the previous session," said Daisy.

A member challenged Daisy more directly. "You have an agenda here, too. It feels like you're hiding something, and you're not giving it to us. I'm waiting to hear what's happening in the session, and I haven't heard it. I can't find Daisy anywhere.

> The halting retentive quality of Daisy indicates that under pressure she regresses to an anal withholding level.

Daisy responded with, "I was anxious after the previous session because of her challenge to me, so this time I decided to bring this issue in and work with it. I was looking for a place where I could tie up with what was happening in this session.

Delores asked, "Why did you feel so pressed about the previous session? Did you feel that you had wrecked something between you, or had done some damage?"

"I felt that I had made a boo-boo," said Daisy. "In the previous session I was defensive and didn't admit to it, and wasn't in touch with my feelings during the session. I wanted to deal with it . . ."

"I see," I interjected, "you wanted to relieve your guilt."

"So I could go on. I didn't want to start the session directly with, 'I'm sorry.'"

I made a technical point here. "When you admit your mistakes to a patient, you are trying to help both of you live with your respective senses of infallibility. If you use it as a confession, you're not helping your patient live better with himself. Here, it's teaching him to confess. The patient wasn't upset with you. She hadn't voiced any complaints. It seems that you were raising an issue that was yours, not hers."

Daisy protested, "Last week she was upset with me and she told me so."

"What was she bothered with you about last week?" I asked.

"That I was reacting defensively!" said Daisy. "And that I didn't really own up to it. She talked about not wanting to be in therapy for a long time, of wanting it to be a pretty quick process. She said that now that she'd decided to do it, she needed help and couldn't help herself."

I tried to help clarify. "But the question she has for you is, 'Do you think you are a good enough therapist?' And Daisy says 'If I didn't think so, I wouldn't be here.' What do you think about that statement?" I asked the group at large.

> I take distance away from Daisy and give her a chance to observe
> the group's reaction to this question. Perhaps it will give her some
> permission to be more comfortable with her agression.

Group members all speak at the same time, the consensus being reflected in the words of one member. "It's a fine statement . . . So what?"

"Well, she questioned whether I was angry," said Daisy. "It felt to me like there was an aggression issue here . . . that when she becomes assertive she is afraid of being attacked. When I was checking myself afterwards, there was a part of me that really *was* angry about the challenge. When I said what I did, it was the right response, but it's the *tone* that makes the difference."

> Honesty with a guilt-ridden patient does not help. It only serves to threaten them with their hostility.

I again addressed the group at large, "Now, if she says 'you know, you're being defensive,' what would you people answer if you were the therapist?"

Delores responded, "So I'm defensive, so I'm hostile."

"Okay."

Rachel added, "I would want to ask him to tell me more."

Daisy responded somewhat defensively, "I tried to get more feelings out . . ."

A member suggested, "Suppose she just owned up to it, said something like 'yeah, I'm defending myself, what does that do to you?'"

A member playing patient responded, "I don't like it."

I asked, "What do you think he would say to that—patient?"

Daisy as patient: "When you're defensive it shows that you have a weakness or have a problem and I don't know if you can help me. I want you to be supertherapist, be supercharged."

Member as therapist: "I guess I felt I needed to defend myself. I'm feeling that you're angry."

Again, being self-revealing does not help the situation. It just deflects the action.

Daisy was confused. "Who, me or patient? I can't tell one from the other." The group laughed. Daisy stepped back into the patient role. "I don't like it. Why would you be defensive? If you're a good therapist, why would you be defensive?"

Rachel as therapist: "Oh, I don't know. Maybe there's more to your question . . ." Stepping out of the role, Rachel noted, "I'm feeling backed up about you as patient, so I feel I've got to get control and turn it back on you. She really backs you up."

Daisy as patient: "But I don't like my question being answered with a question. I want an answer."

Rachel as therapist: "How come?"

Daisy as patient: "I want answers from you."

> We cannot avoid the underlying feeling that behind the demand is a good deal of anger that is ducked by Dorothy, the therapist.

Dorothy as therapist: "I understand that you would like an answer, and I would like to give you an answer, but I have the feeling I'm not getting the whole question, so how can I give you an answer? Give me the whole question and I'll try and answer you."

Daisy as patient: "I just feel I need to be sure that you can help me. It's hard for me to come here, and I want to be sure you can help me."

Dorothy as therapist: "What makes you think that I can't, and what would help you to feel that I could?"

Daisy as patient: "I don't know. In my past experiences, I did feel that I was helped by therapists." Again stepping out of role, Daisy says, "She wants me to be in a good place for her—a kind of exclusive perfect position for her . . . all attending, perfect . . ."

> I was aware that some of the issues that were being explored with the patient were present in the group dynamics. Daisy was going to be very disappointed by being unable to finish her case. I hoped I could serve as a model in demonstrating how to deal with these issues.

I waited a moment and said, somewhat uncomfortably, "The time is drawing to a close, and I'm feeling anxious. I'm feeling it's the end of session and we haven't *given* Daisy enough. I'm wondering if maybe she can walk out of here hungry. I feel like I'm in a double bind. If I try to respond, to give something to Daisy, I'm in trouble. If I try to meet her hunger, I'm in trouble. I *hear* the hunger, and I want to give, but the more I try to give, the less adequate I feel. It's similar to being a therapist with a patient like yours. Part of me must pull back and not get worried about my giving or not giving. I'll take my time, and listen, and explore, and bear the sense of unfulfillment . . ."

"That's so hard," said Daisy, looking unconvinced.

Rachel asked, "What about the feeling that you are not giving *enough*, as opposed to you weren't giving *anything*?"

I responded, "So I may not give you, Daisy, enough, or what I give may be *experienced* as not enough."

Daisy: "I think what happens to me as therapist is that if it's not enough, I don't even see the part that I *did* give."

> This is an important part of the countertransference. The split is both in terms of receiving and giving. It is all or nothing.

"Okay," I said, "Then we move into a central issue of depression. The depressive essentially says, 'If I don't get what I want, I've got nothing. If there is not *enough*, it becomes *nothing*.' And the therapist, if he or she isn't attuned to the depressed person, feels the anxiety and wants to be *enough*. But the fact is, he or she is *never* enough."

Rachel responded, "I feel so *anxious* while you are talking about not giving something to somebody."

I clarified: "Not giving what a patient is hungry for and needing touches your own hunger. By giving to a depressed person, you give yourself . . ."

Dorothy: "I was all set to open next week's session here by saying, 'Daisy, I don't think we finished the case . . .'"

Another member cut in, "And do you know what my experience was when you started that? I thought, 'Holy shit, and you're going to give her more time next week!'" The group broke out in laughter.

"That's not fair. That's it!"

"Yeah, and you're giving her too *much*."

Daisy piped up here, "You know what my reaction was? Again I felt I was expressing my need and it was too much. It was my fault."

I turned to Daisy. "You get stuck on feeling like you got nothing. It's hard for you to realize that you really did get something, but not everything."

"If I knew how to take, then I would get," responded Daisy.

Daisy is only half right. She does take, but sometimes can not be satisfied with just a piece of the pie.

I came back with, "That's right, it's your fault. When you've gotten something, you negate it's being something because it's not enough, and then turn it around to make it your fault. Do you see how this works?"

Daisy: "That's because I can't deal with it not being enough . . ."

". . . So if you get nothing, then it becomes your fault," I emphasized.

Rachel: "Oh, wow. Then you become depressed . . ."

"I don't know what to do about that," said Daisy sadly.

"That's right," I affirmed.

Rachel: "My fantasy was that we would all say really nice things to Daisy before she left . . ." The group's laughter halted her words. ". . . But if we can walk out today and feel that Daisy got something, and not feel guilty, we'll be able to worry about what will happen next time, when we get to it." The session concluded on a note of relief and exhaustion.

THE INSATIABILITY OF DEPRESSION

The depressive patient is a most relentless animal who finds it very difficult to give up secret wishes and hidden dreams. At times, we as therapists are worn down by the utter stubbornness and onslaught of a very harsh superego. In spite of this pressure, we must bear our patients' pain, offer ourselves as constant objects, and help our patients to internalize a more human and accepting self-object in the process, as the archaic superego is externalized in the transference.

From the very beginning, the group set the stage for the dynamics of the case presentation to unfold. The issue of who gets how much, and when, in time and space became the immediate topic of the group. A number of defensive techniques come into play, ranging from mechanical applications to a variety of self-beratings and appeasements. The pain, rage, and helplessness of each member of this group mirrored one another, in spite of a variety of different characterological covers.

Daisy silently accused Dorothy of wanting too much and found it very difficult to own up to her accusation. In turn, Dorothy was riddled with defensiveness and was very angry, but stubbornly held on to her position. There was a good deal of anxiety and sharing in their mutual dilemma of how to give and take with one another within the context of how to receive needed help on supervisory issues. The group negotiated and finally found a solution acceptable to all, allowing Daisy to get down to her case.

Throughout the entire presentation Daisy was bogged down by depression. Her voice kept halting, hesitating, and occasionally trailing off as she found herself unable to finish some of her sentences. At other times she became weighed down by details, unable to face the sheer force of her aggressive need to get help. Apologetically she attempted in spite of herself to fight for her position. At the same time she made very sure that she was correct and exacting in her demands of herself and others.

Daisy was reluctant to display her greed, for it is a forbidden feeling that does not lie very comfortably within the confines of her intrapsychic life. Thus, the irony of the depressive dilemma manifested itself in the dialogue of the case presentation: The group felt weighted down and put upon; Daisy's self-doubting, vacillating style of communication created impatience and criticism with her fellow group members. In turn, Daisy's vacillation between exposure and retention became reinforced, thus becoming a part of a convoluted circle that imprisoned her aggressive self. Yet, in spite of these psychic operations, her need for care and attention came out, if only in a self-punishing way.

The identification of therapist and patient in this presentation was clear. Their defenses mirrored one another in their needs to control through masochistic surrender. We also saw the subtle expressions of hostility being played out by both parties. The crucial issue for both therapist and patient emerged in the dialogue: Can each party accept partials? Perhaps, more to the point, the therapist can be less than ideal and still be adequate. Being apologetic to her patient for not living up to the superhero image of her patient's dreams disguised the true nature of Daisy's unconsious motivations: by satisfying the needy child in the patient, she was, through projective identification, responding to some of her own needs.

Apologizing for one's therapeutic errors seems only to distract both parties from the underlying communications. Confessions can be used as a masochistic ploy by the therapist to avoid being seen as the bad mother. In fact, the expression of humanism—that we are capable of errors—can often be a ploy to stifle aggression and hostility. Guilt and the associated omnipotence that lies behind such accusations as those leveled by Daisy's patient must be handled in a direct manner.

Daisy both enjoys and is frightened of regression with her patients. She seems to say to herself, "What if my need to be a child gets out of hand? Perhaps both of us will run away from reality and never want to grow up." Once again we observe the need for control in order to avoid the fantasied destructive impact of our needs getting out of hand. Again, regression is seen as dangerous, or at best is met with some suspicion. There is need to put a tight wrap on one's inner hunger and rapaciousness.

The group as well as the leader struggled with these issues with both laughter and pain. We were all too aware of the universal issue that touches all of us in our struggle to be grown up in the treatment dialogue. The members acted as a container and shared with one another the shame and anxiety we all feel regarding our hunger. At the end of the session, there was relief, comic mockery, and a grudging acceptance that our session was less than perfect, but perhaps in the end, good enough.

Some concluding points in working with countertransference issues in the treatment realm of depression are worth emphasizing:

1. As therapists, we should be alert to a universal tendency to either *do* or *be* something for our patients, if only as a means of alleviating pain. Disappointment, hurt, and rage are part of the territory in working with depression, whereas the ability to listen and be with our patients is, in fact, the curative agent.

2. Masochism and depression are close friends, and flow into one another, but can also be seen as distinct pathological entities. The countertransference induction will often give us clues as to what is in play. When we feel controlled by pain, more often than not, the affects of self-abnegation and humiliation can be seen as a defensive layering that distracts both parties from feelings of power and aggression. In depression, the archaic superego has completely taken over the patient's ego resources so that there is little hope of ever attaining mastery over an ungiving world. Thus, in working with depressed patients, the therapist more often than not feels equally helpless. In turn, the countertransference defenses may arise to avoid the affects of helplessness.

3. The stimulation of countertransference irritation or sadism is a common phenomenon in working with patients in the depressive/-masochistic range. The dissociation of these affects creates problems in empathy such as those manifesting as reaction formations or an identification with the patient's masochistic issues. Occasionally the therapist attempts to convert a masochist into a sadist because of such a countertransference association. The emotional juggling act for a therapist, then, becomes one of being alive and responsive, in *spite* of the patient's counterweight to be heavy and helpless, without resorting to being either sadistic, or all-powerful. Humor can often reach depressive patients, as it often satisfies both the inner wish for pain and relief. Laughter certainly seemed to combine some of these elements in the preceding supervisory session.

4. We can also view conflicts regarding greed along such issues as bad and good internalizations. The greedy part of Daisy was associated with the father inside of herself, the object of a good deal of criticism and disapproval from the mother. Yet he is also the source of her affective nourishment and engagement, as well as life. This places Daisy in a most conflicted role regarding her use of self-assertion to get feeding and nourishment.

Upon reading this transcript, Daisy confronted me in the group and stated that I was a narcissistic and selfish person who was exploiting the members of the group for his own purposes. She was hurt and furious and felt very exposed by the written material. I, in turn, responded defensively and said that if she preferred not to have the chapter included it was entirely her decision. After I realized what I had said, I bit my tongue and subsequently smiled to myself. As therapist, we sometimes think of great lines after the fact. I told Daisy in a later conversation what I should have said: "Yes, I am selfish and greedy, and I hope some day you will be too." She, in turn, shared her response to my comments regarding the return of the two chapters. All she wanted was a good fight with me, and my submission to her demands made her feel all too powerful with her aggression. We both smiled at one another, somewhat the wiser for the experience.

Chapter 7

DAISY

Exploring the Male Element in the Female Therapist

Women often introduce transferential material to their female therapists that is essentially male or father related. Fears and wishes of penetration, loss of control, body vulnerability are but a few of these issues that can come up in the transference/countertransference relationship. In this father/daughter dyad, the female therapist calls forth the male or father inside of her to respond to heterosexual communications. As Daisy discovers, this can be quite a challenge. Labels like "phallic woman" or "castrating female" come to mind, making the exploration difficult, while issues and fears connected to homosexuality further complicate the picture. Daisy is not alone in finding this realm of exploration frightening. The whole group struggles with the extremely charged area of investigating male or female internal representations.

Two months have passed since Daisy's previous presentation. The same case is presented, but we now take a very different perspective in understanding the patient's dynamics. We see how depression can be a regressive defense from the oedipal level. Daisy's personal dynamics are often reflected in this push-pull from a symbiotic ambivalent relatedness to a more autonomous sexually differentiated role.

A HIGH-FUNCTIONING WOMAN

Daisy launched right into her presentation. "I would like to present a private patient. She is a thirty-year-old and is a high-functioning woman. She has just been accepted in law school. She is pretty articulate, has some insight."

With curiosity written on her face, Rachel asked: "Haven't you presented her before? You have a private patient who is also a law student, right?"

"*Have* I presented her?" Daisy responded with surprise.

Dolores nodded affirmatively.

Daisy, still befuddled, said, "That's interesting, I did?"

Lenore nods: "She was very articulate, yes?"

Dolores commented, "As I remember, she was intimidating you."

Daisy smiled and said, "And I still feel that way."

I feel a familiar accusation. We simply didn't do enough last time.

I reminded Daisy, "It was a while back that you presented her, like six weeks ago or two months."

Daisy, in a slow, somewhat depressed voice, continued her story: Much of the case material that was mentioned in the previous case presentation is now repeated.

Her parents divorced when she was fifteen. She is very close to her mother, and she has had a very bad relationship with her father. He was very humiliating, often making her his scapegoat. She just couldn't do anything good for him.

She's the oldest of four, all three siblings boys, and when she was quite young, she took care of them. She remembers taking them to the movies or to the park. Her mother, who was always the closest person—the most available person—was always there for her, especially when she was sick. (In some ways there are a lot of identification issues for me, because my mother was always very good when I was sick; she was a very good nurse, very giving, very much there.) In her history she describes her adolescence as one long depression. She retreated to her own room, cloistered away from friends. She was obese and has hated her body since puberty. "She has this boyfriend of two years' duration and for the last year, she has not been able to have a sexual relationship with him. In fact, she has no way of interacting with him. It is very troublesome for her, for she doesn't want to lose him, yet she can't have him.

"In terms of therapy, she doesn't want to come for long-term treatment; she wants me to tell her what to do, like behavioral therapy. She wants a quick solution. She'll say to me, 'What can you do for me?' I did bring up the option of seeing a sex therapist with her boyfriend if that's what she really wants. I tried to be very direct in telling her that what I do is psychoanalytic long-term treatment. If she wants to deal with this concrete issue, she ought to find someone else."

"Excuse me," Rachel said with a note of curiosity in her voice, "could I just ask a question? What prevents her from having sex? I don't understand what gets in the way."

"She just loses interest. She doesn't want him."

Rachel persisted, "*When* does she lose interest?"

"They can play, they can kiss, but when it comes to the point of having intercourse, she can't have it. She doesn't want him to touch her and feels terrible about it. Naturally he feels bad about it, and she feels bad for him. There's a lot of talk about how it makes him feel and how she is worried about that, but for herself, she doesn't understand what this is all about."

Rachel, still trying to get a handle on the problem, asked, "Do *you* have any sense of why that is?"

> As per her usual manner, Daisy does not answer questions directly. I make a mental note of this but decide to leave it alone. I am not sure what good confronting such an issue would do in terms of the case presentation.

"One of her problems is concern with health issues, she can't swallow certain kinds of food. She also has this cousin who is diagnosed with AIDS and she's been very anxious about it. When she first talked about him, she was somewhat optimistic. She sounded like a cheerleader saying 'everything will be okay.' She had real difficulty dealing with the loss issue, and I tried to push her to get into the material but she had a really hard time talking about her feelings."

Rachel doggedly held her position and tried to focus on the question: "Is she angry at her boyfriend? There's some hostility in what she's doing."

Daisy continued in the same controlling, somewhat depressed voice: "Last session, we talked a little bit about that, and I also tried to listen to see the carryover with her father, but it went nowhere."

"How does she express anger?" Rachel inquired. "Does she ever express it to you?"

"Very little. I tried to explore how she felt when I asked her to role-play some of her feelings. It felt like she experienced it as an intrusion, but she's a compliant kid, so she did it because I suggested it. Then afterwards I felt that I pushed too hard, that she really wasn't ready for this, so during last session, I tried to explore that with her. She did say that she felt put upon, and that she really didn't want to do it. She didn't feel comfortable with it. Then during the same session, she talked about the fact that there's no movement, there's no change, she wants more. There's this push and pull that feels like, 'I want you to intrude, you must be stronger.'"

> I was also aware that this push-pull characterized our session. I wasn't quite sure of the meaning of this behavior, but I did know that it related to the countertransference.

Dolores, in a soothing voice, said: "It seems there's no way that she is not going to feel bad, that's part of the process. She has you intimidated with the body or the sexual issue and you get lost because she doesn't want you to go easy on her. She gets annoyed with you. You know when you said that you referred her to a sex therapist, I thought, 'Wait a second, what's happening in your relationship with her?'"

Daisy, with a slightly placating tone in her voice said: "I tried for a while to work on our relationship. She had a reaction to my vacation, I could experience it. She said with exaggerated emphasis. 'Oh, have a wonderful time; you deserve it!' I tried to really work with it, but even then it felt that I was pushing too much. Whenever I try to make her aware that something is going on between us, she tells me, 'Oh, no, no. It's not a real issue for me; it doesn't really bother me.' So, almost anything I do, I feel pushed out."

> Delores inquires about the sexual area. Daisy converts this question into areas regarding abandonment and desertion. Is Daisy frightened of dealing with sexual material?

Rachel continued in her role as chief investigator, "I want to know more about her father."

Daisy continued in the same measured, controlled tone: "She doesn't talk much about him. She has one memory of being in the garage. She was trying to get something from the cabinet and he was in the way, he was stopping her. She was really angry and she picked up a screwdriver. She felt like driving it into him. It was a powerful moment. Again, she doesn't know why, she doesn't understand it. This vignette is pretty scary!

"I tried to go back with her to see if she could remember any good time with him. She does remember as a younger kid taking him on long walks, going to the lake, having a nice time with him. She was five, six years old. My sense is that when she approached puberty, he turned away from her, and not long afterwards, her parents were divorced."

"And she got hives right about the same time," Rachel chimed in, "and she got very depressed later?"

Daisy continued: "Yes. She says that she was always very close to her mother. Her parents had a very bad marriage from the very beginning, and her connection with her mother pushes her away from men. Her father associates her with the mother and pushes her away. It may even be that the negatives he feels towards his wife he displaces onto her."

Dolores tried to hold back her pointedness, but nevertheless said what she meant: "I think you did a lot of work since you presented her last time. I'm wondering about where that work went, what happened to all the material that we shared with you in the presentation; that woman you presented before?"

Daisy somewhat apologetically explained, "I think when I presented, we went into a lot of my own issues, and somehow it wasn't carried over into the case."

Rachel readily agreed. "Yes, that's my feeling, too, because I didn't know any of her history."

Daisy continued to defend herself: "Last time, it was helpful, but I don't feel that I really presnted the case."

Rachel asked, more supportively, "What's the issue you're bringing here, now? What do you want from us?"

Daisy made her plea: "I feel stuck with the way I respond to her. I feel stuck with her need for more concrete work and at the same time, I have a long way to go to create a relationship of trust before I can even deal with any of the presenting problems. I feel that the sexual issue is just the tip of the iceberg; there's a whole person behind that with a lack of integration. At the same time, she pushes me with these concrete issues . . ."

Daisy's inability to see behind the defensive aspect of the patient's use of concrete issues points to some of the countertransference resistance. Daisy does not help the patient see what the patient's preoccupation with the concrete issues is doing in terms of her inability to deal with sexual conflicts.

Lenore tried to clarify her sense of what's going on. "Since you're not giving to her, she pushes you about concrete issues. She keeps you in a position of *depriving* her. That way, she can stay *victimized*. It seems that she does that; depriving herself with her boyfriend."

> Perhaps being the depressed, deprived victim becomes a safe retreat from more dangerous material. This may parallel some of the problems of the therapist.

Daisy followed the thinking and added: "She says she loves to start making love, then she stops and says, 'I'm sorry'."

Lenore continued: "It sounds like you try to highlight the problem in the relationship, so I don't know what the problem is, except that it is not all that very bad."

Daisy complained, "I am not sure where to go with her. The therapy is a very intellectual interraction. I find myself explaining to her about therapy, explaining my point of view. Somehow I go away from the *feelings*. In the beginning of my work with her, there was more affect. I remember when she was talking about not feeling her feelings, and I used a lot of the suggestions of the group, accepting the depression, acknowledging the pain. She felt very touched, very understood, and she cried a lot. When we started to work, I felt we had connected on that level, but somehow I lost those feelings; actually, we don't have it between us at all anymore."

> Here we see the difference between depression as the primary problem as contrasted to it being used as a regressive defense. The acceptance of depression, and being with the depression and acknowledging the pain has limited usefulness when it's used as a masochistic defense.

Rachel inquired, "When did you lose it — when you went away?"

"Maybe it had to do with the vacation, but there was a long period when we talked a lot about her applications to the law programs."

Eleanor, in an insinuating voice, asked, "Do you *like* this woman?"

Daisy quickly answered "Yes, I look forward to the sessions with her, but she also makes me very anxious. I really question my qualifications in working with her."

Dolores, in a soothing voice, noted, "She has become much more resistant from what you are describing . . . her asking for solutions . . ."

"Okay," said Daisy, "but I don't know how to *deal* with her resistance. It really gets to me. I feel unqualified, and I don't feel I'm able to understand the *context*, pick it out and use it for treatment."

Rachel, also trying to be supportive, asked, "Do you think you're picking up her anxiety about coming to therapy as she gets closer to things?"

Daisy asked in exasperation, "*What* things?"

Rachel responded directly, "Well, her anger for one thing: the anger that almost killed her father."

Lenore chimed in: "You're invited her to work on her sexuality, and the more you give her permission, the more her anxiety increases because she feels an enormous retribution from her mother."

I joined the discussion. "Let's take a closer look at what's going on between Daisy and her patient. She is saying to the therapist, 'I want you to penetrate me, I want you to break through.' The therapist says, 'I can't, I can't.' In a sense the therapist is saying, 'I don't have one to break through with.' Are we speaking on some sexual metaphorical level?"

> We are still not sure by whom she wants to be penetrated. On a more superficial level, I suspect it is the father. On the deepest level, I wonder whether it is the mother who has the breast/penis.

"We have a father who is turned off by his daughter, and she has an early memory of wanting to drive a screwdriver into him. Now your patient is asking you, provocatively and masochistically, to come after her, to get through to her, and you are in essence saying you don't have it."

Daisy, upon reflection, added: "Earlier on in the treatment, she came dressed all in white. I remember thinking that she was coming to me like a bride: she was totally loving, adoring."

In a provocative tone, I said: "And you didn't deliver the goods. Can you experience yourself as the male part of this relationship? Here she arrives, loving and adoring, asking for the contact with the masculine part of you. Have you ever felt masculine?"

> In spite of the difficulty of the material, I knew this area would be far more accesible to Daisy than seeing herself as a woman with a hidden penis.

"In general?" Daisy asked.

I affirmatively replied and she nodded back. A ripple of nervous laughter went through the group.

I recognized that I was being provocative and penetrating. I wasn't quite sure whether I was acting out some particular conflict of mine in relation to Daisy, or serving as a model in the case. I would have to watch how the material unfolded.

"How would you feel with a male presence?" I pushed.

Daisy looked totally perplexed: "Male, myself?"

"Yes."

She smiled widely and said, "Pretty powerful."

Continuing in this vein, I asked provocatively, "Can a woman be powerful?"

Daisy thought before she answered, "Not in the same penetrating way."

"So," I said, "how could a male inside you be 'powerful and penetrating'?"

A long pause followed as Daisy tried to frame her answer. "My association with penetrating . . ." and her voice trailed off as she struggled with what to say. Then, in all the heavy silence, I asked the group, "Am I getting into territory where everybody is comfortable?" The group broke out in laughter, and I added more seriously, "Can you feel your body as masucline?"

Dorothy complained, "I hate those kinds of feelings when they come up—I can't stand them!"

"Yet," I said, "a patient may want to work with a male rather than a female component in therapy."

Daisy giggled as she spoke. "I don't know how to handle this problem. There are two other women patients from whom I also feel these vibes. One woman came in and said that she had just awakened and had felt she had to put on makeup and dress up to come see me, and she didn't understand why. The other one keeps telling me about her rape experience . . ." Her voice drifted off contemplatively.

Dorothy, speaking agitatedly, complained: "I am sitting here amazed; I never think like that. I can't remember ever having had any kind of thoughts like that in relation to a patient."

"Are there forbidden feelings?" I inquired.

Dorothy and Rachel concurred. Rachel verbalized her thoughts: "It's threatening to me, because I think of a male as having more differentiated thinking; clearer, and that's an area that's hard for me."

I tried to clarify my position: "I don't think any personality traits belong exclusively to males or females. What I'm referring to is a *phys-*

ical presence. For instance, remember your father's body; do you think you could fit into that?"

Rachel said, "Well, it's a foreign concept," and the group giggled uncomfortably in empathy with her.

Dolores took a different position. "Actually, I could fit into his body more comfortably than my mother's."

Lenore agreed with Dolores. Group members laughed at themselves as they tried to find their masculine bodies. Denise commented, "My mother was the more masculine one, so I have something of a reversal."

Eleanor contributed her perspective: "I'm thinking more about my *uncle's* body . . ."

Amid the laughter, Dorothy proclaimed, "I don't want to have anything to do with my father's body; I have my own body!"

Dolores noted, "There are definitely postures I have that feel like my father's, like the way he stands, and I like it."

"You like it," I said. "They're not threatening to you?"

Dolores emphatically stated, "No."

Daisy tried to clarify her thoughts. "It's strange . . . it's also softness. In a more real way, my mother's body was the more invasive one for me. Even now, I hesitate hugging her—it's like there's nothing there."

> I was perplexed by this comment. On the one hand, Daisy sees the mother's body as invasive, but yet also associated with softness. Perhaps she is frightened of envelopment, but at the same time states that it's like nothing's there. Are we touching on some early fusion difficulties?

THE "BRIDAL" PATIENT

I tried to offer a frame for some of the obvious anxiety in the room. "I'm trying to explore the feeling of 'maleness' or 'femaleness.' Daisy, in her presentation, seems to be speaking in male sexual terms, such as that she couldn't 'penetrate' her patient. So, there is a question about the phallic issues connected to this woman; about how she feels about her sexually. Remember the phrases about wanting to break through, her coming in as a bride all dressed in white, and your feeling she was glowing?"

Daisy took this in and added, "And she comments on my clothes, sometimes."

"Then, how comfortable are you," I asked, "in commenting to her about the sexual part of herself that she brings into treatment?"

Daisy quickly retorted: "To *say* that to her? Oh, boy!" A long pause, then, "I don't think she's in touch with it. I think it's totally unconscious for her."

"That's what the therapy is about," Dolores said, "to make the unconscious *conscious*."

Daisy protested: "I have a hard time with penetrating."

"The point I'm raising is your relative comfort in being sensitive to your patient's sexual communication."

Daisy looked rather forlorn as she said: "I have a very hard time, generally, with making direct interpretations or zooming right in. I sit there, I observe, I have analytic understanding, but I have a hard time delivering it or working with it, I'm having a hard time with *all* my patients."

> The countertransference problem begins to open up. Daisy becomes aware of her problem with direct forthright interventions. Does this relate to her problems with the male inside of her?

Lenore spoke with a good deal of emotional fervor: "You describe her as being there with you. She is all wrapped up in a tight package, and she's gung ho. The fact that there's a phallic quality about her presence in the room may indicate she's worried about her femininity, and she wants to be penetrated to be reassured that she is female."

Dolores objected that she had to watch that the masculine part didn't get out of hard.

"But you're comfortable with the male part of *yourself*," I said.

Dolores clarified her thought on the matter. "I think it has a lot to do with my father, who was always pretty direct with me, even if it meant, in some ways, hurting me. I have difficulty with people who are not *direct* with me. In my own therapy, that was an issue. I had a therapist who was very direct and she had to soften it sometimes with me, but I think that because of that, I find that I am not that fragile really. The directness of being able to get through the rough spots in life, knowing that I am okay, makes me feel stronger than somebody who could not do that. My father was always very direct. Even though I might cry, he was very honest, and that's something that I benefited from."

I said, "So that you have a good warm feeling about him."

"Yes," Dolores agreed, "it was always lovingly done."

I tried, then, to sum up what she was saying: "Lovingly done, so that you've taken in a loving extension of him."

Daisy struggled with her thoughts on the matter: "For me, my father was nasty, and the loving part was very evasive, very nonverbal. I know about it, I can experience it, but in a very nonverbal form. He could be very sadistic, but then loving."

> There seems to be a confusion between male assertiveness and sadism, creating a regression to an anal sadistic level. We see plenty of evidence in the way Daisy handles questions.

Eleanor reflected, "This feels very honest [referring to Dolores], while Daisy's relationship to her father *doesn't* feel honest. It feels manipulative, sadistic."

"So," I queried, "how does a woman take on a healthy part of her father and integrate it into her identity?"

Daisy said, "I think I have identified with my patient."

Eleanor asked: "Did you ever have an uncle, relative, or older cousin where you could identify at all with that kind of maleness?"

"I have two; an older and a younger brother, but neither come close to my father as far as a powerful presence."

"A *powerful* presence, but not always a loving presence," I added. "Certainly there's love, but it's mixed in with sadism."

Daisy continued reflection about her father: "He's the one who really cares and worries about me, and actually would do anything for me in the world. If I cry, it hurts him. He's very tuned in, sensitive. He beat up my brother, but never me. I was much more special."

"So there's a loving connection," I said.

"Very loving."

"But also he could be mean," Daisy added, "so there's a certain kind of fear of his kind of directness. It's only recently that I could confront him for being mean to me."

> Upon reflection, I wonder if I was acting out the all-powerful father for this group of women. Was I parading this power by an excessive amount of interventions? I simply didn't know, but went on with it and said,

"This raises an interesting point about female sexuality. Sometimes a little girl learns to have power with her father through a seductive compliance, but with an underlying fear. She learns to deal with a male, but with a sacrifice. Sexuality, then, becomes a means to control, but there's an underlying resentment for the emotional toll that it takes."

"It's a defense, and it's not too good," Daisy added.

"But there's power in that too," I said, "covering over fear. Let's talk," I said, "about the woman's use of aggression." I turned to Dolores: "You seem to have less of a problem with directness."

> By turning to various members of the group, I was attempting to give some type of dimensional perspective to the problem.

"It took me a while to find it in myself," Dolores admitted, "to find my identification with him, because he had become the 'bad' person, so it took a long time for me to find it in myself. It still takes a lot of courage to be able to do it, but it comes easier with time."

Daisy mused: "I'm trying to think . . . there's a lot about my father that I idealize. He's smart, very knowledgeable, but at the same time his kind of achievement isn't simple. He doesn't compete in the world too much. He really does his stuff on an island. Everything is so mixed with him; it's very intense admiration on the one hand, mixed with criticism on the other."

I turned to Dolores: "In your integration of maleness and femaleness, did it all come together as a concept of a separate self in terms of being a woman?"

"It's complicated. I feel okay with the male side of myself, that part of me that can be direct, in charge, and comfortable with ambition. Where I have more trouble is in what I attribute to the feminine, which is vulnerability. My mother always thought of that as this *fragility* in me. That's where it gets very complicated in sexuality . . ."

"One of the traps," I pointed out, "in getting into this discussion is attributing a particular trait to one sex. Obviously there's a difference between the sexes, if only because of body image and the psychic space that connects up with body image. Is it possible, then, to have a masculine and feminine self? I'd think there are different levels of synthesis of these two components."

"They do come together," Dolores said. "I think the 'maleness' has become a more integrated part of me."

Dolores added: "I think I got more of my sexuality, my true sexuality as a woman, from my father. Whatever he projected definitely had a sexual presence. I didn't feel he violated the boundaries, although he was very clearly sexual. With my mother, sexuality was much more prohibited."

"So," I said, "one's feminine identification can be reinforced by either parent.

"With your patient," I added, "she wasn't seen as a sexual person, as with her father, and I believe she wants to punish you."

Daisy looked confused, "I wasn't available?"

> Sexuality becomes a secret that must be acted out through hidden channels and coy seductiveness. Being up front with these feelings is not permitted in the family.

You didn't appreicate what she was doing for you," I said.

Rachel looked dismayed. "Gosh, that's complicated . . ."

"Why is it so complicated?" I asked.

"Just figuring out these ins and outs," Rachel lamented.

"Part of the so-called figuring out has to be your ability to feel the masculine component in the relationship," I said.

"You know, what's happening to me," Daisy said, "is that part of my father's manners were penetrating, but the lididinal part for him was very intellectual. Books, study, knowledge—boom, boom, boom —that's how he approaches it. Maybe there's some part I identify with. What happened to me with this patient is that I shifted. I *did* experience sexuality in my head."

Up to the head rather than letting your body experience what was going on," I pointed out.

"It's uncomfortable for me to feel it," Daisy admitted.

"What's the 'uncomfortableness'?" I asked.

After some deep thought, Daisy spoke: "With the two other patients, especially the one who came very clearly saying 'I came dressed up for you,' I've wondered about the homosexual aspect."

"She may be working out something with her father," I said. "Allow your body to tell you if she's making a pass at you as a man."

> This becomes a rather complicated area of exploration. We don't know whether the patient is really getting involved with the phallic mother or the oedipal father. Again, we will have to trust the patient's associations in order to understand where the material will lead. However, the patient does want to feel penetrated and overpowered.

"In some ways she is," Daisy admitted.

"And as you feel it," I said, "you'll know how to handle it. If she were a man, you could handle it. Is that right?" I asked.

Daisy agreed and said: "I would have a much easier time identifying what was going on."

"And then would you bring it up?" I asked.

"Yes."

"So, what's the difference?" I asked.

"I think I don't trust my own reactions about this."

"If you make a mistake with a man," I noted, "it's no problem. If you make a mistake and you think you see something sexual he denies it, and it's no big deal, but with a woman, that's hard to do."

Lenore now jumped in. "What if you point out to her that she was glowing?"

Daisy looked pensive as she said, "I'm thinking about my own homosexual fantasies about this woman. I like her and I like when she comes."

"And can you tolerate these homosexual fantasies about her?"

Daisy looked somewhat stunned: "My own?"

A few second earlier, Daisy reflects about her own homosexual fantasies about women. Yet she quickly disowns any sexual feelings toward her patient.

"Your own," I said.

Lenore chimed in: "To be able to feel that she is attractive, is touching on that; it's great!"

"Yes," I agreed.

Denise added, "But she's also attractive in the way that your father thought people were attractive. She is your star patient because she is smart, she's going to get her degree; she's got the brains along with looks."

Daisy now got into the spirit. "I like the way she dresses. There's a lot about her that's attractive."

I encouraged her, "Yes, right!"

"And also, she had problems very similar to mine, so that there's a lot of identification with her."

"Okay, what we're touching on are homosexual fantasies, and your ability to access this part of yourself. Intellectually, that's fine. Emotionally, it's another story."

Daisy reflected: "I'm just thinking now, that the way I've experienced her for a while was that I was pushing too much intellectually; I wasn't really meeting her on the emotional level."

> This is the area where Daisy has made most contact with her father's masculinity. The bodily area appears to be forbidden territory.

"You were meeting her on a level that you knew the best." "But it wasn't working," Daisy admitted.

"You know," Dolores said, "I'm remembering our dance workshop in New Hamsphire. *That's* the part of you that needs to come into the session: working with the body, being in touch with what happens."

"In other words, can you ever see yourself walking and feeling like a man?" I asked.

"*Imagine* it?" Daisy repeated.

"Yes."

"Yes," Daisy acknowledged, "But I don't necessarily *like* it. Part of my growing up was trying hard to identify with a feminine part of my mother. My self-image was very plump, a very non-delicate person. When I got feedback that I was *delicate*, I couldn't believe it. There was a lot of discrepancy between how I felt, how I looked, how I adapted other people's experiences and all that."

> Daisy's patient was likewise overweight when she was young. Both patient and presenter may well have problems in identifying with a female persective.

If I asked you to draw yourself as a boy, how would you look?"

"I don't have a problem with that. I think I could imagine having a boy's body, only I don't have a penis."

"Okay, how does it look to you?"

"I don't know, but it's not *me*."

"Not you?"

"Sometimes I would *like* to have a penis," Daisy said. "More, the *concept* of it. Physically I *like* my body, I don't want it to be any different."

Again, playing a somewhat provocative role, I said, "If you wanted to discover the male part of yourself, you would have to grapple with the *fear of being cruel*."

> Here we open up a further dimension of the countertransference problem. Daisy describes her father as a profoundly impotent man who expresses his power through cruelty and intellect. Here, Daisy can explore her fear of the male identification as well as her ability to differentiate from it rather than denying this aspect of herself.

Daisy looked at me in amazement, "Of being *cruel?*"

I proceeded to explain. "Since your father was cruel, I think there may be a fear on your part of getting into this role for fear that it's associated with being cruel."

Daisy quickly responded: "I understand—I don't have control over it."

"You see," Dolores said, "in contrast, I find that what happened to me was that unlike my father who wasn't cruel, I was cruel when I first identified with all that stuff—there was a very nasty aspect to me."

"So when sadism is a substitute for real power, control substitutes for self-assertion," I added.

"It would be safer to be like my mother," Daisy thought, "who can be very powerful in a passive way, so I don't do interpretations, I don't move on."

"So," I said, "let's go back to the session when your patient comes in glowing. Who in this room wants to play this patient? Who looks 'glowing'?"

> After this question, I wonder, myself, if I was getting carried away with myself with all the sexuality floating around the room, and I the only male.

All the members kept their eyes averted. "Glowing . . . oh, God!" someone muttered.

Daisy pointed to Lenore.

Lenore mumbled: "Keep it up, I'll be real."

I intervened, for I knew that Lenore did not want to get into the role-playing. "Suppose it's Dolores, and she comes in dressed in white, glowing. She talks about an interview for a new job and how wonderful the interviewer was. Now, go at it from there."

Daisy, the therapist, said: "You look pretty dressed up tonight —No, this is too much."

"Okay, start again."

"I wonder how you felt coming here today."

I suggested, "Think of yourself as a male. You're not frightened to go after what you want. You feel assured and powerful."

"Boy, this is hard because of my relationship with Dolores."

"It's hard for me, too," said Dolores.

Daisy, as therapist: "That white really looks nice on you." Silence. "I bet you dressed up for me. You almost look like a bride."

"What's going on?" I asked. "Describe your feelings."

Daisy replied: "I'm feeling very embarrassed. I'm jumping on top of myself. This is something I'm not really prepared to deal with."

> Daisy utilizes an interesting metaphor: jumping on top of myself. Does she squelch any self-expressive, assertive role for herself and resort to a childlike seductiveness because of her ambivalent feelings toward her father?

Dolores: "The patient would feel embarrassed—she'd get sort of coy and soft, blush maybe—But I think that would be good if it happened."

Lenore commented: "It heightens her sexuality. She really feels her sexuality."

I know turned back to Daisy to get her back into the role. "Remember, you are your father. Try to be your father really enjoying his daughter."

"Remember," Lenore pointed out, "her father left when she was thirteen or fourteen."

"I don't remember my father saying anything about what I wore, unless he didn't like it."

Lenore asked in exasperation, "Don't you have any positive relationship with an older man?"

"Maybe my older brother," said Daisy.

"Can you do an adolescent girl doing her hair up?" Dolores asked.

Daisy immediately responded with relief: "Yes, I enjoy that—that I can do."

"That's more a *mother* thing," Rachel commented.

"I don't find that's necessarily so for the ones who are really testing their sexuality out," said Dolores.

Daisy agreed. "I have a thirteen-year-old niece, she's fourteen now, and she's starting to put on makeup. I've always responded, always said something about it."

Eleanor noted: "Now that you mention it, I can feel myself responding that way to my patient by saying something fatuous like 'I love that color combination,' or 'That looks really nice,' or 'I like the way you did your hair'—something to make her feel alive rather than this repressed little thing. It doesn't have to be 'Your look beautiful, you dressed for me.'"

Daisy considered, and said, "The fact that my father never verbalized any of this, maybe that's important."

Eleanor querried: "What would you have liked him to say to you?"

"That I look good—that he likes what I wear and thinks I'm pretty."

Lenore suddenly laughed. "What a job you have, Robbins, teaching all these women to be men!" The group broke into laughter with her.

"Okay, why can't you say that to your patient? It's a matter of your perceiving her and feeling her in the relationship," I said.

"As a sexual object?" Daisy asked.

"That's what's blocking you," I said. "It's an inner perception of her; it's feeling what's happening."

"You say it's the father?" Rachel asked, looking perplexed.

"The father is, I think, extremely important in reinforcing and accepting a woman's sexuality."

"Listen," Lenore said, "this patient missed it. Her father left when she was thirteen or fourteen."

Dolores took exception to this. "Except that it wasn't necessarily missed. My father and I had some problems around that time too, but I definitely had him through the oedipal period."

I tried to bring the discussion back to what I thought was the central issue: "Try to feel the masculine side of you with the patient so you know and feel what she is talking about in terms of transference. Otherwise, you may keep on hearing 'Mamma' and it's really her father that she's speaking to."

Apologetically, Daisy confessed, "My trouble now is that in spite of all we have done today, I'm a little worried about what's going to happen."

> I was aware that we had given a good deal of material for Daisy to assimilate. At the same time, I did not want to get sucked in to pushing my point rather than permitting Daisy to struggle with her own confusion and anxiety.

"Well," I answered, "you'll have to let some of these notions settle in."

Daisy went on, in a questioning voice. "I remember I was trying to role-play with Dolores. I don't understand the difference between being seductive and letting yourself feel that masculine part in yourself."

"Well," I said, "how does it sound if you say: 'Look, you know, it seems to me that you're not only glowing, but there's an element of sexuality that you're bringing into this room. I think you want me to be aware of your sexuality. That's a part of you that got lost when you were younger.'"

Dorothy, who had been observing closely, said, "That's a very different statement from what Daisy's been struggling with."

"Yes," I answered, "she was getting too mushy and seductive with her patient."

Daisy said, with obvious relief, "What you're doing is more comfortable for me, because it's coming from on top of it. It's like seeing an overview of what's happening, instead of being mushy."

"That's right."

"I felt," Lenore added, "that your patient might be afraid of homosexual feelings."

"Perhaps," I said, "both parties are threatened by homosexual impulses. I guess the issue is how to be masculine, but not seductive. That means that you have to differentiate feeling direct and pointed from being seductive."

> Here we do not have to concern ourselves with whether we are speaking to the patient as phallic mother or oedipal father. I am simply encouraging the presenter to take on a more assertive role and differentiate herself from her father.

Daisy reflected, "I *think* I'm careful not to be sexy. Actually, I'm kind of numb in the process."

I suggested, "Perhaps you're numb because you have to be aware of the sexuality on one level, and not respond to it on another."

"And to be able to bring it back to her in an observing way," Daisy finished.

"How do you think she'll respond to your interpretation 'I think you're bringing something sexual into the room'?" Rachel asked.

Daisy answered thoughtfully, "I think I would have to put another statement with it—that I think the issue is important because the sexuality got lost. I think that she'd be able to handle that. There's something about her that really wants to work. It would be like a gift. She's really dying to receive something, and this would be something that I could give her."

"So that you're working," I tried to summarize for the group, "on a couple of levels here. One level is to be aware of it yourself; the second is not to confuse maleness with seductiveness, and not to be frightened that when you're aggressive you're going to be hurtful."

Dolores added, "It seems to me that Daisy also needs to get comfortable with the *cruel* aspect of herself. At least, *I* found that when I was testing out that part of myself, I discovered a cruelty I acted out. You have to rework it to be more comfortable with these feelings."

"I have a final observation," I said, turning to Daisy. "It seems to be much easier for you to think in terms of the pregenital issues rather than the genital issues."

"Like the swallowing, the drugs," she said.

"Basically, it's a higher level of the patient."

With these words, the session came to a close, but all left well aware of how much more exploration into these matters was needed.

Varieties of "Performance Anxiety"

Looking back at the session, the fears that were so palpable in the group could be greatly diffused if we clarified such concepts as power versus sadistic control. The notion of "sadism," which is not based on gender, can be appropriately employed by either sex. Following this line of thinking, one can assume that a sadistic controlling stance can be a substitute for power as well as a screen for feelings of impotence. Likewise, such traits as assertiveness, power, ambition can be realized by either sex.

I do want to emphasize, however, that we cannot pretend that there are no differences between the sexes. As stated earlier, the physical difference between the sexes influences the very nature of the psychic representation that is projected into the therapeutic relationship. Discovering an exploring our emotional availability to these important elements in the therapeutic self creates a readiness to resonate with different interiors of our patients' self and object representations.

Now, let's discuss some of the technical issues that are posed by

Daisy's presentation. The ratio of eight women to a male leader becomes an extremely important dynamic. Upon reflection, the leader seems overly active and structuring in the group discussion. Perhaps, on a subliminal level, he plays out the powerful father projected by the presented patient as well as the therapist.

Upon review of the material, the presenter's reliance upon naivete and little-girl helplessness becomes a provocative invitation for the big powerful father to take over. Following this course, however, may well strain the delicate balance of group supervision and therapy and a choice was made to pay less attention to this dynamic.

Daisy is still in treatment and working on such character issues as passivity, tangential communications, and a helpless provocativeness. Direct confrontation with these issues may only serve to increase a negative transference to the group and the leader. Here, then, we arrive at the bottom line regarding these decisions. Maintaining a positive, supportive approach becomes an extremely important part of this type of supervision. At times, group members will go after these characterological problems, and the leader must determine the emotional readiness of the presenter to deal with such issues. In Daisy's case, we stayed on an intellectual level, relying on an assumption that there existed a sufficiently conflict-free part of the ego to assimilate the didactic material.

It will be recalled that in the previous presentation, Daisy's depressive tone became a focal issue for discussion. Here, we see another dimension of the countertransference problem. The depressed, naive, impotent girl makes emotional contact through sadistic provocation. Undermining these defenses immediately precipitates fears of object loss. Consequently, the exploration of countertransference problems become extremely complex: how to be direct, but non-attacking; supportive, but not reinforcing of the little-girl, "helpless" image. In the end, both patient and therapist must face their mutual fear, rage, reactive contempt, and power issues associated with men, and the regressive dependency issues with women. Interfaced with these issues is a lurking fear of attack if one is vulnerable to the male.

For female therapists, experiencing the male part of a transference communication requires some degree of comfort with the male element in a therapist's self-representation. Some of Daisy's problems can be traced to an overidentification with the patient's issues. Both therapist and patient are frightened of the powerful, sadistic male, and both unconsciously provoke others to assume the very role that creates so much anxiety. Yet, the masochism is only a surface surrender, for both parties avoid compliance by playing the game of being passive and helpless but, secretly, immovable.

Let us now explore a more ideal interchange between therapist and patient. First, the therapist must *experience* the witholding, sadistic part of the patient that covers the fear if she is to understand the nature of the patient's provocativeness, envy, and competitiveness. Ultimately, the therapist must rely on the "good" paternal presence, rather than the out-of-control, crazy part of herself that can be direct and interpretive with her patient. The therapist, then, must disengage from the notion that an interpretive, assertive role can be harmful or dangerous, for indeed she must rediscover the male part of herself than can be gentle, supportive, and yet forthright. As the treatment process unfolds, and the patient offers her own associational material, we will get a better perspective as to where the sexual fear lies: with mother and/or father.

Chapter 8

JANICE

Expanding Transitional Space

TO DANCE OR NOT TO DANCE

Janice came to the group with the seemingly innocent technical question of whether or not to attend a patient's dance performance. Behind her question, however, lurked not only the personal issue of her seeking "systems" or "right answers" to avoid her own intuitive responses to her patient, but also the much larger, thornier issue defining the nature and boundaries of a therapeutic relationship. While it is clearly true that the therapist cannot indulge the fantasy of being the good mother, father, or even friend to a patient, it is also true that it is the emotional resonance between therapist and patient that supports the therapeutic process and the restructuralization of the personality organization. The "frame," or "holding environment," within which a patient's developmental issues are attended will necessarily vary from patient to patient. The degree to which the nonverbal versus verbal aspects of this environment is emphasized will depend upon the degree of object constancy in the patient. Let's turn to Janice's presentation to see how the group defines and creatively addresses the interlocking issues.

A few words about Janice and her manner of speaking: She often describes her cases in a dryly intellectual, sometimes sardonic manner, mixed in with some humor. For the most part she is much more comfortable with intellectual material than with the emotional issues that are connected with transference/countertransference material. In this presentation the reader may observe how the material gets quickly bogged down in a dry, somewhat disconnected way. The reader may further observe that Janice never really gets into the heart of any question that is asked of her. Gradually the group becomes increasingly irritated by this approach and the leader then decides to change the level of communication by introducing a nonverbal technique.

In her usual direct manner, Janice began in a clipped, controlled voice: "I have an issue I'd like to present. It's just a technical question, and I don't want to present the whole case. This is a patient I presented a while ago who is a musician. She has given me an invitation to a concert of hers in May. I did talk to her about such implications as why she gave it to me, what she wanted, whether she wanted me to go. She made it very clear that it was important to her to have me there. Now, whenever I've thought about a patient asking me, my stance has always been, of course I can't go, I have my boundaries, and blah-blah, but nobody ever actually asked me. Nobody invited me to his wedding. Nobody asked me to go to her performance. I've never had to deal with what it would do to therapeutic boundaries.

"I think I would feel wrong going to my patient's performance, but I am not quite sure *why*. Even if it's *theoretically* wrong, is there a way it could be *right*, if it's important to her, to her growth, her development? I don't know. I need to throw it out for discussion."

These seemingly concrete questions, I thought to myself, are just the tip of an iceberg. I am aware of my use of the metaphor, iceberg, and suspect that Janice needs to thaw out. I said: "It can't be discussed without getting into the specifics of the case."

Somewhat taken aback, Janice replied, "I'll talk about the case. I really thought it was a straightforward question." She paused thoughtfully and the group waited intently before she continued in measured tones.

"I see this woman twice a week. She is thirty-five years old an single. She originally came to me in a state of confusion as to whether she should stay or leave her boyfriend, a relationship that has gone on for ten years. She went to a Gestalt therapist for three years, and apparently he told her about his personal life, which only made her more confused. Whatever techniques he was using, basically it helped very little.

"She initially came to me for a consultation while she was still seeing him. I said that she had to terminate with him before beginning treatment with me. Apparently she wanted to do in therapy what she was doing in her personal life; she had a boyfriend and a lover on the side, with triangles everywhere.

"She is the first of three children in a wealthy WASP California family. Her father is a doctor. She is thirty-five, the brother's thirty-two, the sister twenty-nine. Three years ago, the brother attempted suicide and got the family to rally around him. The sister, right now, is living with a Puerto Rican and for the past six years has gotten herself kicked out of every college she's attended. She is very bright and as my patient says, figures out the day when you can no longer get your money back, and then drops out the next day. She disappears—whatever.

"Anyway, before this relationship with a Puerto Rican man, my patient had gone out with a very Establishment-type WASP for eight years. Her younger sister had picked up a Haitian. There really is a lot of acting out in this family. It's a very unemotional family, so the sisters are going for the Puerto Ricans and the Haitians who will give it back to them. In October my patient separated from her boyfriend, but as she said, she wants to have her cake and eat it too, She wants the separation, but also wants the option to come back again. She said it was a separation, he said it was a divorce. She went off to Puerto Rico for four weeks with her boyfriend to this little town and had a wonderful time. Her question now is should she go back to her other boyfriend who is real Establishment or should she stick it out with the Puerto Rican. The problem with the Puerto Rican is that she doesn't want to move to Puerto Rico, and that's what she'd have to do."

There was an uncomfortable giggle in the room. Finally Dolores broke the embarrassed silence. "Even if it's Peurto Rico, I'm wondering what you're feeling about the relationship. I just had a negative reaction right away when you talked about the younger sister "picking up" a Haitian and a Puerto Rican. I felt that there was a bias, and it's included in the use of terms like "acting out." I guess I need to hear more about what the relationship is like."

> All of us are aware of the underlying detached, impersonal tone
> of the presenter. We leave the character defenses alone and try to
> give Janice more space to see how she will explore the material.

Janice looked somewhat confused as she asked, "What their relationship is like?"

"Yes!" Dolores emphatically answered.

Janice continued her story in a very measured, thoughtful tone. "She had gone to Puerto Rico one summer as part of a dance troupe. She had affairs with a couple of men. When she came back, she met a man who asked if he could use her apartment until she returned from Puerto Rico. She agreed, and he lived in her apartment for the summer. When she came back again, she saw him once, had a wonderful time with him, and within that year started a clandestine relationship. Nobody knew anything about what was going on because he was having a relationship with a member of the troupe at the same time. So he would secretly come to her house at twelve o'clock at night. I think she was acting out, because she wasn't trying to find out who he was and what the relationship was all about."

Dolores gently persisted in her probing: "It sounds so *judgmental*, rather than diagnostic, although I don't know *why* it sounds judgmental."

Janice brushed the comments aside and retorted nonchalantly "Is it judgemental? It probably is. I think I'm responding to her other relationships. My guess is if it weren't José it would have been somebody else; she can't bring herself to say, 'The relationship isn't working, I can't cope with it, let's discuss it,' or whatever. Inevitably, she has to get *out* of it. The way she gets out of everything is that she gets the person angry by doing something else. She is constantly provoking people to make decisions."

> I am aware of Janice's offhand coldness in describing her patient. Are we hearing shades of her mother?

"Is that what she's doing with you by provoking you to make a decision about the theater ticket?" a member wondered aloud.

Lenore blurted out in a fast, clipped voice, "She knows. She's worked with a therapist, so she knows about the issue of boundaries. She probably picked you because you are different and now she's put you in a bind."

> I felt we were getting bogged down and wanted more information.

I asked, "Tell us more about the case."

Janice maintained her typically objective, informative stance. Although her words came rolling out without too much affect, the group maintained its engagement with the case. "She's been playing the flute since she was five years old. Her early life was made up of music, taking care of her younger brother and doing well in school. She got good report cards and was given big parts in children's performances. She saw her role as taking care of the grownups and making everyone happy. Any time that she came home and did something that was rebellious, angry, or whatever, she was completely ignored. She quickly learned that the only way to get attention was by bringing home goodies."

"Then during her adolescence she drank a lot and was bulimic. Basically, she wouldn't listen to anybody, and nobody set limits. She wanted someone to stop her and say: 'You stay here, don't go out, stop fucking around.' They didn't do anything, except leave her notes in the middle of the night that said things like: 'I'm very diappointed with you. You're not doing what we are expecting you to do. Shape up, and if you don't shape up, we won't talk to you.' She said that the more notes she got, the more upsetting it got, and the more she kept undoing what she had to do. The only time she really got something from her parents was when she completely fell apart. She never went out and attempted suicide, but she'd get very depressed and physically unable to cope. At that point she'd call them up and they'd listen to her. Similarly, with her friends, she won't *ask* for anything, but she *provokes* them."

Rachel pushed for more information: "I have a sense of her relationship with both parents together, but not with them separately. What was her relationship with her mother?"

Janice continued to turn out the information like a fact sheet. "Her relationship with the mother is getting better now. She's described her mother as never showing any emotion to her or anybody else. The arrangement seems to have been 'You do this, I do this, you make me happy.' There was no emotional connection with her. She says that now there is more of a connection, but when she was younger there was nothing."

"Her father was very judgmental. She says he's still very judgmental, very contemptuous. He makes her feel like she's never doing enough, never good enough. He's never satisfied with anybody. There was never a point where she could say, 'Ah! I *did* it!' She's internalized him and now says that nobody is good enough, nobody does enough, nobody is perfect enough."

"And she probably isn't either . . ." Rachel added.

"One of the things that she remembers," Janice continued, "is that as a two-year-old, she carried around the newborn baby. She remembers seeing it on film. She complained to me, 'How could parents let a two-year-old carry a baby and take care of him? Here I am on film walking around with this baby. That wasn't my job. How could I do that?' She thinks that he was cute and people thought she was good at it, so that was her job."

Both with surprise and suspicion, Lenore remarked, "When you think about a two-year-old, something weird must have been going on for her to be so aware of their responses to her and yet make no protest about that, like dropping the baby or something. Really, at that developmental point, you are not interested in pleasing."

"I'm not even sure I believe her," Janice hastened to respond. "I don't know, maybe she was carrying the baby for the film for two minutes and then when she saw it later she constructed this whole picture."

Lenore, with a sudden glimmer of insight, commented, "That's why the memory comes from the film and not from reality . . ."

"Yes, that's a good point,"

> Nothing was very alive in this room. Yet I saw no point in confronting this issue, as I feared that it would only tighten up the presenter. Trying to see the dynamics of the therapy relationship, I asked,

"What goes on between this patient and you?"

"She is an entertainer," Janice quickly and easily responded. She then mechanically offered a list of activities and relationships that her patient flitted through, but all without very much affect. "It sounds boring as shit!" Dorothy exclaimed with humor and an acceptance of background laughter from the group.

Janice continued, "Mostly, I'm kept on the outside. She comes in with a very tight package and wants understanding. She is very smart and knows that she wants control and is being manipulative. She's also afraid of being disappointed. She pulls it all together, but somehow I don't see her as working in treatment. I confronted her on that, and it was a big relief to her.

"Recently she came in and said, 'You know, I started walking over here and realized that I didn't have anything to tell you to entertain you.' It wasn't a sarcastic dumping, it was a 'I really feel that I don't have the goodies that I am supposed to have. I am supposed to bring you stories, and I have nothing to tell you.' We spent a lot of time on how she doesn't let anybody have any true interaction with her."

"How does the patient feel when she is not entertaining you?" Cybil asked.

"It was relief. I felt fine about not being entertained, but anxious. She could sit there for forty-five minutes and not talk, and this isn't like her. When she walks in she's 'blah-blah-blah-blah.' I've never felt gratified from the entertaining, I've felt quite isolated."

"How do you feel about *that*?" Lenore persisted, trying to get some emotional connectedness with the case.

> The lack of emotional connection with the case may well reflect the problem, not only of the patient, but of the presenter. I knew we had to loosen up Janice, but as yet I wasn't quite sure as to which way to go.

In the same matter-of-fact tone that had persisted throughout the presentation, the dialogue continued. "How do I *feel* about it? Whether I like her? She's a nice person . . ."

Dorothy struggled with the same problem, but from a different perspective, and asked, "What's there to like?"

In a straightforward way, Janice responded, "There is a struggle going on that I appreciate in her. She is very likable. Maybe it's the animation, whatever it is that comes out of her. I don't know . . . I don't know what I can tell you."

A lot of perplexed comments from the group ensued. Lenore voiced her reaction. "I feel distant from her, but maybe it's *your* distance from this case I'm feeling."

Janice answered defensively, "Wait a second, are you saying that you're feeling my distance from the case and you're not sure what it's like?"

Lenore persisted. "I can't tell where you really *are* with this case. Maybe this question could clarify the issue: What's your dilemma about attending her recital?"

Janice maintained her objective reporting stance. "Music is the only place where she is authentically who she is. She doesn't bullshit around, she doesn't manipulate people. It's the only safe place she can come out. I don't get the feeling that her attitude is, 'I'm entertaining you out there,' but is more like, 'This is what I want to say, this is what's important to me, because of who I *am*.'

"My question about going is that, given what it does mean to her, is it a slap in the face not to do? If I didn't go, I would feel uncomfortable because I wouldn't know how to deal with it afterwards. I'm not going to watch the dance, I'm going to watch *her*."

"Couldn't talk about how she feels about your being there?" Leonore suggested, trying to be helpful.

The group all joined in, also trying to be helpful, but at the same-time defending themselves from their lack of connection to the case.

> Feeling isolated and cut off is one of the most difficult feelings to contain in a therapeutic relationship. Often we push for related-ness or connection, denying the underlying connection: isolation and lack of connection.

Rachel added, "You could congratulate her. What is so hard about saying something to her after the performance? It could be worked out with her within the session whether she would want you to wait and see her backstage."

Dorothy brought in a different angle. "You made a very positive statement that in the music she is authentic and unmanipulative. How do you *know*?"

"How do I know? Because I know how she talks about herself and because *I* used to be a dancer, and can feel her authenticity."

> I decided to shift the mode of communication in an attempt to by-pass some of the resistances in this presentation. By introducing a nonverbal form of relatedness I hoped to open up an imaginative connection between Janice, the case, and her group members.

"How would you feel, Janice, if all of us draw her mother and your mother? Could all of you draw Janice's mother as you experience her in this room right now, plus this patient's mother? Any reactions?"

"Well, I'm wondering how I experience Janice's mother . . ." a member said, apprehensively.

"You've heard Janice today," I said. "What kind of mother do you think she has?"

"I'm trying to think," Dorothy said pensively.

"I'd like all of you to see if you can feel and depict what kind of "mother" Janice is right now with this patient, as well as how connected she is to the patient's mother."

"I guess that *is* significant," Lenore said in support.

I responded pointedly, "That's right, it's significant." Then, as I looked around at the blank faces, I commented, "If you look at each of us, you can feel the mothers in us in how we deal with others."

Cybil blurted, "My God, I'm sorry to hear that!" and the group broke up in laughter.

"Okay, some of you will have a harder time with this than others," I said, somewhat challengingly.

> The group was intrigued, anxious, and thoughtful. But one change was evident; there was an energy shift. Everyone had felt outside, trying to get focused, and now they were all very much present and engaged. I was pleased, for we had moved away from a controlled, disconnected level to a sensory playfulness that I hoped would open up an intuitive form of connection with one another.

"I don't feel the patient's mother. I feel Janice's mother," Dolores said.

"That's important. You have any reaction, Janice?"

"No, I'm just trying to figure out why *my* mother comes out, and not the patient's."

Again the room filled with laughter, and one of the members chided me, "You just want to meet Janice's mother!" Amid the giggles and laughter, we buckled down to the task at hand.

"On one side of the paper place Janice's mother; on the other side, the patient's mother," I instructed.

Rachel looked upset and said, "I still don't have a *clue* about Janice's mother."

"Take a good look at Janice and feel that mother inside of her. If it's nothing, then put down nothing because that's what you feel about her mother. If she's a question mark, put a question mark down." Reluctantly Rachel turned to the task.

"How can we tell if our pictures are accurate?" Cybil asked.

> I was pleased by this question, for indeed I intended to demonstrate that most of truth had a subjective/objective quality to it and that we should trust our intuitive perceptiveness. I intended to demonstrate that various members of the group have different perspectives both on the case and Janice and yet each one presents a piece of the truth.

"Okay, we're going to get into that."

Again there is laughter and reiteration of the instructions as the group finally settled down to draw. After ten to fifteen minutes of animated discussion and concentrated drawing, we went around the room to look at one another's work.

There was much quiet giggling and anticipation as though each of us were giving Janice a special present and was waiting for her to open our package. Cybil began. Pointing to her picture (Figure 1), she said, "This is Janice with her mother, this is the patient's mother. And the difference is—I'll show you—Janice is trying to dance for her mother and smiling and facing towards her mother. This is the patient's mother, who is very similar to Janice's mother. The difference is that the patient is trying to dance *away* from her mother."

"Dance away?" I asked, to get clarification.

"I see them both in similar relationships with their mothers, but the patient is dealing with her mother by rebelling." Cybil explained.

Cybil's drawings, like the others, illustrate a very deprived and empty psyche. There seemed little to be gained in pointing out these issues, as I was mainly interested as to how these drawings would stimulate the associations of the presenter.

"As you hear this," I said, turning to Janice, "is there anything that strikes you?"

"Well, the part about the rebellion—that you rebel in different kinds of ways. I rebel in the appropriate way."

"How did you 'appropriately' rebel?" I smiled.

"I was smarter than her, so I got the goodies by getting all the smart stuff. It made me feel better to do better than them that way."

"Who is 'them'?" Dorothy queried, somewhat confused.

"My parents," said Janice. "And it's interesting, because my patient does the same thing, she doesn't talk about either of her parents as individuals."

"It's 'them'?"

"And when you presented, it was 'them' too," I pointed out. We were all seated on the floor, thoughtfully looking at our work. I started to frame the material.

Most important, I wanted to reinforce their trust in subliminal intuitive perceptiveness. Many of the presenters had no idea what would come out in their drawings. Yet all of them had something very profound and important to say to the presenter.

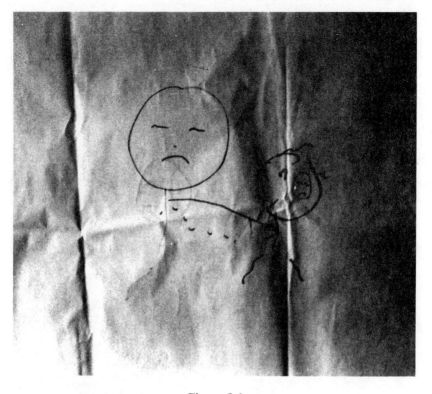

Figure 8-1

"Some members seemed to feel no contact with what was going on, and yet in your drawings, you gave more character to these figures than Janice gave with her presentation."

Eleanor spoke of her drawing (Figure 8-2). "I felt Janice's mother as being very big physically. This is Janice's mother, that's the patient's mother. And Janice's mother is, you know, the stereotype with the finger. Janice is trying to please, trying to be flexible, trying to dance, or whatever. This one is like a big cloud over her head."

> Eleanor makes a very cogent distinction between both mothers in the presentation. The mother of the patient creates more of a schizoid organization, while that of the presenter reinforces a distant, but controlled organization that is more grounded and tight.

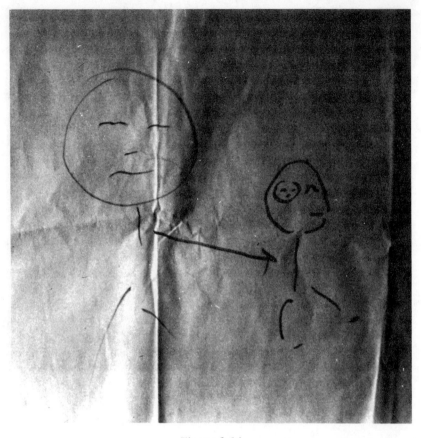

Figure 8-1A

"Oh," I said, "so she fogs it out. She fogs out the connection (the patient), whereas Janice is more confronting, but not touching."

Janice now added in a constrained but very involved voice, "I was thinking, my mother did not give a finger, but we *knew*. She had the eyes, that was it."

"So the eyes were the finger . . ."

"Yes, there were no words about what you were supposed to do, you just did it."

> Again, the presenter's associations are stimulated by the pictures, as she speaks about her own capacity to pick up some very early nonverbal cues from her mother.

Figure 8-2

I pointed to Janice's picture (Figure 8-3), and noted, "You gave the patient an *eye*."

Janice replied, "Her mother *has* an eye." "Her mother looks like a snake!" Dorothy exclaimed.

I made some additional observations. "There's so little connection in your drawings. The question I have, Janice, is why didn't you turn out to be more rebellious?"

"How *come*?" Janice looked confused and a bit defensive. The group looked somewhat anxious as they listened to this dialogue.

"Because you're describing yourself as being so alone," I said.

Suddenly a bit of anger surfaced, and Janice responded with an animated statement. "I'll tell you why. Because my father gave me love."

"So you internalized your father as the 'good mother'." I reframed. "Still, there should be something of a rebel in you."

"Why?"

"If you're so alone, who gives a rap about society? You just go your own way."

"The way I rebel," Janice said, "is first to get *into* the system, then to get what I *want*."

"You learn, then, a kind of manipulation of the system," I said gently.

"It's taken me a while, but I've learned it," Janice responded, smugly.

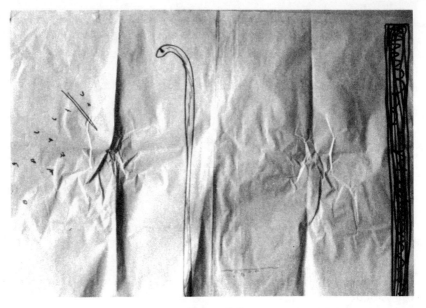

Figure 8-3

Janice is amazingly open in her ability to demonstrate how she has coped with her early deprivation. The sharing and communion with other members can only serve as a support and help in her ability to loosen up some of her compulsive defenses.

I then said with even more gentleness, "Your patient is trying to figure out how to survive in this systems, also."

After a thoughtful pause, Lenore pointed to her picture (Figure 8-4) and said, in a clipped, low voice, "This is Janice's mother and this is the patient's mother. I drew the two of them in relation to one another. The patient's mother is saying 'Do this, do that.' That's supposed to be the phallic mother in the figure."

"You're the second member to draw the mother with the finger," I said. Lenore continued, "In fact, there's a third drawing with the finger. With Janice's mother, there's this steely cold feeling. You know that there's an ominous presence out there, but you don't know what the fuck you're supposed to do. You just don't know whether you're going to fuck up or not. You get the idea that maybe you know

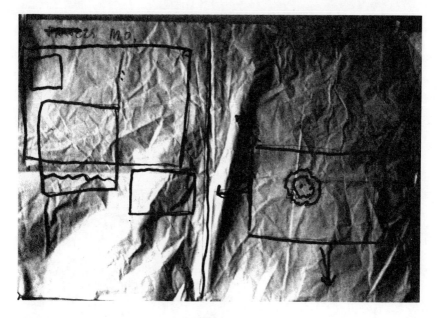

Figure 8-4

what you're supposed to do, but then you really can't tell, it's all covered up."

Janice now responded, trying to elaborate and fill in the story.

"Her mother *is* a lot like mine, but in different *ways*. Her mother is an artist, and my patient's description of her is that she was always in her studio doing what she was doing. The kids always knew she had her own life."

Lenore continued with much animation: "Somehow, if the mother is saying, 'Do this, do that,' she can go off and do her own thing. There certainly is a big presence to reckon with . . ."

"It's like a lot of ice over there," Eleanor added, in a slow, deep voice.

"So far, the faces vary from coldness to sourness," I observed.

I was aware of my early metaphor of touching the tip of the iceberg.

Dorothy jumped in at this point to share her drawing (Figure 8-5), "I was trying to show depression in both members."

Figure 8-5

"But you didn't experience depression as much as *coldness*. Is that the idea?" I asked.

"It's not so much coldness, but *reserve* on the part of my mother," Janice enthusiastically offered more material. "Like the things she says about my son. When I got sick last week, she said, 'It's good you got sick because he has to learn that he can't depend on you being there all the time.' Now, my mother was *physically* always there. She thinks we are crappy parents because we do everything for this kid. She says that he has to learn to be by himself, to learn to play by himself, to be self-sufficient. That's what children are supposed to learn to do, according to my mother. She believes we are indulgent parents."

I could almost hear Janice's mother—not so much from what Janice said, but in the very objective, efficient, matter-of-fact tone of Janice's voice. Turning to Rachel, I now said, "You had a lot of trouble thinking of Janice's mother."

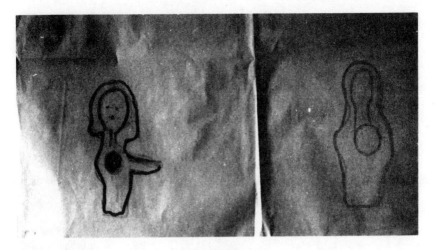

Figure 8-6

Looking at her drawing (Figure 8-6), she said, somewhat hesitantly, "It's a shadowy sort of cold, gray, walled-off ice-blue . . . I saw both mothers as very much the same, but the patient's mother is pushing her away. I can almost see her mother complaining, 'Grow up!'" Muted giggles rippled through the group.

Again the group responds to the theme of coldness and isolation, as well as a demand to grow up and fonform.

"So you were able to experience both mothers," I said.

Rachel nodded in confirmation, "And there's a void inside each of them . . ."

"So some of you are picking up the void, the nebulousness, the coldness, the iciness. What about *you*?" I asked, turning to Dorothy.

"This is Janice's mother." Dorothy pointed (Figure 8-5). "I pictured her as very well formed. I purposely put in a lot of details. A very pleasant woman, well dressed, put together, but this is supposed to be a block of ice. The patient's mother is similar, but she did not have to block herself off because there was nothing to close off."

Dorothy focuses on another difference between the two mothers. Again the patient's mother seems far more impoverished.

Figure 8-7

I turned to Janice and asked her, "How do you feel about what's being said?"

Janice replied in a bitter tone, "My patient's mother needs *her* kids more than my mother needed her kids."

Dorothy continued, "Yes, that was the sense I got, even though I didn't put it down. I remember thinking as I was drawing, that this woman would need her children to give her internal stuff."

Dolores thoughtfully and deliberately spoke as she looked at her drawing (Figure 8-7) "I did the patient's mother first. I saw her as being very together and coordinated, and she expected her daughter to be stylish and together, but unapproachable. This is the patient's mother—*remote*."

"With your mother, Janice, I saw her as having the *trappings* of being the mother—that she would look like a mother on the outside, but really would not be as bright as *you* are in terms of being "together." Maybe she'd be depressed and not very approachable."

Again another possible facet of Janice's mother unfolds. Was there an inner depression as contrasted to the patient's mother who demanded conformity?

"You moan when I mention your mother, Janice, but what could you bring from your mother to a case like this where there was been so much deprivation?"

I recognized that the question was a difficult one. My attempt was one of demonstrating how, even under the most difficult circumstances, there are usually some positives that can be of use in facilitating a healthy internalization. However, Rachel broke in at this point and carried the discussion to a different perspective.

There was a long pause before Rachel broke in and spoke in a confessional tone. "I am sitting on a lot of guilt, because last night I went to a dance performance with one of my girlfriends to see a patient's work. Now I'm feeling a little better because I thought you were all going to say you never go. I also went last year when she gave a performance. She is a choreographer and it seems to further the treatment. She's also a very deprived woman, and I had a very deprived mother . . . But I would not have thought of not going. That's my problem."

In a somewhat cautious voice, I said, "You've had some of your own deprivation to struggle with. It's very easy to act out being the good mother with your patients."

Rachel added, "And avoid being accused of being the steely cold one," referring to her drawing.

By offering very concrete representations of mother that reflect the patient, the therapist, as well as some of the internalizations of the memembers of the group, we begin to have a very clear sense of the variety of defenses that can be utilized in coping with the bad mother inside of us.

I continued cautiously, "So to avoid being the steely cold mother, we sometimes become the good mother with our patients."

"But also, *I* get mothered," Rachel pointed out.

Janice now brought the discussion back to her case, trying to weigh the options. "If I go, and my patient sees it as another offering, another performance, then *that's* wrong. If I don't go, I am being the rigid therapist who is keeping 'appropriate boundaries.' I keep asking myself if I am going for some personal gratification. Am I giving something because I did not get it, so I want *her* to have it? Or is it good because this is where she most authentically *is*, and she is saying, 'I want you to see me, and this is *important* to me'? This is what she actually *said* to me . . ."

> Again we see the rigid parent in Janice asking some very black and white questions. The hope is that we can let Janice struggle and find a solution that comes out of her own sense and feel of her case.

"Can you feel your way through it?" I asked. "Do you feel what could be good for her?"

"No, there's too much guilt about doing the wrong thing."

"That's what we're trying to get at. You're frightened of using your own intuition," I said.

"I'm frightened about boundaries," Janice emphasized.

> The boundaries of mother and child are very clear and defined for Janice. If anything, there is a good deal of anxiety that arises out of a creative state of oneness that is neither antitherapeutic nor destructive in making a very early contact with a deprived patient.

I responded with equal challenge in my voice, "Yes, and as a result you are frightened of using your own intuition, which is nonverbal relatedness. In your picture there's not contact. Intuition has to do with *touching* a person."

Looking confused, Janice asked, "But do you have to go to *performances* for contact?"

"No."

"And does that mean that you're doing the contact inappropriately?"

"No. You are rasing a question that cannot be answered intellectually. There's not a single person in this room, including myself, who will come up with the right answer."

Dolores now intervend: "That seems to be the problem. You're operating under the assumption that there's a right answer. Earlier, we were talking about the Puerto Rican and the Haitian, and it sounded like a right and a wrong. That's where I got the image of her mother being very judgmental. That, plus your attempt, because I feel her inside of you, of trying to figure out what is the right thing to do."

Janice protested, "But it's also a responsibility to the *treatment*."

I spoke with a good deal of intensity, and the group observed with corresponding intensity. "Your responsibility to the patient is to make contact. That is as important as the transference issue. Do you remember when I spoke of limits, in connection with another case, and you vehemently responded to my setting a structure? You were quite clear about needing to feel the humanity of the therapist. So that human contact is important for you, and it can't be figured out in terms of strict rules and techniques. I am not asking you to give up on your cognitive needs, but that side of you is too mixed up with guilt and control. All too often you are living with your mother, trying to figure *her* out."

"What are you talking about?" Janice said with a defensive look.

"I mean, using the technique you learned as a child to cope with your mother. Now, for instance, with your own child, do you consult the good book to figure out which is the right rule for each moment?"

"I try to, but it never comes out at the right time or the right month, so I forget it."

"How does it work out?"

"It's all right, we're surviving." I could hear the underlying pride in being 'good mama,' and said, "I guess you have to trust your own intuition."

"But the other guilt comes in: I really *want* to go to the performance, because I really want to see her dance. I don't know whether that's my wish, or really good for the patient . . ."

Everybody jumped as Dolores blurted, "Wait a minute. That's a very healthy reaction."

"Are you allowed the gratification?" Janice asked, in a quiet voice.

Lenore responded enthusiastically, "But wait a second. If you were to say to her: 'I really want to come and to see you dance, but I am concerned it will get in the way for you,' why wouldn't that be *contact?*"

"That's very nice," Rachel said, pleased with the solution.

I now tried to integrate the drawings with the discussion. "Take a look at all these rigid ground rules, that cold black rigid material. There are more boxes than straight lines or anything else. Everybody is encased in ice. The rigidity keeps you with your mother and prevents you from enjoying your patient. Here contact is an important part of treatment, so let's hear your biggest fear about mushing the boundaries. What is going to happen?"

Janice replied in a somewhat irate tone, "I am going to be like her other shrink who did not give my patient her own space. He was somewhere else. He was eating in her session."

"Did she ask him to eat?"

"She told him not to."

I kept on challenging Janice, "Does this sound somewhat different? She is asking you to see her, but that won't necessarily be over-gratification. Perhaps the crux of the matter is that we are looking for a developmentally appropriate means of communicate. If there is an attachment issue, your level of responsiveness and available warmth would seem crucial."

Janice now addressed her other problem with the case: "If I do something wrong, I'm up shit creek."

"What is 'wrong'?" I asked.

"I don't know what's wrong but, you see, it's not knowing . . . You don't *do* things if you don't know how they'll work . . ."

"So you're figuring out the system all the time," I observed.

"Well, that's right. You get penalized if you don't figure out the system."

Dolores reflected, "You probably learned how to squelch your instincts and not take risks."

> The group acts as a new model of acceptance and connection. They support Janice's right to accept risks, make mistakes, and listen to her inner voice that truly makes contact with her patient.

We could hear the pain in Janice's voice as she spoke. "When you put everything in a pot, the goods and the bads, the rights and the 'wrongs,' there are only a couple of wrongs you're allowed to have."

"It's a very big system to work out," I said. Then feeling that I was being too hard on Janice, I added more gently, "There's no question about it . . . your ability to figure out the system has been very adaptive. You received your doctorate at a very young age; you just plowed right through it. God knows, a lot of people wish they had that ability. I am not knocking it as a negative, all I'm saying is that it interferes with the use of your intuition and instincts."

"I don't trust them, because they're going to get me into trouble," Janice maintained.

"'Getting into trouble.' What *is* the trouble?" Lenore asked in a challenging voice.

"You're projecting the mother onto her. Is she going to come down on you in some way if you do it wrong?"

"No, it's the *global* effect of 'doing wrong'."

Lenore continued, "Yes, this community is going to come down on you for going to your patient's dance performance. Right?"

"No."

I added, "It really *would* be a problem if you didn't want to go, and felt obligated."

"No, there's no question about wanting to go. I am curious and interested."

Dorothy sat back and reflected: "I have been thinking about similar situations with some of my patients. I don't want to get involved with patients outside the office. That's important to me. You still can explore the issue; you still can say 'I'm curious, but I don't think it's good for the treatment for me to attend.'"

Lenore asked, "When do you listen to yourself and work with the patient as one human being to another, and how much do you maintain the analytic structure when there is no risk?"

I laughed, "Since when does analytic work mean no risk?"

Dolores defined her position in the discussion. "If I want to go to a performance, as one human being to another, I go."

"A lot of us at the end of the day just want our own space . . ."

Trying to clarify, I said, "It is all too easy to fall back on some rule rather than ask ourselves where the patient's at, what I feel, what's going on, etcetera. Analysis takes a lot more than following some prescribed rules."

"Have you read any of the material by Langs?"

"I took his seminar," Janice responded.

"You took his seminar!" I said, in amazement.

Janice went on, "I took his seminar. I tell you, he would say things like: 'That's where you screwed up! You screwed up because you looked at the clock or you had your office in the wrong building.' It was a great system because if you could buy it, all the answers were there."

I spoke in a somewhat challenging voice, "He believes in a system. Now, here's an analyst who presents a system. How come you didn't buy his system?"

"Because I did not believe it."

"Since you come from a family of systems like your patient, perhaps you might also see her wish to free herself from the system."

"I don't have a system, so that I don't know the system that I am really following," protested Janice.

I pondered, and said, "It means that you have to use your instincts. It means that you have to use *yourself*. If your theory kills the person *in* you, then there's something dramatically wrong with the theory. A theory gives a structure, an organization to your experience. A patient can tolerate the therapist making mistakes. What is *in*tolerable, however, is if he or she can't feel your presence."

Dolores interjected a technical question: "If you decide that it might be good for the treatment to go, but you're really not up to going, how would you deal with that? What would be your technique?"

> The anxiety of the members has been raised in their identification with Janice's mother. I am bombarded with questions regarding right and wrong under the guise of technique. I try to maintain my position that the best answer is to listen to themselves.

I further defined my position. "Again, it is very much being 'you.' I might say, 'Look, the best way I can help you is by helping you bring your feelings into the office.' I have said this to performers. Just remember, a patient wants you to tell them that you liked the performance. What if you felt it was awful? It makes a lot of sense to tell a patient that you don't want to be put in the position of potentially losing your role as a therapist."

Another member reflected out loud, "It's not being selfish for me to say to the person: '*This* is a place where I help you most, it's not out there.'"

"What is more important," I turned to Janice, "is for you to leave that mother/daughter role and trust yourself."

The "Magic" Mirror and the Mother Within

This session ends with the presenter's question still unanswered. We trust Janice's instinctive good sense to struggle with the "right answer" and come up with a solution that will not be based on technique, but upon a nonverbal relatedness and understanding of her patient.

Shifting to a nonverbal mode by delving into a playful imagery, drawing was the key to opening up an array of connections within the group. At the beginning, the atmosphere was rather dry, cold, and matter-of-fact. Our relatedness was being shoked off by judgments and technical issues. Questions of what was the right or wrong seemed to hide the very life of the case. Here, the leader decided to avoid a direct confrontation with Janice's characterological issues which were so connected to her manner of presentation. Maintaining a supportive holding environment in the group atmosphere by shifting the level of investigation to a nonverbal area appeared to minimize the defense and avoid the destructive building of a negative transference.

The parallel mirroring of the patient and therapist's mothers became a frame for further group exploration. For each member, the drawing became an amalgamation of his or her own mother, the patient's, and that of Janice. Each member, then, became a receptor picking up different pieces of the internalized mother in the transference/countertransference dyad. The sharing of various drawings by different members of the group became a "magic" mirror for Janice to rediscover a piece of her mother. Each member resonated with a particular aspect of the therapist's mother/child dyad. The nonverbal quality gave a shape and frame to this experience which avoided Janice's intellectualizing, defensive posture. Here, then, the group and therapist each gained a better understanding of the term mirroring: It is a reflection that captures the multitudinous levels of perception that are embodied in a psychic representation. Janice stubbornly held on to her survival mechanisms, but occasionally let down her guard to move to a more intuitive level of communication. This was a pragmatic learning experience for the presenter, as well as a means of facing her negative introject that interfered with the playful relatedness with her patient. It also gave us an opportunity to explore mirroring in its full perspective. In this exercise, different dimensions of the mother/daughter relationship are reflected, giving the presenter a far more in-depth perspective rather than a one-dimensional view of her mother.

Nonverbal empathy becomes an important aspect for group discussion. Translating the visual mother image to the psychic representation requires a familiarization with nonverbal language. This representation then becomes a focus to reframe and reorganize a more adequate holding environment for the patient. In the sharing of each member's representation of mother, the tone, posture, and rhythm, along with a number of other subtle nonverbal inflections, become the major organizing force for building a new "holding environment." Janice, by taking a risk and exposing herself to the unfolding images of mother, went beyond her defenses and was able possibly to construct a new conception of empathic relatedness.

Let us turn now to some of the issues regarding group process. Janice, as with many other presenters, often starts a presentation with a seemingly innocent question that will take no time to answer. *Behind* this question lies a plea for help and support that goes beyond the boundaries of a simple inquiry. Here, Janice's need was one of reexperiencing a playful contact between mother and child. The dramatic imaginative play with the concept of mother then became a gateway for touching and connection that was largely absent in the initial part of the presentation. Here, the exchanging of pictures from one member to another became an additional means of support and emotional investment.

The preceding case presentation deemphasized character analysis, both for presenter and patient. In each instance, an unmirrored and unresponded to self required resonance and appreciation. Character analysis with either party, at this particular stage of development, creates a further disconnection to a primary mode of mother/child connectedness. One can also observe how different cases elicit different theoretical frameworks which, in turn, organize case material. As per the case under discussion, a self-psychology point of view seems most appropriate; but somewhere down the line a more classical stance may be more resonant with the treatment process.

Playing with the visual dimensions of form and the organization of energy, space, and affect becomes a frame for Janice to explore, with the group's help, the possibility of discovering a mother inside herself that resonates with her patient. The so-called technical question then falls into place as she becomes more connected to the mother/child imagery.

Some further clarification regarding "the mother inside the therapist" appears to be in order.

1. The representation of mother can be expanded to include any number of mothering experiences other than with one's original mother. To name but a few sources, we can draw upon the mothering elements of a father, teacher, or sibling. Consequently, we are not necessarily "stuck" with our original conception of mother, either within our patients or our therapeutic self. A multidimensional exploration of the internal mother representation can be an experiene of freeing oneself from a fixed perception of an earlier relationship. What therapy offers, in terms of an internal representation, is an opportunity to integrate the varieties of mothering experiences. The various mirrors of mother offered to the presenter were an illustration of this process. In instances where there has been a good deal

of deprivation in the therapist's background, playing out the ideal mother as a means of offering gratification through an identification with the patient can be a recurring danger.

2. Depressive patients, or those with seriously deprived backgrounds, constantly tempt the therapist to live out a gratifying role rather than promote insight and an internal structure. Here the confusion often lies in discerning the difference between empathy and a regressive gratification of infantile wishes.

3. The complex interrelationship of the real with the analytic relationship becomes overly charged with deprived patients. There are few guidelines, except one: balancing analytic discipline with a warm, empathic relatedness that does not violate the analytic integrity of the relationship.

4. *Concrete acts*, such as attending concerts or weddings, are *always* emotionally loaded. The decision as to whether to attend or not becomes highly subjective and often contingent on the therapist's ability to maintain an analytic role, even though the analytic *arena* expands. In this regard, the issue of a transference cure versus a restructuring of the personality becomes an unending one to investigate, as these patients do flourish in a very supportive atmosphere. The question arises, here, whether we are ducking any of the more difficult and charged issues, such as negative transference and separation anxiety, by being overly supportive with deprived patients.

Chapter 9

JANICE

The Therapist as a Whore

A STUDY IN CONTRAST

Janice found in her work with Jim that therapy with a narcissistic patient can be quite a challenge. As an appendage to the patient's internal world, Janice's separate presence in the therapeutic relationship took a back seat as she mirrored, reflected, and supported her patient in the interests of developing a mirroring transference. What arose in the course of Janice's presentation were both the narrower therapeutic issues, such as weighing a supportive versus a more active interpretive approach, and the broader question pertaining to the role of therapist as a masochistic vessel. As the patient paraded his contempt for women through the therapist's office, Janice managed to hold her tongue, but only by becoming overly detached and "objective." Interestingly, the supervisory group, consisting of highly functioning women, responded with disproportionate rage, which in turn caused them to look at political, historical, and cultural issues pertaining to the roles of women.

In her previous case presentation, Janice explored both the mother inside of herself and her objective, reality-oriented stance, which permitted her to navigate the terrifying waters of abandonment. Here, kernels of her unresolved narcissistic issues come to the fore as she struggles with the differences between maintaining an autonomous therapeutic self in the face of very difficult conditions as opposed to utilizing masochistic holding mechanisms to control her patient.

THE PRESENTATION: A "NUMBERS" MAN

In her characteristically direct, controlled manner, Janice began. "Three weeks ago I had more of a dilemma about this case than I have now, but I still want to present this patient. Jim is a forty-year-old stockbroker who originally came to treatment because he was planning to separate from his wife. He was referred by a psychriatrist who had Jim's wife in therapy. They had joint sessions, trying to work through her anger, *his* anger, her wanting him back again. She would literally grovel on the ground, begging him to come back, saying that her life was over.

"After two years of treatment, he decided that he'd dealt with what he wanted. He separated from his wife and moved in with his girlfriend. I recall that while he was still living with his wife, he was going back and forth between home and his new girlfriend as well as having affairs with other women. He couldn't make a commitment to anyone. He called women, 'Kleenex.' 'When I'm finished with them I throw them out,' he'd say. He doesn't talk like that any more, but it was difficult sitting with him and feeling like yet another piece of Kleenex, not quite knowing when the Kleenex was going to be thrown in the garbage.

"After a break of one year, Jim called me and was very depressed over his lousy relationship with his girlfriend. He really wanted to deal with what was going on, where he was going, because he hated going home and he hated being with her. Work was also terrible, which made him more depressed.

"He had a co-op apartment in the city, his girlfriend had an apartment in New Jersey, and they went back and forth between the two. It somehow was okay, until she moved in. The issues around her moving in—he was a little sneaky about it, and she was a little stupid about it. She didn't like the situation. It was *his* apartment, and she was there like a mistress. She had no say in what went on. Their arguments would always be around who had to do what in the apartment. He would procrastinate and procrastinate and didn't care shit about the decorations or furnishings. She didn't want to give him any money for the household expenses. Now, he makes a lot of money, but it doesn't end up being a lot of money, given that a third of it goes to his wife, and he gets a third, and whatever is left over disappears. He thought that she should contribute to the household expenses, and they would get into arguments over who did the shopping, who paid this much money for this, why the other wasn't paying any money for that. The main issue was, who was going to commit to whom? He said he was very committed to her: He wanted to live with her, and he wanted to have a life with her. The problem was, he didn't like the fact that she was forty-five years old. He's forty-two, she's forty-five. I think it was a smokescreen. He kept talking about how he wanted more children; how he loved the idea of a family.

"This man didn't have much contact with his three kids until he got separated and divorced. It was only after he got divorced that he took the kids out and started to have a relationship with them. All of a sudden he's thinking, 'Maybe I want to have another family. Maybe I want to start over, and I don't like the fact that she's forty-five.'

"He has always been concerned with being able to walk down the street, walk into restaurants and into the theater, and have people turn around and say, 'Look at that great couple.' Now, he's a very attractive man, and he is somebody for whom you'd turn around. He is very tall and looks like a real yuppie WASP. What he liked about this woman was that she was understanding and she confronted him about things and didn't just let him go. She was exactly what his wife wasn't. His wife just said, 'Do what you want to do, just be a wonderful loving person with a great job who gives me a great house.'

"Now I'm hearing the same complaints: Nobody was giving enough, everybody was taking too much, so they went into marital counseling. About a month ago Jim told the girlfriend that he didn't want to live with her any more, and basically kicked her out, which was her fear all along the way. She had been pretty bitter and used to complain to him, 'I don't own a share of this co-op, I don't have any savings, I don't have anything. What I'm afraid of is that one day you're going to tell me to leave.'

"I think this age thing was always in the back of his head—he just couldn't forget that she was three years older than he. It always bugged him. First he'd complain she had heavy thighs, then he'd go back over whether it was the right decision or the wrong decision. He'd say things like, 'Maybe there really isn't somebody out there who's perfect and wonderful. Maybe she really is the right person, but I can't stand the fact that she's forty-five years old.'

"He spent a lot of time talking about how important it was to be with somebody who made him look right. His wife was not a very attractive woman, so he bought her beautiful clothes and beautiful jewelry to dress her up. When he'd gotten married, somebody at school had said to him, 'You know, the woman you're going to marry is very nice, but she'd be better if you could cover her face.' He carried that around for a long time—if you put a bag over her head, she looks great."

> The lack of dynamics and emphasis on the transference is a tell-tale sign of countertransference involvement. I am not even quite sure how much empathic contact there is in this case, as the presentation is full of history, but with only a minimum of deep relatedness.

A member broke in and excitedly exclaimed, "How can you *stand* him!"

Janice continued in her typical nonchalant manner. "I'll tell you, the only way I've gotten immune to all this is that he really is a character. He's so narcissistic it's incredible."

"He's kind of a perpetual child," someone else added, with mild disgust.

"He *is* a perpetual child, and he really is a very empty, deprived human being. The only way he gets anything is by having somebody out there. He can sort of pull people in by how they look, except that he doesn't talk like that. He talks like, 'I want somebody who is understanding, emotional,' etcetera, and 'Why can't I find somebody who has both sides?' He's got a list: She has to be thirty-three, but she has to *look* like she's eighteen, but she has to be emotionally like forty-five, she has to want children, she has to be a professional, but she always has to be available to him.

> The volley of complaints continues, with a deemphasis of unconscious dynamics. Where is the complexity in this case? *When the presentation has a sense of flatness, there is usually some form of countertransference involvement.*

"After his girlfriend left, he bought a book and started getting people's names to go out with. He had a list of three people the first week and four people the next week. This was always a problem. He really got depressed and anxious.

"He'd come in and it'd be a matter of my sitting there and just listening. He'd go on about women: This one's too this, that one's too that, this one's ugly because of this. When he was in treatment a year ago, I got pissed, because he was treating women like Kleenexes. He walks in now and complains that he wants someone who is thirty-five and he can't live with someone who is forty-five. It's a real . . . it's like watching a movie, and I don't know whether . . . it feels very seductive. It's not that I'd ever want to be *with* this jerk, because he really *is* a jerk, but there's something about watching how fifty percent of the world's women are attracted to this guy . . ."

> The therapist moves away from the patient's feeling of self-contempt that is projected onto women. What does this say about the therapist's dynamics?

Delores queried, "Do you know anything about his parents, his family, what kind of relationships he had?

"His father was a hotshot doctor, and an alcoholic. The mother was very subservient. You know: 'I have to take care of my husband; I have to do what he wants.' The father would go on rampages around the house when he came home. Jim, an only child, was the one who really took care of the mother, in terms of getting furious when the father would go into his tirades. He'd have to rescue her.

"Jim was a dumpy kid. I think his thighs were so big that they had to get two pairs of pants and put them together . . ."

A member couldn't believe what she was hearing and interrupted: "He was obese?"

"He was fat, and they couldn't get a pair of pants to fit him."

"So he has a defective body image," another member threw in, trying to be analytic and objective.

"He *had* a defective body image . . ." This seemed to set everyone to talking at once . . . "It's inside of him! And what's happening now is that his twelve-year-old daughter is about thirty pounds overweight and doesn't understand that *one* hamburger is what you eat, you don't eat three hamburgers. It's a whole thing that he's going through again with her."

> We see how the patient projects the greedy, ugly part of himself onto his daughter. Again, the therapist's anger interferes with being in touch with this dynamic.

A reflective comment from Lenore moved the discussion to another level. "I was associating, for some reason, to homosexuality. I have nothing to base it on, but I keep thinking that this guy's got a real problem. I don't know why I was thinking that . . . I'm thinking of his one-night stands, his contemptuous attitude toward women. There's a whole lot of stuff involving his sense of himself as a man that he needs to keep repeating to reassure himself. Every time he sleeps with a woman it reassures him that he's a man, somehow."

"This subservient mother, I have a feeling, is some kind of connection for him," Delores commented, trying very hard to keep her analytic "cool."

> Delores attempts to move the treatment onto a more profound level. However, Janice does not buy this contemplative mode and stays on the same level of contact with her patient.

"Yes. It's easier for him to talk about how he has so much contempt for her now because his father keeps drinking and passing out. Still, the mother won't come back from California to visit the grandchildren or him because she's afraid that if she leaves, her husband's going to die. Jim asks why she'd put up with a man like that, or stick with a man like that."

My curiosity was being increasingly aroused. I asked, "How does he treat you in the sessions? What's he like with *you*?"

"At first he'd shut me up or glare at me; now he'll listen, take it in, and sort of spit it out a little bit. He gets to be a king by coming in and saying, 'I have to tell you what happened this week,' and he'll go on with his blah, blah, blah. When I stop him, he'll get upset. He doesn't want an interruption. He's like a little kid who has to say, 'Let me finish my story, or I'm going to forget it.' I feel like I have to start pushing and say, 'Wait a minute,' but it's very hard to get in."

"Do you think he's afraid of your taking over?" Lenore asked.

"Well, he puts me in a dilemma. What he'll do sometimes is to ask me questions that he knows I won't answer, and if I give him one of these 'What do *you* think?' responses, I'll get shit for being psychy and not giving him an answer. Like, 'I asked you a question. Stop giving me that therapist crap. Give me an answer.'

"You see, the problem is that I have this theory that if he lets me in once every two months, I might get in a little more next time. Mostly, though, it's, 'Look, your place is over there, so do what you have to do, and I'll make you feel better by letting you get in once in a while.'"

> The therapist takes a self-psychology point of view where she sees
> herself as an appendage of her patient. There is, of course, an-
> other way of conceptualizing the case. Perhaps the patient is
> frightened of a secret introjection of his mother and a dissociated
> identification with his father.

I felt the need to offer some direction to the discussion and
asked, "Has your stance been helpful?"

"I think it's been helpful up to a point, and it's been helpful only
because he will come back, and he *will* remember things that have
made sense two months before . . ."

"You want to change things?" Eleanor asked, looking a bit confused.

"Yes, I do, because I'm really not quite sure what I'm doing, plus—
there's something that isn't *right* about it."

"Suppose we had a session," I said, "and you're this patient, and
he's going on with all these tactics, and I say to him, 'I'm not sure you
want me to listen to you.' What does he say?"

"I'm listening to you. I don't understand what, uh . . . I heard
what you said."

"It's almost like I feel I'm being dispensed with. Is that the kind
of relationship you would like to have with me?" I asked, as therapist.

"I don't feel that way. I've been coming here for four years. Why
would I come here if I felt that way about you?"

I pushed a little further. "I know that, but there may be a piece of
you that's acting just like your father right now."

Janice, as Jim, said patronizingly, "I don't like my father, and I
don't like anything he does, so what are you talking about?"

"Maybe the way your father was completely oblivious, denied
what he was doing, didn't give a damn about anybody, just rushed in
and intimidated everybody, and everyone would be subservient to
him . . . Some of that can rub off on you without your knowing it . . ."

"You're not making any sense," Janice/Jim responded
contemptuously.

"I don't think your father could have heard that either. I don't
think anyone could *speak* to your father . . ."

> The problem of what to mirror becomes a very crucial issue in
> this treatment. Picking up the father's defense seems to hit the
> mark.

Janice broke the dialogue to say, "You'd get him on that one!"

"What would happen?" I pushed for more information.

"He'd listen to that, because then it wouldn't be *me* anymore, it would be his father."

"Well, I would pull his father into the session. Jim's riding right over you as fast as he can, and you're tolerating it. Do you want to go after his identification with his father? I'd keep after the theme and say something like: 'I think your father was always concerned with himself, everyone else was inconsequential, and you were a victim of it. Sometimes a victim identifies with the aggressor.' I'd keep going after it. Does that approach feel right to you?"

> Taking a rather directive stance with the supervisee always presents dangerous repercussions. The supervisee may well identify with the "aggressor" supervisor mimicking his or her suggestions, and sabotaging the treatment. It's to be hoped that our supervisory relationship will not mirror the subtle unconscious identifications in this case.

"It feels okay, but I'll have to turn into a super tank to do it."

"No, you won't. Why do you have to be a 'super tank'?" I asked.

"Because so much bombastic stuff would come back before I'd get in there."

There was an insistence in my voice and I continued, "Then I go after *that* and say, 'Is that what your father did to you? He's right in this room right now. Do you really want to be like him? You say you don't, but maybe there's a piece of you that's unwittingly like him right now. Do you dispense with me like your father dispensed with you?' Keep right after him."

"I'd have to get my guts together to do it."

"Why do you need guts?" I asked.

"Because he really feels like a bulldozer—a bulldozer that really shoves me over."

"He doesn't seem *that* intimidating . . ."

"You're not a woman," said Janice sharply.

"That's a good point," I conceded.

"*What* did you say?" someone picked up in surprise.

"Art's not a woman. He doesn't hit Art where he lives."

"Let's hear more about that," I probed. "Do you think a woman is more vulnerable to this type of person?"

"Yes," a chorus answered me.

"Why?"

"Does it have to do with sexual excitement?" Lenore looked quizzically around. Janice looked surprised. "What do you mean, sexual excitement?"

"To me he's kind of voyeurish," Lenore said, and Janice, in her nonchalant manner, agreed.

"Where do you want to go with that?" I asked.

Lenore, looking thoughtful, commented, "I was just thinking. This guy strikes me as being so narcissistic. I was wondering if he wouldn't feel injured by what Art was saying."

> We sometimes have to balance empathic contact with our patients versus the possibility that the interjection of fragility by the patient can be utilized as a subtle control of the therapeutic process.

Picking up on this, I raised a theoretical treatment issue. "Does this man respond to a mirroring transference where we emphasize a reflection of feelings and keep the interpretations down to a minimum? If so, when do you go after the character issues? Is the former point of view basically supportive treatment? Can he handle interpretations without feeling too wounded?"

Janice reflected a moment, then spoke. "I think that he could hear it, but I think that he would fall apart—not that there's anything wrong with falling apart."

"I don't think he's ready to hear about the hurt. He's still at the stage where he's visibly angry over his crappy father and that his mother didn't stand up to the father."

I followed her line of thinking, and noted, "The mother not standing up to the father really influenced the lack of involvement in the family. You're on this side when you confront the father inside of him."

> The issue, then, that arises in treatment revolves around domination and submission. Does the therapist become the submissive child who must indeed show the patient how to stand up to the frightening father?

Suddenly the group began talking at once, apparently in response to the rising tension level in the case. When the hubbub died down, Janice went on. "During the time they were together, his girlfriend left him once, and the separation lasted four days. He was an absolute basket case."

"If *he* can leave *them*, it's one thing, but when it's the other way around . . ." a voice cut in sarcastically.

"He felt isolated, lonely, he didn't know what to do with himself," Janice continued. "He didn't know who to call. He was like a little kid who'd had a door slammed in his face and been told, 'Goodbye, I'll see you when the week is over.'"

"Isn't that what his father did?" I asked.

"Yes, and what I was afraid of three weeks ago was that the same thing was going to happen, because he was so fearful of being alone. To my surprise, he didn't fall apart, but I still feel he would panic if I confronted him about his father."

> Again we see a hidden masochistic identification with the mother and a suspicion that he controls through guilt-provoking mechanisms.

I told Janice, "then I would answer him, 'You know, dealing with this father in you may be a way of not being alone; of being able to make contact the way your father didn't.'"

Janice argued, "He would say, 'You're telling me that stuff again, and I don't know what you're talking about. What do you mean, my father in me?'"

I went on, "'Your father was like a steamroller,' I'd say. 'Nobody could speak his mind when he was in the same room.'"

> I use the therapist's metaphor as a fulcrum for my interpretive efforts.

Janice objected, "I feel he'd think I was mimicking, and be hurt by that."

"Okay, let's do some role-playing," I said. "I'll be the therapist, you be the patient."

Art as therapist: "Look, let me explain to you . . ."

Janice as patient: "You know, this is how I see it about this woman over in New Jersey, and I want you to understand. You understand my point of view, don't you?"

Art/therapist: "Now, do you hear what I'm saying? I feel that I'm being talked at. Now I know you don't want to talk at me, but that's what happens between us. I'm being talked at and boomed at. I can almost picture your father doing that to you right now."

"That he could hear much better," Janice said, out of character.

We're beginning to arrive at an interpretive approach to the patient. We must combine a sense of empathy along with our interventions.

The dialogue between "therapist" and "patient" continued as the
group listened intently. "Do you make contact with your father? Do
you speak to your father?" I asked.

"Well, sure I talk to him, but he's an alcoholic now, so he doesn't
want to listen to me."

"He doesn't listen to you. I bet he bellows right over you — That's
the kind of contact you have with him."

"That's not contact, that's nothing."

"Right. Now just remember that. That's not contact, that's nothing. Do you see any piece of your father in you right now?"

"Maybe if I thought about it, but he's so different. I mean, this
guy just falls apart all the time," said the "patient," in a superior tone.

"He falls apart all the time . . ."

"He falls apart. He drinks all the time, he doesn't know what day
it is. I mean, he's a real alcoholic. I'm not like him."

"But how was he when you were younger?" I asked.

"He wasn't even there then. I mean, he just walked in and he
drank, and that was it."

"Sometimes he boomed all over the place, too," I suggested.

"He boomed at everybody."

"Shouted at everybody, gave orders, told everybody to listen, be
little puppets," I said, enlarging on the "patient's" words.

"Yeah."

"If I heard that father in you, would you want me to tell you
about it?"

"You can tell me about it, but I don't see myself as being that
way."

"Just in case it creeps in there without your knowing about it,
would you like me to warn you about it?"

Janice broke character to say, "Now he would be polite and say
yes, but I think what he'd really like to say is that if it makes you feel
better, you can tell me."

I continued in the role of therapist. "Okay. I'll try to say it to you,
even though I know you really don't want to hear it. We can drop it
right now if you want us to."

Empathizing with an awareness of his defense rather than the underlying impulse becomes a very important form of contact with
this patient.

Again breaking from the role, Janice said, "That would work much better. That fits much better with how he is. It's open, in his control this way. If he doesn't want to deal with this, he doesn't have to."

"I don't think you would keep on trying to drive your point," I commented. "You can say, 'Okay, you've had enough. At least we understand each other. You're saying you've had enough, and I can respect that.'" I went on to clarify the therapeutic issue: "The father's got to be somewhere in the room. He's either with you or with him. You may find yourself pushing more than you want to push to get a point across. That's a clue. At that point you're going to have to say, 'I guess I was being a little bit too much like your father.'"

> Here we are picking up a projective identification with the father. Owning up to this induction allows the patient to negotiate a different perception of this imago.

"And that he would be comfortable with," acknowledged Janice.

"Okay, so he'll push you into the other role," I went on, "but what you just gave him was a mirror, and the reflection was part of a corrective experience where he can have the opportunity to tell you to back off."

> A corrective emotional experience does not mean that we can be the father he never had. We are giving him an opportunity to negotiate and speak to that father. That is the corrective emotional experience.

"How would you push or make him aware of the contempt that he must have felt for his mother's subservience, and which he transfers to all women?" Lenore asked, with a look of puzzlement on her face.

I reflected a bit and responded: "I think a lot of it has to take place in the therapeutic relationship rather than in his coming in and dumping his week on you."

Janice commented, "Well, what's been happening that's different is the nature of his first two or three sentences when he comes in and starts, or the last couple as he's walking out the door. For instance, he walked in about six weeks ago and said, 'Coming here is like going to see a whore—you come here for your hour, and pay your fee.'

I said, "So what's it like coming to see a whore?" And he dropped it saying that I wasn't a whore, I was this and that, but I think that I pushed it back on him because it was such a grotesque, disgusting feeling."

"But then," I said, "to follow out the sentimental stereotype, whores are supposed to be sympathetic and understanding." I added, playing therapist once again, "'Whores are always there. You can have them when you want them.'"

> Being free to move at different levels of understanding even with such a loaded affect as contempt becomes an important aspect of transference/countertransference play.

Janice protested: "But there's also the contempt he feels because he has to buy it, and that he can have what he wants as long as he pays for it, as long as he reserves his hour . . . There's no love, no Eros in there at all." A perplexed look lingered on Janice's face as she reflected on this.

"'Yes, the bitterness at having been cheated,' I retorted, with an ironic twist in my voice. You don't make up for what you didn't get as a child. There are scars that the treatment can never take away. But you do get understanding, a form of therapeutic love, that makes it possible to leave the past and be open and available for the present. I could not sit there coolly! . . . again we go back to that woman business— that Art is not a woman, and he can hold all this at a *distance*."

> I knew that the male/female issue would be an important area for exploration. I waited for the group to pick this up. Otherwise I would bring it back myself.

Delores stepped in and spoke intently. "I was thinking about how to use the anger that he stirs up for some interpretative purposes."

Janice protested, "But the thing is, I wasn't angry."

> I was aware that Janice was denying her anger, and I knew we had to go after this.

Delores came back with, "Well, how would *I* use it, then."

Janice exclaimed passionately: "I mean, I've been listening to this stuff for four years . . ."

"You know what? I don't believe you. I think that what you said earlier is probably true. You're numb to it by now. I mean, after four years, what are you going to do?"

Janice stood her ground and replied: "Maybe. I didn't sit there when he said that and say, 'You fucking asshole, don't call me a whore.' But it wasn't that—like, if I weren't sitting in here and you were a man who wasn't a patient of mine, you know what I'd tell you . . ."

Delores tried to hold onto her clinical perspective. "It has nothing to do with being called a whore. What he's saying is that you aren't worth much.

Eleanor protested: "But it's contact for him."

Delores defended her point with conviction. "I'm not arguing with that. All I'm doing is trying to understand how to use the induction. We've been talking about this for weeks now—how patients dump on us, and how their objects touch our inner objects and we need to use it in interpretation. So let's say it happens to make me angry, and the degradation does make me angry, how do we turn it around? I don't have an answer to my own question . . ."

Eleanor continued to take a more dispassionate view of things: "But isn't he saying in a sense, too, that this is the only way he can hold onto an object? It's degrading, but within that, that's his way of trying to hold on to Janice. All right, he has to pay for it, and it's degrading, but it's the only way, right now, that he feels that he can have anything."

> We are beginning to explore the limits of the induction. It is interesting that different therapists will bring a variety of defenses and internalizations that merge with this induction demonstrating that countertransference is always a mixture of both the patient's and the therapist's interrelatedness.

Janice got into the act of trying to figure out the problem: "Okay, but she's saying that he's making contact with an object. What's the contact with the object?"

Lenore blurted out, "It's sadisic. I think we're back to the sadomasochistic themes again that we were talking about for weeks. This is a sadistic contact that stirs up a certain pain in me, and I'm sure the other women in the room recognize it to varying degrees. Why not use that pain?"

I realized I was being provocative, but went ahead anyway: You're angry that you have to sit there and be the receptor of all this, and at the same time, you don't want to hurt this guy, so how would you be able to use it in such a way as it might be useful?"

Any affect can be used in a positive, constructive, playful form. The ultimate criterion concerns the caring input of the therapist. Even sadistic provocativeness can have care as a major part of the communication. On the other hand, it can be a not-so-subtle disguise of sadism and a belittlement of our patient.

"Well," said Delores thoughtfully, "I wouldn't get playful. I would get serious, but I would get . . ." She stopped in mid-air unable to finish.

I continued with the same provocative line of thinking: "I don't necessarily want to get the sadism *out*, I want to use what is going on between us in a therapeutic way. Why is it not therapeutic to say 'So how does it feel to see a whore,' or 'at least as a whore, I'm always there, because you pay me.' Now that's hostile and sadistic, but I'm not sure it's destructive to the therapy.

I'm trying to get some dimension and amplification to the projection.

"I didn't hear it as hostile," Dorothy protested.
"You *didn't*?" Lenore said, in disbelief.

Again, Lenore seems to be caught up in her own intrapsychic issues and may find it difficult to find a range of playfulness with this affect.

"No," responded Dorothy, "but it harps on the point that you have to pay me, because I'm here."

"And *that's* not hostile?" Lenore said, again dumbfounded.

Dorothy continued, "But I don't give it to you for free . . ."

Lenore countered, "That's the part of it that's hostile. He needs you and he has to come and pay you." After pausing a moment, she added, "He needs you, but he's shitting on you!

The group was silent. I could feel the mixture of rage, despair, hurt, and confusion roiling up in that torrent of silence. I finally broke in by saying, "No one can use that feeling. Apparently it's hitting such a vulnerable area, that it is very hard to use it therapeutically. All of you have a commitment to analysis, you've got a commitment to feminism, sure, but since when do you have to put it on the line with a patient? Is he going to rob you of your baic convictions?"

Lenore protested. "You're saying, 'don't dignify the patient by taking his views seriously.'"

I countered, "Don't dignify views that you think are off the wall. But let's deal with where the therapeutic action is!"

Delores now moved away from the emotional issue and became clinical. "Wouldn't the whole idea of being a whore apply to his mother?"

"Sure," I said.

"Delores continued: "And couldn't one bring that in in some way? After all, she's been used and he's been used."

"That's right." I continued, feeling pressed to make my point.

> I was aware that the group required distance from this case, and decided to take a more cognitive approach.

"The mother has been used, and he's been used. He's been used as a confidant with the mother. He's paid the price and didn't even get laid. That's true, so I guess what I'm getting at is that all this is such a tender issue—the masochistic role in woman—that it can't very easily be played with or used therapeutically with any kind of range. What I'm talking about isn't just humor—I'm talking about a range of different ways to use the concept, so that you don't feel rigidly stuck in a fixed role, but can play *with* the communication. The thing is, it's causing so much rage, apparently, that it's hard for you to see the therapeutic possibilities."

Janice, thoughtful, entered in: "But the last piece helped. The understanding that you just gave about his having been used opens the door a little bit in helping me begin to think about how I might make an interpretation. I still don't know what it is, but now I understand what's going on. He is using me, or women, or whatever, in the way that *he* was used. And so maybe that . . ." her voice trailed off.

> Janice can utilize the clear didactic approach and incorporate it as a form of contact with her patient. This is an illustration of how different therapists must find the approach that fits their particular personality.

Rachel now reluctantly entered the discussion: "His father is an isolated, drinking-to-death man, and *he's* screwed because nobody's taken him on, so he's a whore too."

Dorothy continued: "Could be, yeah. And he's living in isolation, and it's killing him . . ."

". . . And that's the other part," I said. "There's a whole family constellation where everyone gets used. I suspect that the mother was far more comfortable with the husband relating to alochol than to her.

Delores, now felt a bit better about our direction: "I *could* play with him, if he'd go with it."

"Go with *what*?" Lenore said, disdainfully.

Delores went on: "So what's it like to come and see your whore every week?"

Lenore objected, "It's cutting too close."

> My job was to find an intervention that could be palatable for the particular therapist. Each of us must find our own way of playing with a given patient.

"Okay," I said, looking for an alternative. "You can go straight back, then, to his mother, and say, 'Okay, you know, this may be a joke for you and you may just want to drop it, but it was no joke in your childhood. People were being *used* all over the place.' If it's too close for comfort that way, then use the metaphor of the family, and get into it that way. Another alternative to follow could be going after 'this is how people really get care—by feeling exploited.'"

Janice reflected, "It's not that I wouldn't care, it's that the only way he can get caring is by paying for it."

I clarified my position. "You can't avoid the anger and degradation. Degradation is his language, his home. Where he comes from, people were devalued and degraded . . . We all seemed to be immersed in judgment, which doesn't go anywhere. I suspect that it was equally present in his family, which likewise cut off any real relating. We have to find a way to enter his world—by a bridge between his metaphors and our own."

Delores spoke excitedly: "There's *something* happening. . . It's interesting to me that we, the women here, are reacting this way, and you're not. I find myself wanting to protect myself a little bit from this guy. Maybe that gets in the way of really being more relaxed with it and more spontaneous with the light touch."

"How do you protect yourself?" I queried.

"I think what I protect myself from is his contempt; I think that I also *identify* with him."

"With his contempt for women?" Debbie looked incredulous.

"The contempt for women, and his wanting to be so much in control," Delores countered.

Lenore was equally confused. "Are you saying that you have contempt for women and that *that's* what you're identifying with?"

Delores gave a quick smile and said, "No. I've had contempt for men. I see it *that* way. So I feel my contempt for him coming up. I have the feeling that I want to one-up him. That part of myself comes out. It's like the sadistic part of me that wants to go on with him, wants to *compete* with him on that level."

"Right," I urged her, "but you put a control on that so that it doesn't come out. So we've got the problem of his creating sadism in you, which you, in a sense, arrest."

I switched gears, trying to give everyone some space in the midst of this hot topic. "I just want to raise this other point. Motherhood is painful, but not necessarily masochistic, at least in terms of what one goes through in mothering a child. Certainly, in terms of mothering, the pain of rearing a child is in the service of freeing both parties. On the other hand, masochistic pain binds both parties to each other and controls them. Do any of you have any thoughts on this matter?"

"No," Lenore said, with a grin. "I'm just trying to get what you're talking about."

I continued, "I'm trying to draw a distinction between masochism and the mothering role. I would like to ask, historical and political issues not withstanding, did each of your mothers sacrifice a piece of herself to make something good happen?"

Lenore spoke with some degree of self-assurance: "Sure I'm giving up a lot of my previous life to do what I'm doing now, but it doesn't feel like I'm sacrificing for my kid. There is something of a martyr quality about sacrificing for one's child."

Dorothy reminded us, "Sacrifice could be used in the service of martyrdom."

"Yes," the group agreed.

Lenore reflected, "It doesn't feel like that now. It hasn't felt like that, but I'm sure that it could get to a point where it would be that way . . . but I made a *choice*, not a *sacrifice*. It wasn't that this kid turned up and said, 'This is what I'm going to do to your life.'"

I now tried to make my point. "So that pain can be used to control people, to provoke guilt to keep loved ones close to you, but pain doesn't necessarily have to be used in that way. So, there's the feeling of being controlled, and the rage and sadism that's connected with it. When you're right in the middle of it, it's hard to loosen up with it, but, let's look at the role of the therapist. Isn't being a therapist similar, at times, to being a mother in that part of the process of accomplishing something involves some pain? I don't believe that it's all joy. If you're upset, you don't necessarily dump it on the patient. There are many painful things we must contain in order to be a good therapist."

Janice now talked with obvious emotion. "The hardest thing for me about being a mother in the first year was that nobody said it was okay to feel pain. The message was always, 'Isn't it wonderful and lovely, you take your kid out in the stroller,' and blah, blah, blah. But nobody talks about the pain. Everybody talks about the joy, but it *wasn't* so joyful."

I brought it back to the case at hand. "So, this patient has devalued you, and that is your pain. It's not masochistic to contain that. In a sense, you're trying to understand and use it, but it is painful for you to want to slug him, and be empathetic at the same time. I know you don't want to do that, but then, you have to transcend the pain and find the appropriate place to use it. Right now you're feeling too personally assaulted by this patient."

> We touch upon a vital point in empathic contact with our patients. Without denial or reaction formation, we must reach beyond the induction and make contact with the patient's center of self.

I went on trying to amplify my position. "This patient, by the act of calling Janice a whore, is getting something—he's getting contact. He's also looking at something he never dared to look at before. He never dared call his mother or *himself* a whore. That's a very positive thing, and if you don't get shocked and upset by it, you could say, 'Hey, that's progress.' Even though it hurts to some degree, he is taking all that on. In essence, he's really bringing his family into treatment in the form of a whole bunch of internalizations. I think he's right in the middle of something. Now you may find it a bit too hot to hear to go directly to what's between you and him, in which case you go into the father and mother metaphor, which should be more comfortable for you."

Janice added in affirmation: "And I think it's also comfortable for him. When I talked to him directly about coming to see a whore, he cut that right off. I was happy it was dropped, too, I have to tell you. I was relieved when he went on with his, 'Tuesday I did this and Wednesday I did this' routine."

I broke in here and said, "It's funny, because I'm listening to all this thing and saying to myself, 'Just replace being a whore with being a therapist, and everything everyone's been talking about could refer to it.' You're containing a part of yourself, you sit in a position where you have to take a lot of shit from people . . . I'm going back and forth thinking that this is just like being a therapist. I have people come in and say, 'How can you sit here and listen to people hour after hour, and take this shit?'"

Delores laughed and commented: "Your fee isn't even as good as a whore's, probably!"

I kept on pushing the dilemma: "How often do you have to contain a piece of yourself to deal with the issues that go on in a relationship? Who the hell is ever free in it?"

Lenore commented, "Well, it's painful, that's true, but in a relationship, there's more reciprocity."

"Okay," I said, "there's reciprocity, but here she's got a fee."

The group laughed. I offered a closing statement. "I think the whoring occurs when Janice takes a fee but can't do her work; when she can't confront the man, not in a sadistic way, but by being playful, or mirroring or supportive, or whatever is going to work with him. All of us need to feel in charge of the treatment by being able to move in different therapeutic directions. Sometimes, as with a mother, we may choose to wait for our child to be ready to take the next step. But that's an *active* decision, *not* a passive or submissive one."

> Here we are separate enough to perceive the developmental needs of our patients appropriately and elect to offer the most available alternative for contact in the relationship.

"There's always the question as to whether you can make a truly objective, clinical decision. More importantly, if you sit, as Janice has done, on your rage, you become paralyzed for fear of your own sadism getting out of control."

Janice listened intently to what I said and thoughtfully answered: "I think both Jim and I have changed since I presented him in this group last year. Maybe we're both ready to take a few more chances with each other . . ."

There was a period of silence as group members mulled over the provocative material. We all left emotionally exhausted, but very engaged with the subject at hand.

"False Self" versus Transcendence

In this session, we touched upon the very essence of creative transcendence associated in performing the job of therapist. All too often, therapeutic inductions are perceived as invitations to act out with patients. In the service of being human, a therapist may share feelings that do little to promote therapeutic movement. Developing a therapeutic elasticity to contain and master the emotional induction then becomes the countertransference challenge. A false containment can be enacted by playing out the role of helpful therapist and thus denying or covering over the wish or fear to hurt a patient. In these instances, a supportive therapeutic demeanor becomes part of a "false self" system that ultimately interferes with the authentic flow of material. As is so true with a mother and child, patients ultimately experience, on some level, their therapist's inner duplicity.

In the preceding case presentation, the therapist plays the role of being both understanding and tolerant. We observe, however, signs of denial and reaction formation creating an impairment in Janice's spontaneity. Janice feels threatened by a loss of control and suspects that her sadistic impulses will leak out. This is not an example of transcendence, but a reaction formation that is shaped by the "helpful therapist" approach.

We refer the reader to Janice's initial supervisory session where we encountered some of the origins and threads of her countertransference history. We observed how the female element in the therapist is neither loving nor present, while the male, though more loving, is passive. By dint of Janice's survival mechanisms, she holds onto her masculine ties even though they are masked by a loving ambivalence. One suspects she resents the male for not standing up to the powerful female imago. Janice's solution to deprivation becomes, then, and objective, intellectual, reality-oriented stance towards the world. Indeed, this approach becomes a "holding environment" for her.

The patient's contempt, however, breaks through the wall and magnifies some of Janice's unconscious fears of femaleness and power. The reactive rage and sadism is at best controlled through denial and rationalization. This control comes at a cost, however, for she truly cannot play with her patient's issues either by mirroring or through humor. Her tightly knit defenses create an enormous barrier to making a truly empathic engagement with her patient.

The group, too, is enraged with the patient. Cultural, historical, and political forces are strongly felt in the group atmosphere.

Eleanor, an older woman with a European background, rises to the challenge. She is less drawn by political rhetoric and is not nearly so threatened by a man who wants to put her down. The group listens to her reactions and ambivalently responds. All, however, want to do their job effectively, and come to terms with female/male identification issues and their capacities to contain emotional assaults.

While the group challenges the male leader with the assertion that he cannot understand and relate to a female issue, he takes the position that all of us have both male and female elements. While there *is* a difference in living out the role of a prejudiced group of people as contrasted with having a psychic element or identification with that class, nevertheless we can stretch ourselves to experience the identification, even though we may not exactly fit their shoes. Still, the issue remains.

The theme of power moves in and out of the presentation. Cold detachment becomes a reaction to combat arrogance in the male patient, with sadism and masochistic fears emerging as a reaction to an assault on the therapist's identification. Releasing oneself from a power orientation can be a very challenging task. We see the beginnings of Janice's struggle in that direction.

As a sidelight, one may note that the group consists mainly of very effective women with the exception of the male leader. There is a good deal of openness, giving, and support among the members, which helps the women tap their strength and reinforce their effectiveness as functioning therapists. This avenue of understanding and support between women therapists may have some bearing on understanding the hidden envy that men feel towards women. Men perceive support as a luxury. Of note, there have always been more women than men interested in this type of supervisory experience. In spite of considerable efforts, no male applicants were forthcoming for this particular group. Men tend to achieve a major part of their self esteem by being driven by the goals of competency and effectiveness. They have little time for such luxuries.

This patient presents a living example of what happens to our perceptions of men and women in culture. He holds a job in society that is highly esteemed, and yet feels woefully alone. His role in life mirrors his early family relationship which was marked by a good deal of humiliation, contempt, sadism, and masochism. There are two sides to this story, however, for while women may become stronger by offering support and help to one another, they also feel a good deal of reactive rage towards men who flaunt power at the cost of emotional relatedness. There is an inability, at times, to perceive the symbol of men's empty contempt as nothing more than a covering for an imbalance in the realms of emotions and love. This imbalance haunts all of us in different ways, and produces differing approaches to male/female relationships. In this presentation we observe how both the group and Janice struggle to extricate themselves from the multiple dimensions of intrapsychic, political, and social pressures that reinforce the imbalances and make it more difficult to meet one another on a simply "human" level in life and in the therapy room.

As we have observed in Daisy's case presentation, the over-invested imbalance of father as a mothering agent generates a number of possible dynamics: On a more superficial level, one can easily observe the overidealization of the male covering an underlying disappointment at his inability to combat the powerful mother figure. Thus, the powerful male can easily fall from his pinnacle to be an object of contempt. In this presentation, we see how the women have very little patience for this "creep"; but behind this contempt lie such issues as the fear of her own sense of power as a devaluation of her emotional strength. Some of these issues become intertwined with the current political and cultural forces. However, the notion of power becomes enmeshed with the notion of maleness and femaleness. Janice's fear that her contempt will get out of control often creates a sense of inhibition and distance. These are certainly issues that will some day be important for her to work out in her personal treatment.

Again, the impact of a male leader in a basically female group of therapists has important implications for the unfolding of this material. Is there a difference in a basically female perspective as contrasted with a male perspective in the way this patient could be approached? Or should the therapist be able to call upon either a male or female image from their past to negotiate the transference? This area is open to a good deal of discussion. We are left with still another question—was the male leader flaunting his power to this group of female therapists? Perhaps some of the members wanted me to be in the father role and were reluctant to take me down a peg or two.

A number of salient points bear emphasis in working with narcissistic patients:

1. Analysts often require an affirmation of their self-worth by being helpful with their patients. Consequently, when inevitable feelings of devaluation enter the treatment relationship, the therapist's vulnerability to injury and narcissistic hurt soon becomes exposed like a festering wound. Investigating the motivations of being a therapist might be helpful in taking a more objective stance with such a patient.

2. The threat of desertion by a narcissistic patient becomes an on-going anxiety in the transference/countertransference relationship. Interfaced with this threat are countertransference defenses of being excessively interpretive or controlling. Hard-nosed confrontational work usually does not work with these patients. Yet, interpretive work must go on in order to accomplish reconstructive organization in the personality. Consequently, the delicate balance of being soft and re-flective, as well as interpretive and firm, while avoiding being either sadistic or controlling, then becomes the therapeutic challenge.

3. The devaluation of the therapeutic alliance must be faced; oth-erwise the very fabric of the treatment alliance will be undermined. When, however, the therapist responds to these assaults in a very per-sonal way, a number of countertransference defenses can be mobi-lized, ranging from attack to an identification with the patient's introject.

4. A narcissistic patient demands involvement and concern. Yet, they easily can cut off a relationship in spite of the therapist's emo-tional commitment. The fear, then, of being deserted and used by one's patient becomes a constant threat in forming a good therapeutic fit. At times we handle this fear by being overly detached or exces-sively active.

5. These patients will invariably attempt to wear down the thera-pist's goodwill and therapeutic concern. This may be manifested through a challenge of the very structure of the treatment relation-ship, such as attacking the fee or scheduling contract. Once again, surrendering to the patient's introject or feeling furious may interfere with taking a more objective interpretive role regarding the patient's fear of attachment. Ultimately, the therapist may well submit to the patient's introject and as a result play out the repetition of the pa-tient's original trauma through a countertransference identification.

6. These patients will occasionally run from the therapeutic rela-tionship. This should not be interpreted as a defeat of the therapist's empathic efforts. At times, patients need to take distance from the re-lationship, for there are both fears of attachment, as well as underly-ing frightening wishes for fusion. Consequently, narcissistic patients occasionally need permission to leave therapy in order for them to return.

Chapter 10

LENORE

Rage as a Screen for Oedipal Guilt

PRELIMINARIES: THE DAY'S WORK AND THE NIGHT'S DREAM

Having felt a lack of closure in the last session, the group comes back to push and pull over the theme of "the therapist as whore" and the wider meanings and implications of the notion of "whoring." The group struggles with this concept from the perspective of exploitation and manipulation, as well as from that of adaptive survival in a difficult world. There is even the suggestion that beneath the ego-adaptive level, we all harbor darker wishes and dreams that reflect this theme. This discussion leads into the presentation. You will see how Lenore's initial feelings of guilt and contempt and her attempts to hide behind a theoretical stance fade away as she looks beneath the surface to discover that within her own secret places, she lives with conflicts and life experiences that parallel those of her patient.

Lenore, a very active and responsive member of the group, has a long-standing professional relationship with the leader. First as a graduate student, and later as an analytic candidate, Lenore has developed into a very insightful therapist. She brings to her work an hysterical personality organization, and typically tends to ramble when she approaches anxiety-laden countertransference material. The leader decides to give her plenty of room to follow her own course of case exploration, for she inevitably arrives at the heart of the therapeutic matter. This case presents emotionally loaded material for the therapist. Lenore's patient has slept with the therapist's minister, who in the past has been both a guide and an adviser to Lenore. The fury and anxiety mobilizes defenses and keeps the presenter and the group away from the countertransference dynamics. Consequently, we stay on a technical, theoretical level and the material does not really flow or become cohesive. We will observe how the group also colludes with the presenter by avoiding these dynamics. Thus, as with George, the reader may become impaitent or bored with the unfolding material, particularly in the initial phases of the presentation. The energy soon becomes organized around dream material. The connection with unconscious material seems to organize Lenore, and the material in the presentation starts to flow. A very active stance by the supervisor could easily close Lenore down, as confrontation can stimulate unconscious fears of assault or penetration. A somewhat scattered presentation ultimately draws the material together in its own pace and rhythm.

THE SESSION: TOO CLOSE TO HOME

Lenore spoke with increasing emotion and tension as she moved into her case.

"This case will dovetail with our discussion. I was saying in the hallway on the way in that there are two feelings I'm having trouble with in this case, left over from the last session. One is contempt, and the other is guilt. I'll tell you the two ways they came up within the session. First, I felt contempt for my patient's *whoring* part. This is the woman I presented here before, who had a sexual relationship with her minister, who has been the head of my congregation, and someone I have turned to in the past for advice and help.

I'm seeing her twice a week now. Anyway, in the middle of the session she was talking about her husband being meek and powerless, essentially a wimp, and I found myself coming out with something about how I thought she was angry with him, that he didn't stop her from 'fucking around' with "O.," her former lover. Of course, that's not the way she saw it."

> One hears the judgmental, angry tone in Lenore's voice. The reader may recall Lenore's position in the previous chapter. Her fury at being called a whore was difficult for her to assimilate.

Perhaps this has to do with the case, and we will see how the material unfolds.

"Her context was, 'Well, I can't get any satisfaction in this house, so I have to go elsewhere,' and nobody at home tries to stop me. The implication was an affair, although her perspective was that she was looking for any kind of diversion, contact, or intellectual stimulation. She was talking on the level of, 'I might go on a trip, or whatever. I'm going to have to go outside of the house.' And then she made this comment about sexuality, about her husband being impotent, and I brought in sexuality, saying, 'There is a question in your mind that you might have another affair, go outside the house, and your husband won't say anything?'

Then she said, 'Yeah, I suppose that too.' And that's when I said, 'Yeah, I think you really wish he's stopped you from fucking around with "O." And when it came out, it was like, 'Oh, shit!' Fucking with . . . for one thing, he clearly seduced her . . . I mean, she clearly seduced him, but he clearly capitulated, and she's having a lot of trouble dealing with her guilt about her sexuality. I've got a lot of comtempt for her and her use of sexuality. That's one of the problems I want to deal with."

> What hidden conflicts does the contempt mask? At this point, I could only guess. I'm aware that this material is emotionally loaded for Lenore, but decided to give her plenty of space and room to investigate the case.

Rachel asked in a low, soothing voice, "How does she react, by the way, to you saying, 'You're fucking around?'"

Lenore, in a direct and open way, responded, "She kind of looked at me hard, but then she just went on. It wasn't a problem for her. She was involved with this guy for years, and it's one of the best parts of her. In a way it was a coup for her to have this relationship with this man, who had an authority position in her community, and for her to find an outlet for her sexuality in a way that was satisfying. Actually, it *wasn't* satisfying, that's the masochistic part—but for her to find any outlet is a positive thing, so *I've* got the problem."

"It's *your* problem?" Rachel inquired, looking for more information.

"Oh yeah," Lenore went on, visibly upset, "I've complimented her about it, in the past, too. There's a piece of me that can see how it's good for her, but then there's this other piece of me, the guilt. I've been feeling guilty about this, of course, but then at the end of the session, I also felt contempt for her in her depression, in her masochism."

> We are beginning to unravel the puzzle. Contempt is but the top
> layer covering over the therapist's guilt.

"She sounds so defeated that I feel that I have to give her something, that I'm supposed to produce the results. At the end of the session, she said, 'So this is it for today? What am I supposed to do? This is supposed to help, right?'"

"So this is all part of her dynamics with me in the transference. Her mother was all wrapped up in want ing to see her child be the way mother wanted—she was very narcissistic."

> I saw that Lenore has moved away from the countertransference,
> but decided to see what would happen.

"If she's not satisfied with what you're giving her, will she go elsewhere?" someone quietly asked.

Lenore defensively replied: "I work to keep my mouth buttoned, and it goes better when I do. She looks to me to give her the answers. She kind of invites intrusion. So this goes on, and if I stick with her quandary and her denial . . . (long pause) The tape's bugging me. Do you change names?"

I realized that this is very loaded, and wanted to proceed with some gingerliness. "No names. Nothing will be put in without your approval."

Group members were sitting forward and listening intently. Lenore resumed her presentation, the material flowing out in a gush. "Okay, she has trouble knowing herself, she loses what she thinks, and she talks about that dynamic having existed with her mother. That carries over into therapy where I will give an interpretation and she'll say, 'Oh that's it, that's *it!* I should have *known* that,' and then she loses what she's thinking. It's like I steamroll her and she loses herself. So when that happens, sometimes I say, 'Whoa, wait a minute! Something just happened there. We were having an exchange and all of a sudden I said something and now it's like I'm there and you're gone. I want to know what you really thought.' And she can come back with that."

We see another layer of this case unfold. Placation of the therapist covers over the guilt revolving around hostile impulses. Does
the therapist see this, or is she subtly ignoring the implications?

"So in the transference it's like I can steamroll her like the
mother. She *wants* me to. The sequence is: She gets demolished, we
look at it, she comes back out of it. My stance has been pretty much to
try to be supportive, but this last time, when she got into a tirade de-
molishing her husband, I felt that it was so destructive to her that I
had to confront it somehow. It was just amazing. You know: 'It's all
his fault. He's worthless. He's hopeless. He's such a nerd. He's such a
wimp; he doesn't watch out for my son.' She thinks of her father in
the same way. She has more sympathy for him now, but there's no relationship there—he's basically unavailable and weak. And she sees
her husband that way, too. Actually, alternately as that, and as the demanding mother.

"You know, he really *does* sound very demanding. He is kind of
narcissistic, like Denise's patient from last week, but in a much less
sensitive way. He'll taunt to get a response. He'll say to her, 'Why *can't*
you do such and such?' Everything revolves around something being
wrong with her. She's defective. Then *she* talks about herself feeling
defective. Now she says, 'I thought it was all my problem, and now I
see that it's him. He's the ogre, and now I'm afraid we're going to get
divorced. I can't get anything from him. It's hopeless. I'm suffering.'"

It sounds like the presenter wants to get out of the case before she
really gets into it. What areas does she seem to duck?

"Did I give you enough? I think I've given you enough history,
and I think I've given you enough of a feel. . . . *Have* I given you
enough feel of what goes on between the two of us? I get to feel guilty,
which is typical with a masochistic patient, I understand. I think
that's the paradigm that's *supposed* to come up, but now I'm stuck with
where to go with it. I don't want to explain myself; I don't think that's
appropriate. Challenging her, on the other hand, is very difficult, because she takes it in as an intrusion if it's not couched exactly right.
Then I think a self-supportive stance isn't going to help her in the
midst of her trashing everything that she's got, including her husband
and family. When she goes out the door she trashes the whole session,
like, 'Is that it? That was shit!' I really want help in finding help . . ."
The rushing stream of words came to a halt.

The patient attempts to control the therapist by regressing to a demanding helpless child position and placing her adversary in an omnipotent position. The therapist does not know how to get out of this trap, but can only feel contemptuous and angry. Again, we see how both the therapist and patient avoid the underlying guilt.

"Help with what?" Denise asked.

"With how to confront this depreciation of what goes on between us, and of what she's got," responded Lenore.

I saw that Lenore was being overwhelmed, and decided to stay on a cognitive level until I was fairly sure that she was in control.

"How would you describe her dynamics?" I asked.

"You're not getting it from what I've said?" Lenore queried, a bit confused.

I persisted, "I understand the character structure, but how would you describe her dynamics?"

"Is what you mean by 'dynamics,' ego/superego?"

"No," I said, "I'm referring to the infantile issues that are being covered over by the character structure and being acted out in the transference."

Lenore spoke rather hurriedly. "It's a feeding issue. The infantile issue is that she doesn't have a complete sense of self. She feels she can't get an adequate response from the outside world to confirm her. One of the positive things she did get from her past therapy dynamically was that . . ."

I was feeling Lenore's overwhelming anxiety, but still decided to keep it on a very safe level.

I broke in and said: "Okay. Let me introduce a structure. You can look at a case on at least four different levels: from a self-psychology point of view; from a structural point of view, in terms of ego/superego; from an object-relations point of view, looking at introjects, or from an ego-psychology perspective. Now you're looking at her strictly from a self-psychology point of view. Is that how you want to investigate this case?"

"No," replied Lenore, "because the piece having to do with masochism I understand from a structural point of view."

"What's that?" someone asked.

"She has a sister who is sixteen months younger than she, which means her mother got pregnant when my patient was seven months old. Her father wasn't there to offer her any support and her . . . it's difficult for me to look at it structurally, you're right. Let me think. . . . She feels guilty when she gets any of her drives or needs met. And there's a whole issue around her devouring, and her lustfulness, and her father being such a weak figure in terms of not protecting her from her own sexuality, which came up about two sessions ago. It seems her whole sexuality went underground as a result, hence she has never been able to have a good sexual relationship in her marriage. Good sex has always been found outside home. She had good sex with her husband before she married him."

I spoke in soft, soothing tones to clarify my position. "If you see this case in terms of a structural theory, you would deal with this piece of information very differently than if you frame it in a self-psychology point of view. That's why you have to arrive at some kind of diagnostic understanding of what's going on."

Lenore paused thoughtfully, and then elaborated. "Well, I think what's happening at the moment is that she is inducing guilt and contempt in me, and I suspect *that* has to do with the economic problem of masochism, and I don't really understand that . . ." She looked perplexed as her voice trailed off.

Delores responded, also rather thoughtfully. "I was just thinking back to a time when I had a masochistic client. I'm remembering the abandonment issue. Is what your patient goes through a fear of losing the object?"

> Delores describes an earlier form of masochism. Usually, in these instances, the therapist feels the depressive core in the patient. In the oedipal form of masochism, the therapist feels worked over and angry.

Lenore responded quickly to this: "I thought she was angry at her husband for not protecting her against her sexual drives, but when I offered her that interpretation, I felt anxious. Something felt wrong about it . . . Or it may be the way I did it, *that* was wrong."

> Interpretations of this nature outside the transference do not usually work. They are too disconnected from the patient's level of consciousness and the poor timing usually reflects a countertransference issue.

"You know," Lenore offered, "I felt my session with her was an orgy of rage and contempt, like there was sexuality in the room. It's not that I felt aroused, but it felt like she was wallowing in an orgy of defeat." After a thoughtful pause, she continued, "There are some memories that she has come up with that I think relate to the impulses not being dealt with. I have been affirming her sexuality as a good part of her, as a part of her where there is life. There's this memory she has of being eyed by some boys at school and complaining to her mother about it, and her mother says, 'Don't worry, your father will tell them off.' My patient thinks to herself, 'That wimp, he'll never come to my assistance.'"

Lenore became emphatic: "But at that point it went underground. Like all teenagers, there was this period, around twelve or thirteen when her sexuality was really popping—she put up sexy photographs of male movie stars in her closet, and that kind of thing."

> I was beginning to feel increasingly uncomfortable with the emotional disconnectedness of the case, but still stayed on a theoretical level, and I tried to clarify the dynamics:

"Your patient presents material that in essence says, 'My father didn't protect me, woe is me, poor little person.' Now she never admitted that she loved the boys eyeing her; she liked to present herself as the victim as a means of avoiding the feeling that she got a bang out of having those boys eye her."

The group broke into laughter, perhaps in identification with the patient. Lenore continued. "Actually, my patient was quite mean, and nasty and was quite a cut-up in the community, and her mother never confronted her on this, and in a sense defended her acting out."

I continued to try further to clarify some of the dynamics. "With so little guidance, most likely this little girl felt she could get away with murder. I suspect that there was a good deal of development of a grandiose core with an awful lot of guilt that is associated with this fantasized power. A good intervention regarding her protests over the boys eyeing her might have something to do with her distracting herself from getting the pleasure of boys looking at her and finding her attractive."

Lenore responded, "There have been ways I have been supporting her sexuality. I've encouraged her to have fun with it. Now she comes in more and more with complaints about her husband.

'The man in my life is impossible, I can't stand him, I hate him, I can't have it there, etc.' I seem to be stimulating more defensiveness."

Rachel seemed perplexed. "But what about this affair with the minister? Maybe *that's* why she's feeling asexual and depressed."

I said, "You have to look at it within the context of what is going on, but yes, she might only be able to enjoy sex on the sly or where she feels somewhat debased and used. But could she enjoy it more positively and openly? No, because *that* would bring up feelings that she's going to be punished. The trick in masochism becomes looking for things that you both want and feel uncomfortable about, because getting it in the right way, or free way, or good way, would open the person up to the possibility of punishment."

Lenore was now very confused. "Why is there dread of punishment when she doesn't have any model of that in her family?"

> I answered the question, but knew that we had to get to the countertransference material sooner or later. This cognitive approach was starting to offer diminishing returns.

"My guess is that the punishment is more fantasized than real," I responded. "If she received an appropriate response from her parents, she would have less fear of punishment. Usually kids fear punishment when there is a lack of appropriate structure within the family."

"Do you think that's why she came to you after her affair?" Rachel asked.

Lenore replied in a tangential way, "She's very good at hiding the affair."

Daisy asked: "And how do you see the therapist's position?"

I replied, "The therapist's position is to go behind the character structure and help the patient have a more realistic acceptance of her drives and reduce feelings of guilt or reprisal.

> I observed that Lenore was becoming more reflective and more in charge of the case, but I stil held off from going into the emotional material.

Lenore reflected, "I wonder if I wasn't acting out some of my contempt for her when I referred to her 'fucking around' with her minister."

"That's the point," I said. "This kind of patient will induce criticism and judgment, and you will want to bawl them out and lecture them, tell them to fly right; do all the things that a moralistic parent might say to them. All of us act these things out. It's inappropriate, but sometimes we do put our foot in it."

Daisy asked, "But isn't it also a wish to obtain a realistic authority?"

I was starting to feel impatient, and I quickly countered: "The realistic authority has to come within the context of the transference/countertransference. It doesn't have to be taught; it has to be lived out."

Daisy protested: "But it *was* lived out here . . ."

"How was it lived out?" I challenged.

Daisy replied, "I'm not sure . . . was it going too far, the response? Was Lenore's reaction all contempt or was it also the patient wanting to hear what Lenore really felt about this experience?"

> If you recall Daisy's position in her own presentation, she uses some of the same self-revelation approach to soothe her patient. This patient does need a realistic authority, but it comes out of an appropriate interpretive approach to the dynamics. I hoped, by opening up a session, we could get to the countertransference material, and so I said:

"Let's hear a session to get a feel for what really goes on . . ."

Lenore offered a session that occurred right after a dream.

"Okay," I said, "But first, let's hear the dream."

"It's a great dream," Lenore enthusiastically replied. "This is the patient's dream from the session before:

> I was a little girl in the dream—maybe five or six. I was playing on the floor with a boy, horsing around—maybe with my brother. A man was watching me from the corner. I was rocking on a horse, bouncing on the floor, and tumbling around with the boy. My skirt kept flying up. I thought about the man watching. I wanted him to come in and catch me, but make it look like an accident. I didn't want him to think I really wanted him to catch me. He must have been my father—but he looked more like "O."

"I should tell you, Lenore continued, "what I did with it, but it's so down the line. What she came to was—and this made it kind of old stuff, so I'm not sure it's right—she made it a dream about "O.", the minister, ex-lover, and how, although she had thought she wanted to make sexual contact, which she had already said, and which it became, what she really wanted was the contact with him, the affirming mother type contact, and not the sexuality. That's the tack I took, and I think it's a much earlier thing."

> The reader may recall that Don, in a previous presentation, demonstrated a similar countertransference issue. Lenore goes to the safer mother position, as the father dynamics are full of anxiety.

I commented, "She *did* want the sex, and maybe the husband is also father, and therefore she has to knock it. So, she comes in the next session and says that her husband's the biggest jerk going, but in the meantime, she's frightened of her sexual impulses toward him, that came up in that thinly disguised dream."

"Husband is like father." Lenore was following my thinking.

"That's right," I affirmed. Looking around at the intent faces, I asked, "What's going on?"

Denise said, "I'm just trying to digest it."

The dream material seemed to speak to Lenore, and she appeared more centered in her discussion. She enthusiastically added, "I think it's got to be there, the positive sexual attraction to her husband."

"Right," I said. "And she's frightened of the positive sexual attraction."

"She's really holding off," another member added. "She hasn't had sex with him for years and years and says she hates him and she won't have sex with him."

Now Lenore reentered the discussion. "This is my question: "If you go with affirming the attraction to the husband, you're denying her real hatred of it, of his criticism, and he really is bombastic. They both are bombastic and they laugh about it and *that* brings them closer."

I countered, "Perhaps if they fight enough, some sexuality can be released. In some respects the man she really wants is the man she can't get, and that's the father; so she has to denigrate the husband, whom she can get."

> As soon as the man is available, he no longer can become the father, and then become an object of contempt. This issue perhaps cuts across the dynamics of both patient and therapist.

"And was the father also the minister with whom she was fooling around?"

"Yes," said Lenore. "And she'll even say that. But," she protested, "If I said to her, if I confronted, as a defense, her denigration of her husband and her defense against her sexuality . . ."

"Perhaps," I quickly answered. "You have to do it in a supportive way." To myself I said, maybe I was also speaking to Lenore.

"However I do it," Lenore persisted, "she's going to knock it, no matter how supportively I do it, building up her confidence, about her sexuality not being so awful . . ."

I added: "Towards her father . . ."

Lenore echoed my statement: "Towards her father . . ."

> I now switched to a deep personal level, feeling it was time to go beneath the theoretical verbiage:

How do you feel about sexual feelings towards a father?

> I bit my tongue after this remark, and realized that it was too penetrating for her to handle.

Lenore shot back quickly: "That's okay . . . yeah, I mean I can work with that." Then she went back to a technical issue: "If I'm denying her view of her husband as a critical ass, which at times, he is, am I being like the mother who denied her view?"

I replied, enjoying the back-and-forth dialogue: "This is not a psychotic patient. You do not need to give her an idea of reality, because that's not where her trouble is."

Lenore protested: "She's not functioning very well."

"But she's not a psychotic," I countered. "What she is, is somebody who acts out a lot. Her problem has to do with her impulse life. If she can accept her impulse life, she may well come to the conclusion that she can live with her husband and enjoy him, even though he is sometimes a schmuck."

Denise added: "I mean her husband's a schmuck, but she might also want to fuck him . . ."

"That's right," I agreed, "and she can enjoy it, too, even if he is the son of his father."

Rachel said with a grin, "Get that in too!" and we all joined her in laughter. "I *would* fit that in, too. Her mother never really permitted this to go on. She never really felt comfortable about sexual impulses.

And so now it's still easier for my patient to knock her father than feel good about it. The dream is speaking the truth; she *is* saying, 'I want to get near my father.'"

"Can we talk transference?" I asked, hoping that this would open Pandora's box, hearing full well the use of my metaphor.

Lenore was quick to say, "No, that's not where I want to go."

> I knew I had to wait it out. If given enough room, Lenora would come to the issue on her own steam. This is usually the case with people who have hysterical character structures.

She then launched into her concern. "What has been the impact of her sexual relationship with her minister? I remember her saying now her heart would jump as he started to unzip her. All she wanted to do was to kiss him and hug him, but then when she'd see that it was getting down to fucking, she would panic. "Okay," I said returning to my former question, "so what's the transference and countertransference in this?"

Delores, being protective of Lenora, steered us away from the countertransference material and said, "She wants to do the dream."

"Okay. Let's have the dream," I said, acquiescing.

"This is a month ago.

> I was on a boat. It was night, there was a full moon. A man came towards me . . . looked like my father . . . he whirled me around to face the railing of the boat and pinned himself against me . . . he had an erection . . . and I was so scared I called for help, but we were all alone.'

She said she needed the contact and the confirmation."

I interjected: The price of self-affirmation is loss of control and abuse. These impulses Are partly exhibitionistic, and anal erotic, but yet seductive."

Lenore added, "This patient speaks in terms of, 'I haven't got my energy. I don't have my energy up. I'm burnt up.'"

"I also wonder," I mused, "if there was some sexual acting out with the father . . ."

Lenore frowned: "I don't know . . . I don't know. Apparently he used to give her a bath and tuck her in when she was three or four, perhaps five. She remembers how he would bounce her on his lap and caress her. I suspect there was a good deal of sexual excitement."

I persisted in my attempt to focus the discussion on the transference:

"Could the transference be one of mother-daughter; that she has to punish herself before you, or humiliate herself before you, or induce contempt from you?"

I pointed out: If you only look at the session where she's ripping the husband apart and don't look at the dream she gives the session before, then you don't make the connection from one to the other. You've got to put things together and keep your eye on the whole sequence of material."

Lenore reflected, "It seemed like a reactive session to me. There was an onslaught of lambasting. I remember her saying at the end of the session: 'Is that all there is?'

I now took over the therapist's role and answered, 'No, there's much more. There's a whole lot of positive stuff that you're not about to look at; you can use the whole session as a way of avoiding it, but we can look at it next time.'"

"That's quick thinking," Lenore blurted out. "I was very distracted by her rage, raging at the husband's impotence."

"I'm thinking of the countertransference," Cybil added, finding the right tone to open this up. "I mean, you're being pulled in so many directions. You're involved with the minister, I don't know what you're up against here. You must feel awful."

Lenore looked up in surprise. "Feel awful? No, I don't feel awful. I'll tell you, it's more realistic to have seen these people."

"Do you enjoy being the recipient of all these secrets?" I asked.

"It's very stimulating," Lenore readily shared.

"Right, so is there a . . . seduction going on . . ."

Lenore now becomes surprisingly frank and straightforward: "It's really tapping into my sexuality and power issues. *I'm* the one who knows all the secrets."

The group became hushed. I asked, "How do you feel about being the one who is the mastermind behind this?"

"I don't feel like that," Lenore quickly protested. "I feel that I have to contain all this and keep it as neutralized as possible. But if you're asking about my personal countertransference stuff, it's very stimulating, and I wish they'd go away with it."

We see how a therapist with an hysterical character structure can be prone to make "unpleasant material" go away.

I persisted: "What's stimulating about it?"

"I don't want to *know* these secrets. I want them to go away and just clean it up."

"What is the secret?" I pressed.

"The secret involves my knowing she had this affair with the "O." that she's now having this huge reaction to."

"What is it doing to you, the affair. You have no use for the minister. Anything else?"

"Yes," Lenore said in a thoughtful voice. "I just think it stimulates issues about the affair."

I knew I was on to something and kept moving in the same direction:

"How much does this stimulate your own fantasies with other male authorities in your life, say, a therapist?"

"With my therapist? Which one?" (Lenore had two therapists.)

"Take your choice," I said.

"It's in my dreams," she said. "I can tell you, it's been in my dreams during the last two nights. Two nights ago I had insomnia after having had a dream that involved the most recent therapist. I often think about my last therapist at this time of year, in my dreams, so that I could say that it *is* stimulating . . . It stimulates a lot of sexual oedipal strivings."

"So perhaps your patient lived out some of your unconscious wishes," I said.

Lenore spoke with deep emotional intensity: "It's very frightening to me, because my father is overstimulating, so this has been an issue for me. Earlier on he had affairs, and that was sort of cut off as a way to deal with that sort of impulsivity . . ."

"So sexuality was dangerous for you, too," I said. "If he was having affairs with a whole bunch of women, he could have one with you."

"Yes," Lenore readily agreed, "and at the same time I hated him because it wasn't with my mother. I mean, he would sing these little songs to me that inferred that I was the number one, and I would love it, but be scared at the same time. He still does inappropriate things, bordering on . . . I could have the same dream she had, wishing it were all true—I could have been in the position of wishing it to be sexual, and it's still about this far" (she indicated with her hands a small distance) "from exploding with my father. He knows where to stop . . . but just barely. Whereas with my patient's father/minister figure, it *didn't* stop.

"That schmuck minister, by the way, is a very attractive tall, blond, tanned, handsome guy. So it's unbelievable that he would look at this woman, who's short, skinny, and mousy, and I'd try to figure out how she'd pulled it off. On the other hand, I find myself hating his guts and thinking he's a slime-bucket, and not wanting to be attracted. It's all there."

> We see how hate and contempt can cover over sexual guilt around competitive drives.

"What are your feelings about how she pulled it off?" I asked.

Lenore's words poured out: "It's a great relief to talk about it. In my dream my therapist was . . . I went to this outpost, like in the country, and I was staying in this house with him and he was there with some woman who we used to know in . . . sexual issues, boundary problems, when my husband was in graduate school, which ties us in with the past therapist I suppose. I thought, 'So this is what he does with his free time, he stays out here in his country house and runs this little place here. He takes money for it, whoring . . .' Yeah, I think that was there, and I didn't think I could stay there over the weekend. He was running an inn. I woke up from that dream feeling very anxious and then started to obsess about my contempt and my guilt over this patient."

"That's a displacement," I said.

"I knew it, even at the time. When I obsess about my patients I always know it's something going on with *me*. It's something much more immediate when my anxiety is all over the place . . . It's always much closer to home . . ."

"I think you're in a tough position," I said, empathically.

"You seemed very alive when you were just telling your dream. There was tremendous excitement in you," Delores said in a supportive voice.

"It felt calmer than at the beginning of the session when I felt anxious discussing the material of the case."

"Well, you're just a little more connected," I said, "and when you're more connected you're less anxious."

"Yes, that's how it works, doesn't it?"

"It *does* work." The group broke into nervous laughter.

"That's theory for you, boy. I'm about to get intellectual and ask you for readings," Lenore continued our bantering. More laughter ensued. "Maybe I could start fantasizing about my father in the sessions, and that way be able to contain it."

"At any rate," I went on, "The minister, and your therapist have been 'father,' It's too scary when it's acted out and not seen as something that is safe; and that's really where the issue is. It's not safe, for you *or* for your patient, although for different reasons."

> Here we see how guilt and power are very interrelated. Experiencing one's competitive and sexual drives as dangerous becomes the basis for a good deal of anxiety and guilt.

"Those were issues in my analysis in both cases. If there was any variation from the structure I got very frightened with both analysts and would accuse them of not being able to hold to the limit. It scared the hell out of me."

I looked at the time and noted: "We've got around three or four more minutes. Do you people have any reactions, or want to sum up."

"Maybe I feel that it gives me more permission to be with some patients," Daisy said, thoughtfully.

Lenore sarcastically quipped, "Do you think I'd have brought this in if I knew we were going to get this far?" (Laughter.)

"That's my ongoing worry," Rachel said. "It always gets so *deep* in this group . . ."

Denise responded with a sarcastic, "Gee, *why* do you say *that* . . ."

A more relaxed ripple went around the group as we cooled down emotionally. We moved to references in the literature about the paranoid-masochistic character, and then, exhausted, the members trooped out of the office.

THE VITAL "CONNECTION"

The group had moved into some deep emotional levels, and Lenore had taken a most courageous stance in investigating the parallel between the patient's and her own experiences with their respective fathers. With the emerging material clearly touching sensitive areas, the group at first fell into condemning the moral conduct of the patient and her past lover. At the same time, the discussion stayed on a theoretical/technical level, avoiding the transference/countertransference issues. We see here, once again, how similar we are to our patients, and how difficulties in keeping the therapeutic process moving often reflect the therapist's becoming bogged down in countertransference reactions.

The case discussed presents a tangled web of complex issues. It well depicts our dilemma, which can be masked by looking for *the* "truth," particularly when there are so many different theoretical stances that can apply to the case. The "truth" in this case cannot be divorced from the emotional issues of the countertransference. However, from the very beginning, the theory did not become alive until it was connected to the affective aspects of this case. As we review the material, we see that Lenore, having taken a self-psychology position with her patient, found she was making little headway.

The therapist reframed the material in terms of exploring the subtle nuances of the masochistic character with its push to defend itself against a direct expression and integration of drive material. The conceptual framework superficially helped us sort out the developmental material and the different theoretical perspectives in the case. It also gave us breathing space until we were ready to approach the countertransference dynamics. The patient did not require reality testing, as would a psychotic, nor did she have problems in boundary issues. While there were, as there are in any case, issues that pertained to the self, the palpably sexual and aggressive dreams made the libidinal area stand out as the area for intervention.

The group members supported the presenter's reluctance to face the very hot countertransference problem. Ultimately each member decides how the case proceeds by the type of intervention that goes on in a case presentation. The group flirted with the countertransference issue, but it was only when Lenore bravely came out of hiding to talk about her sexual feelings towards her last two therapists, and her relationship with her father, that the group, visibly relieved, was able to explore the guilt and fear associated with these forbidden impulses and her countertransference identification with the patient. In the end, we were all spent, but more connected to one another.

A number of issues have been raised by this presentation and require some degree of clarity:

1) Feeling powerful, all-knowing and wise, yet impotent and helpless, are some of the countertransference landmarks in working within the masochist psychic territory. In feeling both powerful and helpless, we cajole, support, and confront our patients in their self-defeating operations. This type of intervention only serves to reinforce the masochistic pattern, for it reduces the patient's guilt

through moralistic castigation, and by so doing, it rarely offers a patient insight into the dynamics buried behind the character structure. In the case under discussion, for instance, sexual impulses are associated with fears of punishment, more specifically with object loss, creating a regressive recuperative pull to recapture the object by appearing helpless and needy, and demanding succor. Interpreting these issues requires a clear, centered stance by the therapist, where the inductions are processed rather than identified with.

2) When the therapist is induced into a seemingly powerful role by the patient, while at the same time openly denigrated, a reactive sadistic response by the therapist can easily obscure the patient's fear of attack and punishment through object loss. Interpretations should be cloaked in supportive terms as the fear of punishment in masochistic patients becomes a formidable barier to utilizing new information. Along similar lines, penetrating interpretations can create subliminal fears of sexual assault.

3) In the case under discussion, though narcissistic trends are evident, the transference and countertransference matrix appears basically masochistic. The presenter, obviously more comfortable in exploring the self issues, takes distance from a defined, interpretive stance that promotes autonomy strivings.

4) In spite of a careful interpretive approach, our patients can easily submit to our interventions rather than finding them as sources of integration. Buying the patient's idealization or acting out the induced sadism can be a by-product of this tactical problem.

5) A therapist's unresolved sadistic impulse can sidetrack the treatment goal by attempting to convert the masochist into a sadist.

6) Pain is not always associated with masochism. There is an enormous emotional suffering in our patients that can be neither controlling, distracting, nor manipulative, but represents part of the human condition. Masochistic pain manipulates, controls, or binds another. Confusion regarding the differences may represent a therapist's fear and misidentifications of human pain.

7) As therapists, when we become caught up in rage with patients' masochistic maneuvers, an inspection of some of the guilt-inducing aspects of the case is in order.

8) Though social and political forces may have relevance to a particular case, being overly attentive to the outside at the cost of the internal dynamics again must be viewed as a potential source of countertransference involvement.

9) The notion of "whore" can be an emotionally loaded expres-

sion. For Lenore, ultimately the label has its origins in her fears and fantasies regarding sexual power with the father. Here we observe how sexual power can be subverted into a mutual transference/countertransference moralistic dilemma, rather than form of creative self-affirmation. Greed and lust then become contaminated with a moralistic indictment. Even self-protective aggression can be suspect, for the inner judgment regarding oedipal material is relentless and finds but a brief respite in directing itself towards an external target. Expanding the imaginative symbolic capacity of the patient, which in turn becomes realized in the outside world, offers another way of discovering and utilizing power. This notion has little to do with concepts of masculinity or feminity, but as demonstrated by the foregoing presentation, transference/countertransference anxiety can easily be subverted in the masochistic arena.

10) Behind a masochistic character structure lie omnipotent fantasies, reinforced by an absent, overindulgent, or excessively punitive parent. Pain for self-denigration can easily distract the therapist from the patient's inner voice of power, particularly when the former has similar unworked-through issues.

11) Therapists and other important leaders in the community can easily take the transferential imparting of power as something very real, creating a master/slave relationship. Exploitation and dehumanization are not strangers in this society and can very easily enter into a treatment relationship. The loss of an objective distance furthers a sadomasochistic approach in the transference/countertransference relationship.

Chapter 11

IN SEARCH OF A HOME FOR THE SOUL

INTRODUCTION

Creative arts therapists often work with multiple levels of consciousness. In so doing, they bypass, and yet relate to, the cognitive, while working through the sensory experience. Thus, the very nature of their medium stimulates a spatial, motor sensory way of interaction in the therapeutic relationship. Both parties in the therapeutic relationship share the common thread. They are drawn to the space of the known/unknown, temporarily suspending boundaries in their expressive therapeutic endeavors. Consequently, at the very essence of this relatedness is a form of fusion state, where both therapeutic parties can easily lose their sense of separateness. In terms of counter-transference then, the challenge for the creative arts therapist is to understand both the strengths and obstacles created by their powerful mediums. The therapist walks a delicate line in balancing oneness and separateness through alternating ego states of contact. Even as both parties are propelled into a state of being and joining through art and dance, they cannot lose sight of meaning and an awareness of therapeutic process. Often, the creative arts therapist experiences a state of virtually living inside the patient. When this occurs, it is immediately essential for the therapist to be aware of what has happened. Then, in this state, the expressive therapist must from time to time combat overwhelming and possessive demons that are projected from their patients through art, or in the relationship, that rob them of their ability to be separate and autonomous. This can occur even though much of the therapeutic action is filtered through the third party, the expressive medium.

The group I will discuss has met continuously over a ten-year period on a once-a-week basis. During this course of time, changes have taken place as some members have dropped out and others have replaced them. There are still two original members remaining from when the group first met ten years ago. The constellation of creative arts therapists consists of two music therapists, one dance therapist and six art therapists. All of them have developed a deep personal contact with one another that has accrued from a good deal of personal sharing and resonance. Jessica, the presenter, is an important member of the group; she is often perceived as the leader; taking charge and is fearless in confronting group resistances. At the same time, she joins in when the group becomes excited in discovering something new about a particular transference or countertransference problem. Her infectious laugh permeates the group atmosphere and she takes enjoyment in our mutual stumblings and bumblings and is equally aware of the variety of sexual innuendoes that are connected to case presentations. She is creative and self-assertive and like so many other practitioners, is torn between making time for her personal art making and the stresses and realities of earning a living. We go now to the case at hand.

The session started by my speaking about the last session. This is quite unusual, as it has been my custom to wait to see how things developed. I shared with the group some of my reflections about the last presentation. I felt that I was not very clear or precise in my thinking. I described the patient, who had more than her share of masochistic relationships, as someone being caught between the boundaries and restraints of her own particular character organization and the underlying fear of loss and separation. I cautioned the group that it would be very difficult to go after her character structure until the underlying issues were sufficiently worked out. If an early confrontation were made regarding her character defenses, she would simply go undercover for the fear of being chained or attacked was quite prevalent. Underneath her character structure, I pointed out, there was a good deal of deprivation and feelings around loss. Encountering this patient, her pain was palatable. Feelings of loss and deprivation were very near the surface. The real challenge for the therapist, as well as the patient, was not to get inside her pain, but to remain separate as well as related. The group proceeded to discuss the problems of sharing artistic work with their patients. Some either drew or sang alongside their patients as they started to investigate a particular problem. They realized that this could further fusion or losing a degree of boundaries and professional objectivity. This was certainly true with masochistic or borderline conditions. The members of the group all seemed to agree and understand these issues and Jessica then proceeded to say that she was ready to start her case.

Jessica then started to speak, "Even when you participate by not joining the patient in art work, but simply looking at their artistic products, there is a good likelihood that you may encounter a strong force to join them in a fusion state. I have a case that illustrates this point."

The group nodded and encouraged her to go on.

She continued, "I want to talk to you about a fifteen-year-old adolescent who came to the hospital presenting symptoms of an eating disorder. I will pass her art work around and I want to draw your attention to the first two pictures. When I look at those two pictures, I seem to get lost right inside of them."

She then proceeded to pull out the pictures and place them on the floor (Figures 11-1 and 11-2).

Figure 11-1

Figure 11-2

"This patient, " she continued on, "was admitted to the unit three or four months ago. I recall seeing her coming out of the recreation room, and I was behind the nursing station, observing her. She was dressed in a pair of jeans, which were probably a size five, which is probably two sizes too big for her. There was a flaunting of her hipbones and midriff. I took one look at her and I said, 'Oh God, this kid's going to be doing this for twenty years.' I turned around and I shut her out of my consciousness. I had just completed therapeutic work with an eating disorder kid and I wanted a break from working with these patients. Within three or four days, I received messages from five or six different people on the staff drawing my attention that this kid was writing poems and drawing pictures. The mother was running around frantically trying to draw attention to a poem that was suicidal. Everyone told me I should work with her because she was an artist. She wouldn't show this poem to anyone and didn't like her present therapist, who was a verbal therapist. So I said, 'O.K. I'll work with this kid, even if she is suicidal.' I immediately made contact with this kid, who agreed straight away to work with art. She was a little bit hesitant at first, but then something suddenly happened. That 'fusy' state that you referred to immediately entered the picture. I might add, that this is an intensely beautiful girl, even with her loss of weight. She has that mergy, seductive, 'fusy' energy that just captures you. It's difficult to explain this, but it does feel like you're drawn into her world. At the same time, you feel like you hit an inevitable glass wall and you bump your nose against it. You don't even know that it's there, but you hit it nevertheless. The first time she worked, she did a self portrait and handed it to me (Figure 11-1). She kept on repeating it and repeating it. And then we discussed, 'well what part of this is you?' and that kind of thing. It felt very wordy. I tried to open up the issue of her loss of hope and it just didn't seem to go anywhere. I didn't feel she was that suicidal. Later on I found out that someone had gotten their hands on this poem, the poem that I have never seen, and they felt it was more the mother's invention than anyone else's."

The group proceeded to pass the pictures around and there was a good deal of silence as they each felt the impact of this material. Jessica went on to describe the kind of media that were open to her. "She had many choices, but would only work with pencil and paper."

Maxine added, "that seemed to be associated with a lot of anorexic cases that I've worked with. They just like to use pencils."

Another member chimed in that she didn't find that to be true.

"In any event, " Jessica added, "it certainly applies to this kid."

At this point, Maxine diverts the attention of the group. She makes the following statement. "I want to say something right now. I need to bring this to the group, and I'm sure I was late today for this reason. My fourteen-year-old niece was just diagnosed with anorexia last Thursday, and I'm devastated by it."

Maxine has several brothers, and she identified her niece as "the daughter of the brother I feel closest to."

She continued, "The first thing I said to my brother was that you really have to look at what's going on in the family. This is not just about your daughter; it's about the whole family. Look at what just happened in Colorado with the school massacre. It's the same dynamic, you know, but all this anger and rage is going inside instead of out."

(I recognized that Maxine was also talking in a sense about herself. But I saw no reason at this time to interject this issue as it would doubtless emerge with the process of the case.)

The group then returned to the case. I thought it was interesting that they did not pick up on Maxine's issues, but left them alone for the time being.

Jessica proceeded with her presentation. "I became intensely interested in this patient very quickly. This was a red light to me, because it's what I tend to feel with kids who are traumatized. There was a sense that I was rushing in to fix it, rushing to save her. She also seemed to be holding a secret, which was ready to burst. As she was drawing, the room went from an empty space to a place that got so packed with tension that you thought it was going to explode.

"I find these two pictures very entrancing, " she said, pointing to the drawings. "She was practically non-verbal in her capacity to process them. Instead, she would draw, then sit back and look at them, like a reflection or a mirror. Then, each time, she started to cry. I've developed a way of working with her. The 45 or 50 minute session just doesn't work. To be perfectly honest, 20 or 30 minutes twice a week is just about what we can take. Otherwise the energy gets too complicated. It's the best frame to work with her, and certainly it is for me."

A member of the group inquired, "What happens after twenty minutes?"

Jessica responded, "She draws a picture and wells up. She gets so intense and starts to implode. I ask her whether something happened, but she says no. She doesn't know what happens. When she drew, I pointed out her sense of isolation. I said, 'It looks so lonely. It's like something has happened that you can't share with anybody.' Then she would say, 'That kind of loneliness is like, it's too much.' I think this is so overwhelming to her, it is too much to bear – and yet she reports that nothing has happened. This experience can really be described as 'Come in, come in, no, don't come in.' It's a constant tease back and forth.

"After these two pictures, I became very hesitant. I thought, 'Oh God, I don't want to see this kid again. I don't want this right now. I don't need my guts churned by a lawn mower.' I get this feeling in twenty minutes. I feel like there's so much fusion that I need to take even more emotional space. The next time I asked her to title her image. She named it 'Innocence.' So I asked her what she knew about innocence. But meantime, I'm dissociating and it's very difficult even to hold on to the content of what's happening. She says that innocence is purity and truth. She keeps going back to truth: the inner truth and the complete truth, as if truth is a core concept.

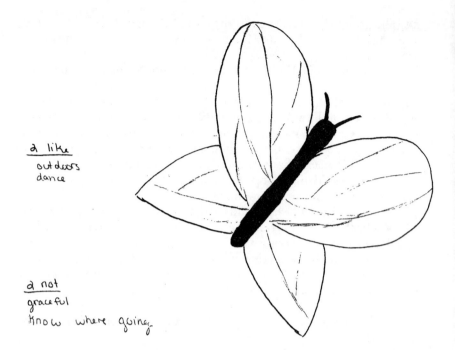

a like
out doors
dance

a not
graceful
Know where going

Figure 11-3

From a family perspective, I don't even have a full history. It's clear to me that one reason is my resistance. The other is that unfortunately, she's one of those kids who is getting almost no verbal therapy, because she's being bounced from Fellow to Fellow and we have a particularly poor group of Fellows on staff this year. I know she is the oldest child in a family whose father is a recovered alcoholic. He recovered a year ago, I believe, which is when she started getting sick. And there is a younger sister, who has a brain tumor. They live upstate, and they come down specifically for treatment. This is my patient's second hospitalization. They travel down here once a week for a family session. Today was the first time she responded, regarding her art therapy session, with the complaint, 'do I have to come?' And I said yes. I was very clear about it, but there was the underlying feeling that the patient was communicating, 'I don't want to come, I need to escape.' I repeated that she had to come, but I'm aware that if I'm not careful, I'm going to set up this polarity dynamic. She could create a power trip between us, which is very provocative. So I asked her this time, 'What do you want to do; do you want to just make a picture, or do you want me to help structure it?' This is a question I frequently ask these kids. They have a chance to either play with an idea, or process something that is already presented to them. She said that she wanted structure. I asked, 'What animal would you like to be if you could be an animal?' She drew a butterfly (Figure 11-3), and I asked her to tell me about it. She said that it could fly away. I then said, 'So you want to fly away today?' I said to her, 'You know, everybody needs a day to fly away.' And I thought that was more useful than anything else was. At least it seemed to resonate with her, and I thought we had reestablished our relationship. And then we went back to this playful back and forth yo-yo: very flirtatious. I don't know where to take this from here. There's a piece of me that wants to walk away with disgust and disinterest. And another part that wants to dive into that tree and take it apart limb by limb (Figure 11-2).

One of the members commented, "Everything the patient does is so controlled. It's like she sucks all the life out of it."

As the leader I wanted to open up the area, for I suspected this affect could lead us somewhere.

I then asked her about her disgust. "It's an interesting word, " I reflected. "It's kind of provocative if you get right down to it." I asked Jessica what she thought about that.

Jessica took a little while to think and responded, "I've had lots of contact with disgust. I think of how much energy you invest in a patient, and you invest and invest and pour it in like a sieve. The container is open and doesn't seem to hold anything. It feels like an absorbent sponge."

"And then, " she continued, "when I ask her what's happening, she says I don't know. She looks at you as if you have two heads, like you're speaking Chinese. She keeps on reiterating the phrase, 'I don't know what happens, nothing happens'."

I then commented to Jessica, "You know, you're asking too much for an explanation, and it seems as a result you're just cutting off the processing."

Jessica agreed, "But on the other side is this: it's like being overwhelmed. Because, frankly, she uses the word overwhelm a lot."

"Let's see how she uses it, " I suggested.

Jessica offered an example. "I said to the patient, 'Tell me what's inside and when you say I don't know, just look around a little bit at what's happening.' And she responded, 'I'm overwhelmed, I'm overwhelmed.' The clearest she could get from one week to another was the flower she drew (Figure 11-4). Then she was silent for a long time. I said to her, 'I notice that you're shutting down and closing off.' Finally she replied, 'I don't want to talk about it.' This was probably the clearest thing she could possibly say and even the healthiest!"

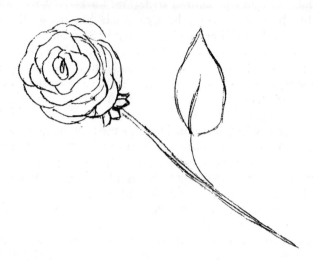

Figure 11-4

A group member then asked her, "Jessica, do you think that she consciously withholds information?" And Jessica replied, "I'm not sure."

But another member said, "When you're fifteen, what is it that you do or don't know? You're not even sure what your deepest secret is."

Jessica went on, "I'm not sure she knows anything about what secrets are all about. There's part of me that thinks she doesn't know, and then there's another part that feels she really does know something about some real secret."

I pointed out to the group that when a person gives this kind of "maybe yes and maybe no, " equivocal answer, it's probably an avoidance of something much more profound.

Jessica volunteered, "Somewhere along the line I hold my breath and pull back. The tension is tremendous, and then I realize I'm having as much trouble tolerating this tension as she is."

A member of the group contributed, "You know, maybe there's too much talk going on. Maybe you should just stay in the non-verbal mode and find out how the tension ultimately channels itself into an image."

Another person queried, "Is it your tension or her tension?"

Jessica reflected a while. "It feels like it's coming from her. I think it belongs as a projected identification. But it's so mergy and fused."

I tried then, as the leader, to help Jessica explore the feeling inside her. "Do you know anything about merging? Describe, " I said, "how it feels in your body."

(I often find it's very helpful for supervisees to explore the feeling in their body when they feel so disconnected. I encourage them to walk like the feeling, dance like the feeling, and see where it lodges inside the therapist. Ultimately the body tension transforms itself into a feeling state or image.)

Then Jessica replied, "I could be hurt."

"How?" I asked.

"By having the merging cut out from me." But then Jessica reiterated, "Of course, that energy doesn't belong to me."

I said, "O.K., would you like to describe her energy?"

Jessica then recalled a situation that embodied the patient's energy. "It's 2 a.m. and she's huddled over her diary. That's her energy. That's the intensity she gives you; it's also present in her art work."

I pressed the point: "Jessica, see how it feels in your body. See what your body is saying." Jessica was unable to do this. So I turned to Maxine, who has worked with eating disorders, and had spoken earlier about her niece. I asked her to take the patient inside of her and become her. Maxine requested a few more clues besides being huddled over her diary at two in the morning.

Jessica said, "She's deeply self-absorbed and her body is very intense. And everything seems to be perfectly controlled in the art form; everything needs to be perfectly controlled."

Maxine picked up the image and mirrored it in her body.

(Maxine appeared hunched in, controlled and taut, with energy moving inward. Her body was sucked in, yet so compelling.)

Jessica replied, "That's it, that's the patient."

"How does it make you feel?"

Jessica responded, "It makes me nuts. I can barely breathe. It makes me feel so uncomfortable. I see this child so totally alone and there's no response from her parents. She just seems to be so lost in her world with no contact. I feel sad and rejected." Jessica added, "As I watch this figure, all I want to do is stroke her hair. I want to offer her something soothing."

(I thought it was time to offer her a model that would be far more present and grounded.)

I then interjected, "Perhaps I can offer you an alternate point of view. I don't want to stroke her hair; I just want to be there. I don't want to ask her to do anything for me. I just want to wait and see what happens. I want to relate to her without being absorbed into her world.

Granted, she looks sad, but I'm not about to completely get lost in her sadness."

A member asked if those were my feelings, or if I was responding to what Jessica had said.

I said, "That was me as the therapist, and I was trying to contain the kind of feelings that Jessica described."

I reflected to Jessica that I certainly could feel the pressure inside to do something, to put aside your role as a therapist. "But all that is required is for you to remain present in a non-verbal space, bearing testimony or witnessing what is happening."

"It seems rather peaceful, " Jessica replied, "and I'm attracted to that space, but then, soon after, I just want to go off and do my own work."

I countered, "But then you are going away from her, " and Jessica agreed.

I then asked Jessica, "Does she look at you?" Jessica nodded and I replied, "Seeing that would probably be enough for me."

Jessica then observed, "I start thinking that I can see myself working with this patient for twenty years, and then maybe another twenty years. And it doesn't matter what I say or do, she's just going to do this stuff for twenty years."

And then I replied, "And so what happens to you, Jessica? How do you see yourself then?"

Her answer: "I question what the hell I'm doing here to begin with."

I replied, "That's the question you ask yourself, but what does it feel like?"

Jessica retorted, "It's a mix; there's something merged in it. I feel a sense of disgust. I want to say to this patient, 'Don't play with me, just don't play with me. If you're going to do this for twenty years, do it.' And then I feel angry. And then I say to myself, 'Come back after twenty years, and make me a picture.'"

(I decided to become more didactic and less emotionally confrontive. But I suspected that we might be touching on some upsetting material that is very overwhelming to the therapist.)

I went on, "Suppose you don't know, Jessica, whether it's going to be twenty years or twenty minutes. You're just being there without any expectations for change. Suppose you'll never know what's going to happen in the long run."

Another member chimed in, "And that's the truth."

I went on, "And that means giving up the wish to cure her or change her. Let me tell you a little bit what I feel in imagining working with this patient: there is something so compelling and so beautiful about her. And just watching her and never being able to touch her is tremendously painful. The beauty is something I want to touch, I want to possess and hold. Yet I know I never can have it. There's an incredible sense of loss and emptiness, and I have to sit with that and then recognize what's going on inside me."

(I wonder to myself, 'Am I describing something that is highly personal and charged for the therapist?')

Jessica, after listening to me, thoughtfully replied, "You know there's a question that I often wonder about. It's something I've never really asked other children, but I asked her. 'What did you give up, in order to come to the hospital? Did you have to give up ballet, art or poetry?' She answered immediately that it was all three, and then sat there in silence."

I asked, "When she said that to you, what was going on inside of you?"

"Nothing, " Jessica responded, "just a feeling of loss."

"And do you have any associations" I said, "with loss?"

"My mind goes to sitting in the medical rounds and hearing what is going on. There is so much negative energy in people. I think about this stupid Fellow spurting out all he knows. All this textbook crap about the family; all that fix up crap. I just want to stand up and say, 'Listen, she's going to be here for twenty years. Sit back and relax. Take your salary and go home. Take care of your house, take care of your kids.'"

I replied, "There's something very sad in what you say, and I think that you're not really paying enough attention to it."

Jessica said, "There's a lump in my throat when I put it into words. It's one step removed, but I think about my art that I walked away from around twelve years ago."

And I said, "And what part was that Jessica? What did you search for in your art?"

Jessica thought and said, "The word that comes to me is the holiness of it. There's a prayer in it."

And I said, "Did you have a love affair with your art?"

Jessica responded immediately, "Oh yeah. That's a good way of putting it."

I continued, "It sounds like your art was very healing and reparative."

Jessica replied, "I felt and did my art work all the time. It didn't matter where I was and even if I was doing some clerical work, I was still painting. I was still living and breathing it."

And then I said, "Living and breathing it?"

Jessica responded, "Yes, the creative process."

I retorted, "And getting lost in it?"

Jessica replied, "Yes, getting completely lost in it."

I then observed, "It sounds like it was a highly lustful and erotic affair."

Jessica said, "Can I ask you how you put all those pieces together and arrived at that comment?"

I thought a while and then said, "I was reminded of two members of this group, who have shared some similar experiences with us. And in each memory that they shared here, as they spoke, there was a faraway look in their eyes that is similar to your presentation today. It felt both erotic and loving and yet, behind this sense of beauty, there was a glass wall. It seemed that they were only chasing something and were ultimately left with a feeling of impotence, because the hole inside was never fixed. Sometimes the art repairs this empty hole, but it really doesn't do the whole job. It can be deceptive. The art feels very complete and seems to fulfil a yearning, so you're ready to dive into the next canvas only to realize that it simply keeps your head above water.

Jessica and another member both agreed, and Jessica added, 'Yes, it's like chasing a moonbeam."

And I added, "It's like drinking in something when you're parched. And it feels very healing on one level, but compulsively you must go on to the next piece. Certainly it is better than nothing": your music or your dance or your art, but it really doesn't quite change the problems with people. It's that faraway look, that yearning, that never seems to really be satisfied. These yearning eyes seem to say so much, and I realize that this yearning touches so many of you. The greed, the hunger gets partially satisfied through artistic expression, but as soon as you leave your art, the ache comes back. It doesn't really do the job of repairing the problems that arise with people."

One member now interjected, "I feel very sad, as if you were talking about me."

And I went on, "What often happens is that the art only brings me closer to the realization that I will never be able to fill that empty hole. And then there is a sense of loss that I have seen in myself as well as in others. It's sometimes very difficult to share with people, and that is the sadness of it all. And if I really get into it, I can understand why some people become addicts. For you would do anything rather than feel that painful loss – whether it be an addiction to love, alcohol or whatever it takes to avoid that pained feeling."

One member chimed in, "Are you referring to the loss of mother?"

And I went on, "That very early sensuous touch of holding, the sense of perfection. The flower that we see here exhibited that gets lost in a tree (Figure 11-2). The need to have a sense of control and order so that the feeling doesn't get out of hand. I'm sure that some of you who have children recall the experience of looking into your baby's eyes and getting lost in the holding and touching. One could describe it as a form of ecstasy.

Another member spoke up: "Yes, I have it with my child. She starts kissing me and we both get a little scared. She gets so passionate as she starts kissing me on the mouth, and we both kind of look at each other and move away. And then of course there is my younger child, where I completely get lost in the merger. And it feels so much like ecstasy."

It was rather hushed now, each member moving into private thoughts about the yearning for holding, and the empty space that lies inside of us. The big black hole.

And I began to speak soothingly: "We have to honor and respect it. Hopefully, we will have the space and time to find our own solutions for it. Certainly I would find it very difficult to be part of a therapy relationship in which I see a strong, young, beautiful adolescent girl at the very beginning of life, that nonetheless is on the verge of dying. She's very slowly committing suicide, and all I can do is watch. I cannot do anything but be there. I am just a witness as her waist gets smaller and smaller, her eyes growing blanker. I just have to bear testimony to it. It almost feels like I'm in a concentration camp, not being able to help, or do anything about it."

"But, of course, you're doing a good deal by just being present. It is a tremendous gift in fact. You are, in effect, saying that I will be with you, share and accept what you're feeling, even if it is your wish to die. You feel such a sense of pain that it becomes difficult to handle, to control and manage."

Maxine talked about the yearning that feels so central to her. She was aware of what her niece was going through, the need to merge, to get lost rather than feel the pain of emptiness. Maxine and I noted that we have both been in touch with that hole inside of her over the course of our relationship.

I then continued, "I recognize that you cannot ask a patient to give up that painful yearning. The best you can do is observe from the outside, asking nothing of her. This is very difficult to do. But it's offering her a good deal. Of course, you want to shake her and say, 'Don't you want to live?' Particularly when you're very fond of the person and see something beautiful."

Maxine then said, "I recall hiding in the closets as a child, removing all the clothing. And still I could never get rid of that feeling of emptiness that you're referring to."

And I replied, "And, of course, that's where the tears are." They all agreed. "And you can cry and cry forever, because there is such a yearning and sadness about the hole that can never be filled, and you need to control everything, for there is so much pain. And so you are constantly saying, as this patient is saying, merge with me, be with me, be inside. And yet I am frightened to take responsibility for that feeling. There is so much sadness, but the patient is cut off from it. It just feels like too much. True, in some respects the artwork helps to work through the emptiness. But the crucial point, Jessica, is the artwork cannot really work through all the issues that stem from early development. Somewhere you had recognized that you needed something more to fill the empty hole. And now you find it's all a dirty trick, because still you are very much aware of that painful hole."

At this time, the group was very connected and the members felt joined, reflecting upon their own emptiness that was being mirrored to one another.

I went on, "We've been working on this issue for a number of weeks, collectively as well as individually, as we've been presenting each case revolving around a facet of this problem. We're trying to understand the whole notion of closeness, fusion, separateness and loss."

Jessica chimed in, "The piece that is really touching me was when you were saying it was so hard to watch this girl slowly killing herself. And as you began to describe the physical wasting, I was thinking about the AIDS kids that are also wasting away. But that didn't bother me as much as the situation with this girl does."

And one of the members said, "I don't understand."

Jessica replied, "Because I'm not afraid of physical death. It's the spiritual death that concerns me and that relates to my own struggle. It's that polarity between eternal beauty and spiritual devastation that I find in the extreme, in working with this child. She's the person-ification of melancholy. I think of a swan, a dying swan."

The music therapist said, "Of Swan Lake. The woman is under a spell and she can't get away from it."

The dancer member said, "I saw a dance where the woman came under such a spell, and I can actually still see the image. I have danced this many times. I actually experienced it when I was very young."

Jessica returned to speaking of her patient. "What is the meaning for me of working with her? Right now there is no meaning, and I feel like it's being shoved down my throat. And yet, somehow, it's interesting, today I see all these pieces come together. I find myself wondering if we can reframe what we're doing. Can we combine the languages of spirituality and developmental psychology? You know, in some respects, you explore the limits of each language to ultimately make it your own. That's where I am right now. I guess I don't know how to make both languages quite come together."

I responded to her, "Some of us go back to these starting points and face them every time a crisis arises. In many respects, what we face in today's presentation is a spiritual crisis around the body. We all wonder whether this body can hold this patient's spirit and pain. There has been so much violation of the patient's soul. She may question whether she can dare to invest in relationships any more. I wonder at the start, if her mother celebrated her birth, the entrance of her soul into her body. It's a big job for us, as therapists, to do some repairing of this very big deficit."

I referred now to a comment Jessica made in the last session, when she spoke about her mother, who is so unpredictable that Jessica never knew whether she would be angry and out of control, or calm. She described how difficult it was to work through some of her early connection, and that indeed her artwork was an attempt to repair the deficits of her early symbiosis.

"You came to art therapy, " I said, addressing Jessica, "with the hope that there could be even more of a repair in this big, empty hole. This patient represents a big challenge, for she is bordering between life and death. You are very identified with the loss of the soul of this patient, whom you want to save and rescue. At the same time, you don't want to be put through her torture and her sadism and her need for perfectionistic control.

"And so we are all faced, " I said to the group, "with the struggle Jessica sees with this patient, the struggle of her soul to find the self that can give her some entrance to life, some way to express herself. Try to separate your struggle from hers, for you cannot repair that hole of yours by rescuing her."

Thus the session ends on a very thoughtful, though sad note. In reflecting upon the session, I am reminded that in the field of art therapy we encounter a split in the profession between art itself as therapy, and psychotherapy through art. I find this split distracting us from the real issues. Art can be singularly reparative and healing. It certainly goes beyond the verbal and touches the very soul and essence of our being. In this way, art can be a vehicle for the expression of the soul and partially repair its wounds. Yet ultimately, a self must develop that is resonant with this soul and gives it some entrée into the real world of interpersonal existence. In order to do this, the empty hole that we encounter with the patient, and often in ourselves, must be mourned and honored. This pain and mourning are important to repair the deficits of our early symbiosis.

The answer to the secret for this case presentation may well be discovered in the area of sexual abuse. Certainly, there are hints of this throughout the discussion. Evidence of dissociation, sexual provocation and an enormous need for control are consistent with sexual trauma. As in many cases of this nature, the spiritual-artistic, with a de-emphasis of the transference/countertransference, may well be the safe therapeutic road to travel before we open up an articulated expression to the patient's wounded self. The countertransference issues regarding trauma may well need investigation in Jessica's personal psychotherapy.

In many respects, the spiritual expression that we encounter through art offers us a sense of oneness that cannot be reached through the language of dynamic psychotherapy. Yet, art and other spiritual experiences unfortunately cannot restore the self. There are some patients who may need to stay in the spiritual world of expression. For others, the reverse is true, and they cannot go near spiritual experience for it is all too mysterious and frightening. As a profession, we need to heal our own splits and understand that there is a synthesis between the soul, the self and our interpersonal relationships. Art is not only a soulful experience, but can also be utilized as a bridge to make the spirit alive in our relationships with people. But in order to do this, we may well have to meet the pain of mourning regarding the empty hole within us.

A FAREWELL NOTE

The preceding presentations are a testimony to the courage and responsibility of the group members who have met the challenge of countertransference supervision. Each group has evolved and developed a basic trust and rapport among the individual members. The acquiring of this trust has not come easily, for there are particularly in the beginning, enormous struggles regarding the extent of self-disclosure.

This problem mirrors the issues of the overall profession. We are all aware of this disparity between the professional self that is shown to the public, and the actual practitioner self that enters the room with our patient. Our articles and presentations more often than not demonstrate our successes rather than our human foibles and lapses. As students in training institutes, we subtly doctor our presentations so that we will move through our various levels of training with a minimum of emotional complications. By the time we are in an institute, we are smart enough to pick up the prevailing mores of the institute and leave our private exploration for only our closest colleagues or at such a time when we are safely graduated.

As I draw an end to this text, pieces of the history and drama of past presentations cross my mind, but because of the limitations of space an exhaustive treatment of the subject is impossible. I recall the uproar, but 10 short years ago, that took place in one of my groups when a young mother nurses her baby while we discuss our cases. Members wonder out loud whether she is being provocative or exhibitionistic. Ten years later, in the same group, with some of the same members, another member comes in nursing her baby with hardly a ripple. Perhaps the times have changed, or maybe we all have grown and matured.

Pregnancy, birth, child rearing, the attendant problems of integrating a practice with being a parent, all have filtered into our discussions. They are the very tangible facts of our lives that affect our practice. Our patients have an uncanny ability to tune into these events, if only through their dreams, and we soon learn that there are no secrets between the therapist's private self and patients' conflicts. Often the question arises as to what should be shared with patients and in what time frame.

When we become physically ill and must take leave of our practice, how much can we share with patients, and more important, in what form and in what manner? Much of this has to do with a personal inner sense of responsibility and our guilt in requiring separate time and space to attend to these real-life issues.

When we grow older, we may perceive our skills slipping away as we observe our memory becoming blurred. Rarely do we talk of the older practitioner whose practice falls off as he feels defeated and unwanted.

A frequent presentation focuses on the borderline patient. Here, the presenter often requests help in the containment of primitive affects projected by the borderline patient. We are beside ourselves with rage and guilt and consequently seek some form of nurturance and solace from our colleagues. Regaining, then, the rhythm of empathy and structure that is so necessary with borderlines, becomes one of the goals of case presentation.

Therapists also struggle with their identification with their own analysts, and are particularly thrown into conflict when their cases call for a different manner or approach than is experienced in their personal treatment. The painful recognition that their own treatment cannot be a model for all future treatment slowly and grudgingly enters their awareness.

I remember a particularly touching presentation where the male therapist struggled to find a "soft" male inside of him that was both supportive and yet nonseductive to a frightened female patient. The group came up with the model of Mr. Rogers, which seemed to be a marvelous fit for both the therapist and the case.

Finally, I remember the lament of a presenter whose patient was dying of AIDS. Her patient needed to cut off from the relationship and be very much alone with his pain. The therapist felt robbed of the opportunity to mourn with her patient and finally was left with her loss and aloneness.

Obviously, another volume could be filled describing group explorations of an entire set of new issues, other than those described in the foregoing chapters. The treatment of this material is inexhaustible and, with each problem, the solutions are both unique and contingent on the therapeutic mix of the patient's and therapist's psychic constellations.

We are then left with the continual balancing act that crosses over into our social, private, and political lives. We leave these groups in process; the character nature of them will change in time, but the struggle never ends.

BIBLIOGRAPHY

Adler, G. (1994) 'Transference, countertransference, and abuse in psychotherapy'. *Harvard Review of Psychiatry*, September/October issue.

Alexander, F. (1935) 'The problem of psychoanalytic technique'. *Psychoanalytic Quarterly 4*, 588–611.

Balint, M. (1937) 'Early developmental states of the ego'. In *Primary Love and Psychoanalytic Technique*. New York: Liveright, 1965.

Balint, M. (1968) *The Basic Fault*. London: Tavistock.

Basch, M.F. (1983) 'Empathic understanding: A review of the concept and some theoretical considerations'. *Journal of the American Psychoanalytic Association 34*, 101–126.

Baum, O.E. (1969–1970) 'Countertransference'. *Psychoanalytic Quarterly*, 621–637.

Benedek, T. (1953) 'Dynamics of the countertransference'. *Bulletin of the Menninger Clinic 17*, 201–265.

Beres, D. and Arlow, J.A. (1974) 'Fantasy and identification in empathy'. *Psychoanalytic Quarterly 43*, 26–50.

Berman, L. (1949) 'Countertransference and attitudes of the analyst in the therapeutic process'. *Psychiatry 12*, 159–166.

Biancoli, R. (1998) 'The "idologic" view of transference'. *Journal of the American Academy of Psychoanalysis 26*, 1, 15–28.

Bion, W.R. (1955) 'Language and the schizophrenic'. In M. Klein, P. Heiman and R.E. Money-Kyrle (eds) *New Directions in Psychoanalysis*. London: Tavistock, 220–239.

Bion, W.R. (1959) 'Attacks on linking'. *International Journal of Psycho-Analysis 40*, 308–315.

Bollas, C. (1983) 'Expressive uses of the countertransference'. *Contemporary Psychoanalysis 19*, 1–34.

Bollas, C. (1987) *The Shadow of the Object*. New York: Columbia University Press.

Bouchard, M.A. (1995) 'Countertransference as instrument and obstacle: A comprehensive and descriptive framework'. *Psychoanalytic Quarterly*, October.

Buie, D.H. (1981) 'Empathy: It's nature and limitations'. *Journal of the American Psychoanalytic Association 29*, 281–307.

Burke, W.F. and Tansey, M.J. (1985) 'Projective identification and countertransference turmoil: Disruptions in the empathic process'. *Contemporary Psychoanalysis 21*, 372–402.

Chediak, C. (1979) 'Counter-reactions and countertransference'. *International Journal of Psycho-Analysis 60*, 117–129.

Cohen, M.B. (1952) 'Countertransference and anxiety'. *Psychiatry 15*, 231–243.

Cutler, R.L. (1958) 'Countertransference effects is psychotherapy'. *Journal of Consulting Psychology 22*, 349–356.

Daskovsky, D. (Win. 1998) 'The abuser and the abused: Sources of resistance to resolving splits in the countertransference in the treatment of adults who were sexually abused as children'. *Psychoanalytic Psychology 15*, 1, 3–13.

Deutsch, J. (1926) 'Occult processes occurring during psychoanalysis'. In G. Devereux (ed) *Psychoanalysis and the Occult*. New York: International Universities Press, 1953, 133–146.

Edelson, M. (1984) *Hypothesis and Evidence in Psychoanalysis*. Chicago: University of Chicago Press.

Eisenberg, A.M. (1997) 'Institutional countertransference: The matrix of social structure and psychic structure'. *Journal of the American Academy of Psychoanalysis*. Summer.

Eissler, K.R. (1953) 'The effect of the structure of the ego on psychoanalytic technique'. *Journal of the American Psychoanalytic Association 1*, 104–143.

Epstein, L. and Feiner, A. (eds) (1979) *Countertransference*. New York: Jason Aronson.

Erikson, E. (1958) 'The nature of clinical evidence'. *Deadalus 87*, 65–87.

Fairbairn, W.R.D. (1946) 'Object-relationships and dynamic structures'. In *An Object-Relations Theory of Personality*. New York: Basic Books, 1952.

Ferenczi, S. (1919) 'On the technique of psychoanalysis'. In *Further Contributions to the Technique of Psychoanalysis*. London: Hogarth Press, 1950, 177–188.

Finnell, J.S. (1986) 'The merits and problems with the concept of projective identification'. *Psychoanalytic Review 73*, 103–128.

Flarsheim, A. (1972) 'Treatability'. In P.L. Giovacchini (ed) *Tactics and Technique in Psychoanalytic Psychotherapy*. New York: Science House, 113–134.

Fliess, R. (1942) 'The metapsychology of the analyst'. *Psychoanalytic Quarterly 11*, 211–227.

Fliess, R. (1953) 'Countertransference and counteridentification'. *Journal of the American Psychoanalytic Association 1*, 268–284.

Franch, N.J. (1996) 'Transference and countertransference in the analysis of a child with autistic nuclei'. *International Journal of Psychoanalysis*, August.

Franko, D.L. (1996) 'Countertransference in the treatment of patients with eating disorders'. *Psychiatry*, Spring.

French, T. (1958) 'The art and science of psychoanalysis'. *Journal of the American Psychoanalytic Association 6*, 197–214.

Freud, S. (1910) 'The future prospects of psychoanalytic therapy'. *Standard Edition of the Collected Works of Sigmund Freud 11*, 141–151. London: Hogarth Press, 1953.

Freud, S. (1912) 'Recommendations to physicians practicing psycho-analysis'. *Standard Edition of the Collected Works of Sigmund Freud 12*, 111–120. London: Hogarth Press, 1953.

Freud, S. (1913) 'The claims of psycho-analysis to the interest of the nonpsychological sciences'. *Standard Edition of the Collected Works of Sigmund Freud 13*, 165–190. London: Hogarth Press, 1959.

Freud, S. (1914) 'Remembering, repeating, and working through'. *Standard Edition of the Collected Works of Sigmund Freud 12*, 146–156. London: Hogarth Press, 1953.

Freud, S. (1937) 'Analysis terminable and interminable'. *Standard Edition of the Collected Works of Sigmund Freud 23*, 209–253. London: Hogarth Press, 1953.

Fromm, E. (1941) *Escape from Freedom*. New York: Avon.

Fromm, E. (1947) *Man for Himself*. Greenwich, CT: Fawcett.

Fromm, E. (1953) *Collected Papers, Vol 1*. London: Hogarth Press.

Fromm, E. (1955) *The Sane Society*. Greenwich, CT: Fawcett.

Fromm, E. (1962) 'The future prospects of psychoanalytic psychotherapy'. In *Standard Edition 11*, 1919. London: Hogarth Press.

Frost, J.C. (1998) 'Countertransference considerations for the gay male when leading psychotherapy groups for gay men'. *International Journal of Group Psychotherapy*, January.

Gill, M.M. (1983) 'The interpersonal paradigm and the degree of the therapist's involvement'. *Contemporary Psychoanalysis 19*, 200–237.

Gill, M.M. (1984) Discussion of 'Projection and projective identification: Developmental and clinical aspects', by O. Kernberg. Presented at annual meeting of the American Psychoanalytic Association, December 21.

Giovacchini, P.L. (1972a) 'The analytic setting and the treatment of psychosis'. In P.L. Giovachini (ed) *Tactics and Techniques in Psychoanalytic Psychotherapy*. New York: Science House, 222–235.

Giovacchini, P.L. (1972b) 'Technical difficulties in treating some characterological disorders: countertransference problems'. *International Journal of Psychoanalytic Psychotherapy 1*, 112–128.

Glover, E. (1955) *The Technique of Psychoanalysis*. New York: International Universities Press.

Goldberg, A. (1988) *A Fresh Look*. Hillsdale, NJ: The Analytic Press.

Gorkin, M. (1987) *The Uses of Countertransference*. Northvale, NJ: Aronson.

Greenberg, J.R. and Mitchell, S.A. (1983) *Object Relations in Psychoanalytic Theory*. Cambridge, MA: Harvard University Press.

Greenson, R.R. (1960) 'Empathy and its vicissitudes'. *International Journal of Psycho-Analysis 41*, 418–424.

Greenson, R.R. (1967) *The Technique and Practice of Psychoanalysis*. New York: International Universities Press.

Greenson, R.R. (1974) 'Loving, hating, and indifference towards the patient'. *International Review of Psychoanalysis 1*, 259–266.

Grinberg, L. (1962) 'On a specific aspect of countertransference due to the patient's projective identification'. *International Journal of Psycho-Analysis 31*, 81–84.

Grotstein, J.S. (1981) *Splitting and Projective Identification*. New York: Jason Aronson.

Guntrip, H. (1971) *Psychoanalytic Theory, Therapy, and the Self*. New York: Basic Books.

Hanna, E.A. (1998) 'The role of the therapist's subjectivity: Using countertransference in psychotherapy'. *Journal of Analytic Social Work 5*, 4, 1–24.

Heimann, P. (1950) 'On countertransference'. *International Journal of Psycho-Analysis 31*, 81–84.

Hendrick, I. (1950) *Facts and Theories of Psychoanalysis*. New York: Knopf.

Hoffman, I. (1983) 'The patient as interpreter of the analyst's experience'. *Contemporary Psychoanalysis 19*, 389–422.

Hunt and Issacharoff (1977) 'Henrich Racker and countertransfernce theory'. *Journal of American Academy of psychoanalysis 5*, 1, 95–105.

Issacs, S. (1939) 'Criteria for interpretation'. *International Journal of Psycho-Analysis 20*, 148–160.

Jaffee, D.S. (1968) 'The mechanism of projections: Its dual role in object relations'. *International Journal of Psycho-Analysis 49*, 662–676.

Kernberg, O. (1965) 'Notes on countertransference'. *Journal of the American Psychoanalytic Association 13*, 38–56.

Kernberg, O. (1975) *Borderline Conditions and Pathological Narcissism*. New York: Jason Aronson.

Kernberg, O. (1976) *Object Relations Theory and Clinical Psychoanalysis*. New York: Jason Aronson.

Kernberg, O., Burstein, E., Coyne, L., Appelbaum, A., Horwitz, L. and Voth, H. (1972) Psychotherapy and Psychoanalysis: Final report of the Menninger Foundation's Psychotherapy Research Project. *Bulletin of the Menninger Clinic 36*, 1–275.

Kirman, J.H. (1998) 'One-person or two-person psychology?' *Modern Psychoanalysis 23*, 1, 3–22.

Klein, M. (1946) 'Notes on some schizoid mechanisms'. *International Journal of Psycho-Analysis 33*, 433–438.

Klein, M. (1955) 'On identification'. In *Envy and Gratitude and Other Works, 1945–1963*. New York: Delacortte Press, 1975, 141–175.

Kohut, H. (1959) 'Introspection, empathy and psychoanalysis. An examination of the relationship between mode of observation and theory'. *Journal of the American Psychoanalytic Association 7*, 459–483.

Kohut, H. (1968) 'The psychoanalytic treatment of narcissistic personality disorders'. *The Psychoanalytic Study of the Child 23*, 86–113. New York: International Universities Press.

Kohut, H. (1971) *The Analysis of the Self.* New York: International Universities Press.

Kohut, H. (1977) *The Restoration of the Self.* New York: International Universities Press.

Kris, E. (1952) *Psychoanalytic Explorations in Art.* New York: International Universities Press.

Kubie, L. (1952) 'Problems and techniques in psychoanalytic validation and progress'. In E. Pumpian-Mindlin (ed) *Psychoanalysis as Science.* Stanford, CA: Stanford University Press, 74–89.

Lakovics, M. (1983) 'Classification of countertransference for utilization in supervision'. *American Journal of Psychotherapy 37,* 245–257.

Langs, R. (1975) 'Therapeutic misalliances'. *International Journal of Psychoanalytic Psychotherapy 4,* 77–105.

Langs, R. (1976) *The Therapeutic Interaction: Volume 11.* New York: Jason Aronson.

Langs, R. (1978) *Technique in Transition.* New York: Jason Aronson.

Liberman, D. (1978) 'Affective response of the analyst to the patient's communications'. *International Journal of Psycho-Analysis 59,* 335–340.

Little, M. (1951) 'Countertransference and the patient's response to it'. *International Journal of Psycho-Analysis 32,* 32–40.

Little, M. (1957) 'R' – The analyst's total response to his patient's needs'. *International Journal of Psycho-Analysis 38,* 240–254.

Livingston, M.S. (1995) 'A self psychologist in couplesland: Multisubjective approach to transference and countertransference-like phenomena in marital relationships'. *Fam Process,* December.

Malin, A. and Grotstein, J.S. (1966) 'Projective identification in the therapeutic process'. *International Journal of Psycho-Analysis 42,* 26–31.

Meissner, W.W. (1972) 'Notes on identification III. The concept of identification'. *Psychoanalytic Quarterly 41,* 224–260.

Meissner, W.W. (1980) 'A note on projective identification'. *Journal of the American Psychoanalytic Association 28,* 43–67.

Meissner, W.W. (1982) 'Notes on countertransference in borderline conditions'. *International Journal of Psychoanalytic Psychotherapy 10,* 89–123.

Mintz, J., Luborsky, L. and Auerback, A.H. (1971) 'Dimensions of psychotherapy: A factor analytic study of ratings of psychotherapy sessions'. *Journal of Consulting and Clinical Psychology 36,* 106–120.

Moeller, M.L. (1977) 'Self and object in countertransference'. *International Journal of Psychoanalysis 58,* 365–374.

Offerman-Zuckerbert, J. (1998) 'Contact, care, and countertransference: Some critical incidents'. *Contemporary Psychoanalysis 34*, 1, 133–142.

Ogden, T.H. (1982) *Projective Identification and Psychotherapeutic Technique*. New York: Jason Aronson.

Ogden, T.H. (1985) 'On potential space'. *International Journal of Psycho-Analysis 66*, 129–141.

Olinick, S. (1969) 'On empathy and regression in service of the other'. *British Journal of Medical Psychology 42*, 41–49.

Olinick, S., Poland, W.S., Grigg, K.A. and Granatir, W.L. (1973) 'The psychoanalytic work ego: Process and interpretation'. *International Journal of Psycho-Analysis 54*, 143–151.

Racker, H. (1953) 'A contribution to the problem of countertransference'. *International Journal of Psycho-Analysis 34*, 313–324.

Racker, H. (1957) 'The meaning and uses of countertransference'. *Psychoanalytic Quarterly 26*, 303–357.

Racker, H. (1968) *Transference and Countertransference*. New York: International Universities Press.

Reich, A. (1951) 'On counter-transference'. *International Journal of Psycho-Analysis 32*, 25–31.

Reich, A. (1960) 'Further remarks on countertransference'. *International Journal of Psycho-Analysis 41*, 389–395.

Reich, A. (1966) *Psychoanalytic Contributions*. New York: International Universities Press.

Reich, A. (1973) *Annie Reich: Psychoanalytic Contributions*. New York: International Universities Press.

Relk, T. (1937) *Surprise and the Psychoanalyst*. New York: Dutton.

Relk, T. (1948) *Listening with the Third Ear*. New York: Farrar, Strauss and Young.

Ricoeur, P. (1977) 'The question of proof on Freud's psychoanalytic writings'. *Journal of the American Psychoanalytic Association 25*, 835–871.

Rodewig, K. (1995) 'Physical illness in the transference and countertransference'. *Psyche Stutg*, June.

Roland, A. (1981) 'Induced emotional reactions and attitudes in the psychoanalyst as transference in actuality'. *Psychoanalytic Review 68*, 45–74.

Rosenbloom, S. (1998) 'The complexities and pitfalls of working with the countertransference'. *Psychoanalytic Quarterly 67*, 2, 256–275, April.

Rudge, A.M. (1998) 'A countertransference dream. An instrument to deal with a difficult transference situation'. *International Forum of Psychoanalysis 7*, 2, 105–111, July.

Rychlak, J. (1968) *A Philosophy of Science for Personality Theory.* New York: Rieger.

Sandler, J. (1976) 'Countertransference and role-responsiveness'. *International Review of Psycho-Analysis 3*, 43–47.

Sandler, J. and Rosenblatt, B. (1962) 'The concept of the representational world'. *The Psychoanalytic Study of the Child 17*, 128–145. New York: International Universities Press.

Sandler, J., Holder, A. and Dare, C. (1970) 'Basic psychoanalytic concepts: IV. Countertransference'. *British Journal of Psychiatry*, July, 1970, 117, 83–88.

Schaeffer, J.A. (1998) 'Transference and countertransference interpretations: Harmful or helpful in short-term dynamic therapy?' *American Journal of Psychotherapy*, Winter.

Schafer, R. (1954) *Psychoanalytic Interpretation in Rorschach Testing.* New York: Grune & Stratton.

Schafer, R. (1959) 'Generative empathy in the treatment situation'. *Psycho-Analytic Quarterly 28*, 347–373.

Schafer, R. (1968) *Aspects of Internalization.* New York: International Universities Press.

Schafer, R. (1980) 'Narration in the psychoanalytic dialogue'. *Critical Inquiry 7*, 29–53.

Schafer, R. (1983) *The Analytic Attitude.* New York: Basic Books.

Schafer, R. (1984) 'The pursuit of failure and the idealization of unhappiness'. *American Psychologist 39*, 398–405.

Schafer, R. (1995) 'Aloneness in the countertransference'. *Psychoanalytic Quarterly*, July.

Schafer, R. (1997) 'Vicissitudes of remembering in the countertransference. Fervent failure, colonisation and remembering otherwise'. *International Journal of Psychoanalysis*, December.

Searles, H.F. (1965) *Collected Papers on Schizophrenia and Related Topic.* New York: International Universities Press.

Searles, H.F. (1975) 'The patient as therapist to his analyst'. In P. Giovachini (ed) *Tactics and Techniques of Psychoanalytic Therapy, Vol. II.* New York: Jason Aronson, 95–151.

Segal, H. (1964) *Introduction to the Work of Melanie Klein.* New York: Basic Books.

Shapiro, T. (1974) 'The development and distortions in empathy'. *Psychoanalytic Quarterly 43*, 4–25.

Simmel, E. (1926) 'The "Doctor Game": Illness and the profession of medicine'. *International Journal of Psycho-Analysis 4*, 470–483.

Singer, B. and Luborsky, L. (1978) 'Countertransference: The status of clinical vs. quantitative research'. In A. Gurman and A. Razin (eds) *Effective Psychotherapy: A Handbook of Research.* New York: Pergamon.

Spence, D.P. (1982) *Narrative Truth and Historical Truth.* New York: W.W. Norton.

Steingart, I. (1998) 'The analyst's noncountertransferential love (and a footnote on hate)'. *Issues in Psychoanalytic Psychology 20,* 1, 5–16.

Stekel, W. (1911) *Die Sprache des Traumes.* Wiesbaden.

Sullivan, H.S. (1930) 'Socio-psychiatric research'. *Schizophrenia as a Human Process.* New York: W.W. Norton, 1962.

Sullivan, H.S. (1931) 'The modified psychoanalytic treatment of schizophrenia'. *Schizophrenia as a Human Process.* New York: W.W. Norton, 1962.

Sullivan, H.S. (1936) 'A note on the implications of psychiatry on the study of interpersonal relations for investigators in the social sciences'. *The Fusion of Psychiatry and Social Sciences.* New York: W.W. Norton, 1964.

Sullivan, H.S. (1938) 'The data of psychiatry'. *The Fusion of Psychiatry and Social Science.* New York: W.W. Norton, 1964.

Sullivan, H.S. (1940) *Concepts of Modern Psychiatry.* New York: W.W. Norton.

Sullivan, H.S. (1953) *The Interpersonal Theory of Psychiatry.* New York: W.W. Norton.

Tansey, M.J. and Burke, W.F. (1985) 'Projective identification and the empathic process'. *Contemporary Psychoanalysis 21,* 42–69.

Tauber, E.S. (1954) 'Exploring the therapeutic use of countertransference data'. *Psychiatry 17,* 331–336.

Thompson, M.G. (1998) 'Manifestations of transference: Love, friendship, rapport'. *Contemporary Psychoanalysis 34,* 4, 543–561.

Tosone, C. (1998) 'Countertransference and clinical social work supervision: Contributions and considerations'. *Clinical Supervisor 16,* 2, 17–32.

Tower, L.E. (1956) 'Countertransfernce'. *Journal of the American Psychoanalytic Association 4,* 224–255.

Winnicott, D.W. (1936) 'Appetite and emotional development'. In *Through Paediatrics to Psychoanalysis.* London: Hogarth Press, 1958.

Winnicott, D.W. (1945) 'Primitive emotional development'. In *Through Paediatrics to Psychoanalysis.* London: Hogarth Press, 1958.

Winnicott, D.W. (1949) 'Hate in the countertransference'. *International Journal of Psycho-Analysis 30,* 69–75.

Winnicott, D.W. (1960) 'The theory of the parent–infant relationship'. *The Maturational Processes and the Facilitating Environment* New York: International Universities Press, 1965.

Winnicott, D.W. (1965) *The Maturational Processes and the Facilitating Environment*. New York: International Universities Press.

Winnicott, D.W. (1971) 'The place where we live'. In *Playing and Reality*. New York: Basic Books, 1971, 104–110.

Wolf, E. (1980) 'On the developmental line of selfobject relations'. In A. Goldberg (ed) *Advances in Self Psychology*. New York: International Universities Press.

Wolstein, B. (1959) *Countertransference*. New York: Grune & Stratton.

Zetzel, E.R. (1965) 'Depression and the capacity to bear it'. *Drives, Affects, and Behavior 2*, M. Schur (ed) New York: International Universities Press.

INDEX

Acting out, 20, 64–65, 70, 151
Aggression, 111, 116, 125, 126, 138
Agoraphobia, 27
AIDS, 55, 129, 222
Analysis, experience in, 15–16
Anxiety
  defensive, 81
  homosexual, 62
  in therapist, 31, 62, 205, 210, 215

Borderline patient, 221
Boundaries, 35, 61, 150, 167–168

Cancer, 43–59
  and personality types, 47–48
Character structure, 16
Cohn, Ruth, 9
Communication, 17, 22
  barriers to, 61
  erotic, 40, 136
  in group sessions, 17, 149, 150,
    156, 173

nonverbal, 18–19, 41, 78, 149,
  150, 156, 173
of pain, 64–66
patient-therapist, 14, 18–19
sadomasochistic, 79, 190
supervisor-supervisee, 17
Consciousness, levels of, 18, 38
Container-therapist, 13, 18, 79
  and erotic transference, 40
Contempt, 147, 192–193, 196–198,
  201–205, 207, 208–209, 210,
  215
Controlling, 30–31, 37, 154
Countertransference, 9–11, 22–23,
  40, 78, 121, 142, 150
  anxiety, 40, 219
  and authority, 209, 219
  and autonomy, 92
  in case studies, 30, 33, 37, 72, 74,
    136, 189, 213
  and female element, 186
  in group sessions, 14, 58, 60, 62,
    130, 201, 216–217, 220
  in illness and dying, 20, 47, 52,
    56–58

Countertransference (*continued*)
  and masochism, 217
  and mirroring, 100
  and narcissistic patient, 179, 188,
    199, 218
  principles of, 41
  resistance, 131
  and sexual power, 219
  signals of, 40–41

Death, 57
  and countertransference, 20
  and imaging, 43–44
Defenses, 16, 26, 93, 96, 120
  in group leader, 60
  masochistic, 64
  paranoid, 74
  in therapists, 31–33, 38, 39, 69,
    167
Depression, 123–126, 128, 175
  and countertransference, 124–126
  as defense, 127, 132
  and greed, 123, 125
  and masochism, 125, 132
Divorce, 46, 48
Dreams, 61, 87, 93–94, 95, 209, 212,
    214, 215

Ego strengths, 15, 16
Emotional splitting, 19

Fantasies, 15, 219
  homosexual, 140
  rescue, 43, 53
Father, relationship with, 74, 130–
    131, 133, 138–139, 144, 180–
    183, 186–187, 198, 210–211,
    214–215

Grandiosity, in therapists, 20, 24, 35,
    37
  and guilt, 37

Group sessions
  atmosphere of, 15, 21, 22
  and characterological issues, 16
  composition of, 21
  as container, 17, 27, 124
  as form of learning, 14, 15, 16,
    22–23
  leadership of, 16, 39, 62, 147, 201
  and transference/countertrans-
    ference, 14, 16, 17, 38, 60, 62,
    201, 216–217, 220
Guilt
  in group sessions, 109, 110–114
  and illness, 50, 52, 56–57
  and power, 66
  in therapists, 96, 201, 203, 204,
    206, 216, 221

Healers, therapists as, 45, 58
Homosexuality, 75–78, 127, 139–
    140, 145, 180–181
Hostility, 35–36, 38–39, 106–107,
    120, 190
Humor, in depression, 125

Identification, 52, 79, 90, 101, 183,
    221
  female/male, 139, 141, 197
  projective, 61, 124, 187
Illness, 43–59
  and countertransference, 20, 47,
    52, 56
  and guilt, 50, 52, 56–57
  and imaging, 43–45
Image dialogue, 19
Imaging, 43–45
Intrapsychic representation, 18–19,
    173
Introjection, 24, 173
Isolation, 155–156, 165, 191

Male/female components, 18–19,
    134–139, 141–142, 144, 148,
    197, 221

Masochism, 79, 114, 125, 147, 191,
    202–204, 218, 219
    and mothering role, 193–194
    oedipal form, 206
Maternal role, 18, 19, 24, 32, 91,
    94–96, 167, 174
Mirroring, 82–102, 104, 117, 124,
    173–174, 176, 182
    in supervisory relationship, 183
Mother-daughter relationships,
    156–169, 173–174
Mr. Rogers, 221

Narcissism, 79, 176–179, 203, 218

Paranoid personality, 72, 73–74,
    75–76, 78–81
Playfulness, 39–40, 190
Polarities, psychic, 18–19
Power, 20, 35, 58, 65, 197, 219
    fantasized, 207
    through guilt, 66
    and sexuality, 142, 207
Projection, 15, 17, 24, 35
Psychoanalytic Institute, 9–10
Punishment, 33, 40, 114, 208

Reaction formation, 194, 196
Regression, 117–118, 124, 205
Role-playing, 15, 36–37, 70–71, 78,
    120–121, 142–143, 182, 185–
    186

Sadism, 137, 146–148, 189, 190, 193,
    197, 218, 219
Separation-individuation, 48, 52, 81,
    93
Sexuality, 20–21, 25, 34, 101, 116,
    127–131, 137–147, 207–216,
    218
    and control, 138
    and guilt, 202, 206, 208, 215
    metaphor, 133
    and parents, 138–139, 143–144
Sociological/cultural issues, 20, 82,
    90, 93, 100–101
Stress, and illness, 44

Therapeutic truth, 18, 157–158, 217
Transcendence, 196
Transference, 16, 17, 28, 40, 204–
    206, 212–213
    and authority figures, 219
    cure, 47, 175
    and merging, 90
    and mirroring, 100, 184
    projective, 15
Twinship, 82–100

Unconscious, 11, 43